HUNAN

Hengchow

Yungchow

Kweilin

KWANGTUNG

Wuchow

Yunghui

Shumkai
Jungyun

Kongmoon

CANTON

HONG-
KONG

MACAO

CHINA SEA

NO SECRET IS SAFE

By Mark Tennien

CHUNGKING LISTENING POST

NO SECRET IS SAFE

No Secret is Safe

BEHIND THE BAMBOO CURTAIN

by

FATHER MARK TENNIEN *of Maryknoll*

FARRAR, STRAUS AND YOUNG · NEW YORK

All photographs courtesy of The Maryknoll
Fathers except the photograph of Dr. Wallace,
courtesy of the Knoxville, Tennessee,
News Sentinel.

To Maryknoll Bishop Francis X. Ford and Southern Baptist William Wallace, M.D., who died in Communist China jails. And to the millions of other martyred or agonizing victims of Communist cruelty now dead or dying in the battle for faith and freedom. News of Bishop Ford's death came on September 2, 1952, though he died February 21, 1952.

Contents

Introduction

Some months ago, I looked across the barbed wire barrier
into Communist China and wondered about what was happening in that country that I had visited just after the
Japanese surrender in 1945. We were then rejoicing in our
hard won victory and were praying that a world-wide peace
with justice would follow that victory. In 1948 I again
visited China just as the iron curtain was clamping down
around the people of that country who had been our allies
in World War II and our friends for generations. But now in
1952 neither I, nor any other American, could freely and
safely cross that narrow bridge from British Hong Kong
Territory into what is now Red China.

Americans and citizens of other countries of the free world
who have been expelled have given us glimpses of what has
been happening in China but for more than three years no
free-world reporters have been permitted to enter and circu-
late in that unhappy land. From expellees and from refugees
we have had incomplete and second-hand reports. But now
Providence has favored us with the account of a trained
observer who states facts, describes experiences, and gives us
a panorama of Communist China from 1949 to 1952. This
account is from the talented pen of Reverend Mark Tennien,

American Maryknoll priest, who wrote a day to day diary, even during his months in jail, noting what he saw and recording what he heard during those bitter years.

"No Secret Is Safe" is tragic history. It tells the story of Communist aggression and domination. It recounts the methods of Communist indoctrination. It explains how fanaticism is stimulated and mob hatreds aroused. It describes Communist procedures in obtaining confessions of guilt. It demonstrates how Communism works!

The methods of the Communists are most efficient and alarming especially because of the thoroughness of their attempts to destroy all religions and to root out of men's hearts a belief in God. Father Tennien describes in detail this ruthless campaign and also tells us of the inspiring fortitude with which the Chinese Christians cling to their faith even to the sacrifice of martyrdom.

Father Tennien's years on his native Vermont farm, and later in finance work, gave him an unusual background to evaluate the Land Reform Program of the Communists. He observes and faithfully records grassroot reactions to government "reforms" and the government's many desperate measures to cope with economic crises, which is euphemistic for famine and starvation.

The facts themselves are sensational and Father Tennien's calm, straightforward style of reporting lends credence and force to his story, the story of tyranny, brutality and terror, yes, but also a story of heroism, sacrifice and hope on the part of Chinese; and a warning and an example to us Americans to cherish and preserve our faith and our freedoms.

F. Cardinal
Spellman

Part One

CHAPTER I

Enter the Communists

THIS STORY begins in November, 1949. China's entire
mainland, except a small corner in the southwest, had
fallen to the Communist armies. Their conquest was
certain. Effective resistance by the Nationalist army was
broken. Retreat with rear-guard action was carried on while
the Nationalists evacuated what troops they could save to
Formosa.

Parts of the southern provinces of Kwangtung and
Kwangsi were all that remained of Free China on the mainland. Communist armies from three directions were now
sweeping into Kwangsi Province which had been my home
for over twenty years.

Dead leaves were flying by in the November wind, summer was passing, winter was walking in. The retreat of this
last body of Nationalist troops going by the mission was the
end of the old regime and the entry of the new.

I found myself thinking of the years since 1928 when my
life began in China. They had their ups and downs, their

pleasure with success, their tears with failure; their harrassment of bandit attacks, civil wars, bombings and the Japanese invasion during the World War. There was a gap of two years, 1933-34, when I was carried out of China with T.B. to a California sanitorium. Going back to finish the span — for mission work is a life work — I had learned to eat Chinese, think Chinese and live Chinese in a slower, pleasurable way. Hard going in those early days had planed off the rough spots to fit the groove of Chinese life. China was now home to me. My heart had sunk deep roots into the land of China and belonged there, and I wanted to grow old and leave my remains in the earth there.

Communism was closing in and this new era was coming fast. It might uproot and cast me out, though I must try to weather it.

In the garden there in South China where we plant with the fall, I let the good earth squeeze through my fingers. The mountains and the loam that a farmer's son loves reminded me of the farm in Pittsford, Vermont, where I spent my boyhood in the marble and granite hills.

The days in China had been good days. There were only four American priests with their two hundred converts when I got to Kwangsi in 1928. Now there were over fifty Maryknoll missioners, eight Chinese priests and over thirty thousand converts. We had grown up through blunders, failures and tries, and had gotten experience and maturity. Since 1946, our efforts were answered by five thousand converts each year in Kwangsi. Would this all stop with the entry of the Communists? What would happen to us? What would happen to our people?

Communism in China did not die when Chiang Kai-shek broke with the system nearly twenty-five years ago. Communists went underground and worked to honeycomb the nation and undermine the government in power. War favored them. They got control of large areas, consolidated and built up their armies and power.

· 4 ·

A stream of civilians and missioners had escaped from Communist-governed areas to tell us their grim story. Frankly, it was hard to believe, like all unbelievable stories. Communist propaganda was hurled over the curtain as dust in our eyes. Newsmen and writers of the proper complexion were invited on a tour behind the curtain. Their accounts contradicted the words of men who lived there, who had escaped to tell the facts. News accounts and propaganda were in conspiracy to confuse us.

Disaster in the distance often fails to move us deeply. I could not fully believe the horrors escaped men were telling. Somehow I believed like other deluded people "It can't happen here." Now, however, the time had come, and I was about to see Communism for myself.

Just before I arrived in China, Chiang Kai-shek had broken with Russia and the Chinese Communists. His government had been tolerant and kindly toward missions. Our stations multiplied until missioners were located hardly thirty miles apart in many areas. Freedom in China was much the same as it was in America. We worked, traveled and visited at will. Roads were built and the unification of the country was progressing. Schools were established and helped by the government. A modern system of education was built up for the masses, and even the girls, who had been so long ignored, were now going to school to learn the elements of education. No one knew what effect the new regime would have on all these changes.

The station where I had been since 1946 was a county seat, a town called Shumkai. A pointer on the map at Hong Kong tracing up the West River two hundred and fifty miles will it will come to Shumkai. Here in the interior, about three find Wuchow, then southwest toward Indo-China fifty miles, hundred miles from Hong Kong, I was about to see the end of the Nationalist regime that I had lived under for twenty-one years and then to experience Communism in practice for two years. In these pages I shall try to describe the things I saw with the Communist take-over, their methods and rule during that time. We were committed to stay and see it through until we were forced out. That has always been mission policy towards changing regimes.

By the end of November, 1949, the war to control China was close to our town of Shumkai. Tension was high and was increased by the many frightening rumors. Villagers along the highway and the nearby places were locking their homes and skipping off to relatives or friends living in the mountains. There was rush and confusion everywhere. Straw-sandled coolies wearing umbrella-shaped bamboo hats, with baskets of luggage slung from their shoulder poles, hustled by. Barefoot farming women with their baggage or babies strapped to their backs plodded off through the dry rice paddies to a safer refuge. Merchants cached their wares or carried them off to the hills.

Retreating Nationalist troops trailed by the mission. The iron shoes of their pack mules clanked over the stones. When the tired soldiers stopped to rest, I asked them if Wuchow was still in Nationalist hands. "It was yesterday," they answered, "but it will be abandoned soon." This might be my last chance to see fellow missioners in Wuchow. I started out by jeep, weaving over the fifty miles through groups of retreating troops and refugees toward Wuchow. By keeping a sharp eye ahead, I hoped to be able to turn back if the Communist flag or troops showed in the distance. When I arrived at Yunghi six miles up and across the river from Wuchow, I stopped to judge my prospects of getting into Wuchow city. Troops straggling out of Wuchow said it was now impossible to get in. There were machine-gun bursts and shell blasts in the distance. The soldiers urged me to return home to Shumkai while I could. Before I left Yunghui I talked a few minutes with Father Joseph McDonald of Boston who was stationed there. The rat-tat-tat-tat of machine guns and exploding shell blasts hurried our conversation. He was left alone to face the Communist army first.

On the road home I filled the jeep with retreating Nationalists. These boys had been fighting and retreating for the last year, all the way from North China. They were worn out and dispirited, but there was good order and discipline all during the weeks we saw them in retreat.

The last day of November brought the end of Nationalist troops passing by. That afternoon the last company of retreating soldiers crossed the wooden bridge leaving Shumkai. They gathered rice straws from the recently harvested fields, and piled it over the planks. When the rear guard passed over, torch bearers kindled the fire and the last troops plodded down the road out of sight.

Father Arthur Dempsey from Peekskill, N. Y., who came to China in 1929, was my nearest neighbor toward the west — fifty miles away. I thought maybe I could phone him at his station, Jungyuen, since retreating troops were marching that way. At the telephone exchange men were feverishly dismantling the place and carrying equipment off to the hills. They had left one phone to give the final message. The manager got me through. Father Dempsey talked with a strange excitement in his voice, for he could hear the rumble of exploding shells in the distance. Communist troops had cut into the flank of retreating columns and they had to fight their way through. A few moments after our talk, business was finished, the last phone unscrewed from the wall and carried away.

The deserted town was lonesome as a cemetery. The alleys were deserted and the doors of the empty shops were locked. Battle had bequeathed the town to me, it seemed. People had urged me to take refuge in one of the remote villages, away from the path of war. They said I could wait out the fight there and return when it was over, but I chose to stay.

At the convent were two Chinese sisters and two lady

teachers I had asked to stay with them. I told them to bolt and bar the doors, answer no one and stay out of sight when the Communist troops arrived. Teacher Paul Chau and my cook Martin Neep volunteered to stay with me at the mission and see it through.

Three days of nervous waiting followed. The market was abandoned, so we lived on canned goods. Silence had dropped over the whole valley. Here and there a rooster crowed, a dog barked, or a whiff of smoke rose, showing that a few watchers had stayed and locked themselves in their homes. Bright-feathered birds sallied from bush to bush or skipped over the dead grass.

The desert solitude of the valley was broken now and then by someone hurrying back from the hills to get more baggage. That night two looters, thinking no one was at the mission, came prowling around the place. Sleep came hard those nights so I heard them. Jumping up I shouted from the upstairs porch:

"What are you doing around here? Who are you?"

"Looking for a stray pig." Then they dashed off into the darkness. With government, police and soldiers gone, and people away, they were taking advantage of the times.

December 2 was the third day of anxious waiting. I finished Mass and knelt in prayer. Sister Theresa ran back from the convent to announce in a frightened whisper:

"The Communists are here, peeping at the town from the hill down the road."

I went up on the porch to look. Before long half a dozen crouching soldiers came running along in spurts, dropping behind the trees for shelter. They motioned me to lie flat. They dropped behind a bank near town and set off a squirt of machine-gun bullets. No answer came so they got up and walked cat-like into the deserted town. A group carrying radio equipment soon followed them in.

When the sun was low that afternoon, long columns of General Lin Piao's troops reached the town and started to

· 8 ·

tramp by on their forced march. Soft caps with ear laps tied over the top held a star pinned on the front. they wore new green uniforms stuffed with cotton against the winter cold. Their legs were wrapped in winding puttees and their feet were shod with tennis shoes that hardly disturbed the silence or scuffed the dust. Only when the pack mules paraded by did the gravel crunch and clink with the blows from their iron shoes.

No harm or special attention was directed toward us. Right now the hare and hound race was on, and the hound held to the scent rushing by. We breathed easier, but sleep came only in snatches. The mission was the first building at the edge of town, and passing troops banged our doors all night long. Sometimes it was to ask directions and to find out where they were, sometimes to ask for drinking water, sometimes to borrow the stove to cook a meal, and sometimes it was the intelligence men to get information.

Next morning I nearly lost the cook in the first clash with them. Each company or battalion was seizing a local citizen as guide. A column appeared just as my cook came from the brook with two buckets of water. A soldier dashed in to take him along as a guide; but Lin Piao's soldier found me rushing out the door to hold onto the cook. I pushed the cook away from him and started a stiff argument in his own Mandarin language. In the local dialect which the soldier did not understand, I told the cook to skip out back and hide while we argued. When the soldier looked around the cook was gone, and he had to run to take his place in the column disappearing down the road. After that my cook was out of sight to every passing column.

For ten days and nights troops tramped past, detouring upstream from the burned bridge. By counting the number passing each hour, I estimated that around 100,000 were in this army. A bottleneck foot bridge got the troops slowly across while the mules waded, feeling their way on gravel three feet under the rapids. The flat stretch of road in front of the mission was a tempting resting place and many companies called a halt. I talked to groups of them each day, when I saw they were not hostile and not friendly, but something in between. They were suspicious and grim and seemed afraid to talk much with me.

One officer asked about the diocese, the bishop and Church in terms that gave him away. I said, "You are a Catholic, aren't you?" He answered with a slight nod which those around did not see. When they were billeted in nearby villages, a soldier or two stole in at night for the sacraments. One youngster told me his brother was a priest in North China. All said they were not permitted to practice their religion openly.

During their rest by the roadside the tired soldiers often unwound their puttees or took off their shoes. Their morale was high, and now, flushed with victory, they were jubilant. Although under forced march of forty miles a day, none of them would admit he was tired. Each carried his rice ration strapped across the shoulder in a bag shaped like a long stocking. Their rice was cooked twice a day. Some carried the leftovers in a tin cup and they munched the cold rice during rest. One officer showed me his carbine and said:

"This came from your country. All our good weapons are American made, taken away from the defeated Nationalists."

The first division of troops to pass was well equipped, but those coming after were too poorly armed to be called a fighting force. Time and again I counted, and on the average only one soldier in ten carried a gun. These masses of men depended on capturing equipment or picking up the guns of fallen comrades.

Another officer who was quite friendly said, "You won't have much trouble with the fighting men, but those who come after and the political men will be difficult. Your troubles with them will be many."

After ten days the Communist army had passed, and there was silence again. People who took flight stayed away for months in spite of attractive posters to call them back. Communist soldiers felt hurt because the citizens ran off and no one was here to celebrate their entry. Baffled to find me at the mission, they often asked, "Aren't you afraid?"

Christmas was desolate. A few people stole out through the deserted valley for the feast. One asked me to come to his village five miles off the road for Mass. While I was away a company of engineers came back to rebuild the burned bridge.

Sometime during the dark rainy night they reached Shumkai and pounded on the mission door. No one heard them. The cook slept soundly in his room at the garage. They climbed to the upstairs porch and broke the door into my room. No one was home so they hesitated to take over then. Shortly after I returned next day and found the door bashed in, a petty Communist officer pushed in to announce:

"We must take over your house for officers quarters."

"No, you will not," I answered him; "I have read the posters your army put up around town."

The posters, signed by Communist leaders Mao Tse-tung and Chou En-lai, guaranteed the protection of foreign nationals and their property. One of the passing soldiers had also exhibited his copy of regulations stating they could occupy no church or any mission building without permission of the man in charge. These I quoted with the comment:

"You will not have my permission!"

He insisted on looking over the house and when we came to the smashed door I pointed, saying, "Your men broke down that door; is that your protection of foreign nationals?"

He ignored the accusation and pressed his demand for the house. Heated argument followed for two hours. I stuck to my refusal, so he went off grumbling and mumbling; but the siege was not over.

Communists sent on any mission are disciplined to attain their objective at all costs. In their own eyes and in the view of the party, they are failures if they cannot attain what they are sent for. They use every argument and every means to weary you and wear you down, so they may report "mission accomplished."

Next morning the officer was back to renew his attack. Hours of altercation followed. Finally he threatened:

"If you do not give us the house we can station guards around the mission and make it most unpleasant for you."

"Go ahead, but that will not make me give permission."

"We can move in anyway, what can you do?"

"You can take it by force, but . . ."

"Do not say by force; Communists are not allowed to use force; you must grant permission."

"But if you use force," I said, ignoring the interruption, "I shall write to Mao Tse-tung and your General Lin Piao."

"You cannot send a letter to them unless I censor it first."

"Oh yes, I can. You do not cover all the post offices in Kwangsi."

My antagonist dropped his bullying shouts and remarked, "You must not write; if Communist soldiers disobey regulations they are finished," and he drew his finger across his throat.

That just about concluded the day of exhausting argument and he went back to report no success from the day's work.

Next morning he came back to prod me for the third day. He had a new angle now. After repeating his shouting arguments without success, he concluded:

"Very well, if you will not lend us your house we must have the convent."

"Communist China wants recognition by America; she wants to be admitted to the United Nations."

"Yes, of course, she wants what is right," he asserted.

"It is not going to help China, nor will it help you, when Mao Tse-tung hears you are trying to take over foreign mission property by force."

"You must not say I am using force."

"Then put away the gun you are using to slap on the table. America is not requisitioning Chinese nationals' property there, and you have no authorization to take our property here."

"Chinese in America are not real Chinese; they must all be brought back here and indoctrinated."

This confirmed a Communist viewpoint on just who is one of the Chinese people. Mao Tse-tung in his book, *On Peoples Democratic Dictatorship* published in July, 1949, writes:

" 'You are not benevolent.' Correct. We definitely have no benevolent policies towards the reactionaries or the counter-revolutionary activities of the reactionary classes. Our benevolent policy does not apply to such deeds or persons who are outside the ranks of the people, it applies only to the people."

The officer pulled a badge from his pocket with the name Chang to prove he was political advisor to Captain Lee of the engineers. They called him departmental chief, not captain. Chang boasted:

"Whatever I say goes."

"Not with me," and I handed back his dirty cloth badge.

"I have been a Communist twenty years, and never found a person so stubborn and unco-operative as you!"

Next he started to plead. How could he go back and report failure to get housing from me, was the problem troubling him now.

Dealing with passing troops, I had learned Communists hate to give their names or sign any agreement.

"Very well, I can ask the sisters to move into rooms back of the church, but first I require every officer coming here to sign an agreement guaranteeing me against damage or loss, and fixing the time of stay."

"We are not allowed to sign any agreement," and with a string of curses for my mother and grandmother he marched away.

A few days later Political Advisor Chang came to demand

the jeep for a trip to Wuchow. No buses were running. Three bridges were destroyed on the route, but a jeep could ford the streams during the winter dry season.

"No, you cannot take the jeep; but if you pay for gasoline, I am willing to drive you and the officers down."

After some argument he settled for it. Carrying their officers through Communist troops along the route would be a through ticket and I wanted to go to Wuchow for supplies. They were cold, suspicious and unfriendly toward their "fellow traveler" driving the jeep. But it was worth fighting them because the missioners who gave in had them living in their houses, tormenting them day and night.

CHAPTER II

The Local Red Regime
Is Installed

NEXT the political functionaries arrived by bus to set up the local government. They came two months after the invasion to take over from the Communist army. It was February 1, 1950. Along with them the Communist system began creeping into every phase of life and movement. Each week brought new regulations that gradually pruned away man's freedom. Travel permits were required for every move. Forms had to be filled in and a report brought to the police for any guest that was to stay overnight. Mobs were being trained in spy work. They slunk up to folks in conversation or sneaked up and sat under windows to report any shadow of complaint against the regime. Dissenters were warned and soon after, they began to disappear.

But changes were gradual during the first six months of Communist rule. They boasted continually of all the freedom they brought, even freedom of belief. The restrictive measures were creeping in almost imperceptibly, and reasons justifying each move were cleverly spread about.

As with everyone else, the wool was pulled over our eyes by their mildness and ready assurance that only necessary restrictions would be made in this land of new "democracy" and "freedom." Missioners were lulled to believe they might be allowed to continue their work in this Communist state. People thought the new government was not so bad as expected. "Chinese Communism, after all, seems different. Maybe it is really different," most people reasoned.

A sudden change from tolerance to terror, however, came right after the beginning of war in Korea. Chinese opponents, coaxed back from America, Formosa and Japan by rosy promises, now saw Communists with their masks off. Doubters lured back by the mildness of Communist rule during the first few months were jolted to the realities of terror. I copied out the following from the new sets of regulations, promulgated in the newspapers: "Death penalty for bandits who are armed, for espionage rings and assassination gangs operating with counter-revolutionary objectives and for the murder of public servants and people in general, the sabotage of factories, mines, warehouses, etc."

The retreat from tolerance started wholesale arrests. Guilty or suspect, masses of people were thrown into jail and heads began to roll in July.

I was also required to get a permit before going out to any village for sick calls or Mass. The mission dispensary was functioning every day so I could occasionally get a permit on the excuse of going out to treat the sick. People in the villages talked to me like hunted criminals. They would look out the windows and doors to see if there were listeners, then speak their opinions in whispers. In the open they would first glance over both shoulders, then in a low voice tell me of the conditions and of their sorry plight. This atmosphere of freedom dying and tyranny spreading is something that is felt rather than seen. There was sorrow where there were smiles; fear and caution where there was frankness.

The new regulations were published in the newspapers each day and new taxes were imposed. With each day new pressure and demands were carried to our door; with each night came troubles, searches, inquisitions or some other new annoyance. The crunching gravel would startle me out of a worried, waiting sleep; and when guns banged the door I could feel myself go faint and pale. It might be another demand, an accusation, another battle or perhaps only a group of lost soldiers asking the way. We lived not from day to day, but from crisis to crisis.

Each new step in government policy was evident from the increased terrorism of local officials who received their orders from the Central Government. Then some days or weeks later the official regulations were published in the newspapers.

In July, 1950, after the United Nations had taken action in Korea, a wave of arrests came. On July 23, the local newspaper published "Regulations for the suppression of Counter-Revolutionary Activities," from which I quoted above, explaining the arrests.

In December, 1950, after China joined the Korean war, a new policy of severity was in evidence. Foreign missioners were put under house arrest or in jail. The purge was stepped up. Fifth columnists who were liquidated, were called the "agents of the American invaders who prevent the Chinese people from carrying out more effectively the struggle to resist America aid Korea." The local newspaper printed this and two pages of new government policy to correct "deviation" which had crept in.

Six months later in May, 1951, the purge had reached gigantic numbers. The newspaper then published the Central Government's pleasure:

"Now the deviation toward inordinate magnanimity has

been rectified in general. As a result of the persistent suppression of counter-revolutionaries the people are rejoicing and eulogies are uttered by every mouth . . . "

In March, 1951, when I was moved from house arrest to jail, the local newspaper printed at length the extension of their purge from "the actual active opponents of the Chinese government to potential enemies."

This brief chronology of the changes in government policy may help the reader to understand the detailed events that I describe later.

The second serious clash with police came in sultry July, 1950. The police had evidently received new instructions, and a new policy of severity and terror was in practice. This clash brought me mighty close to a prison cell. The Communists planned a fiesta for their six months' anniversary of the new government in our town. They wanted a movie, projector and microphone. Chief of Police Chee sent a pressure squad to urge me to go to Yunghui and borrow Father McDonald's equipment.

The only way I could get a travel permit was on errands for the Communists, so bargaining was the order of the day. A travel permit got me away from their prodding, and I agreed to go. First we argued for hours. The Chief wanted to grant me only a two-day permit; I held out for three, to give me a day in Wuchow to buy provisions. We compromised by verbal agreement (always a mistake in dealing with Communists). If I could borrow the projector I would return next day. If not, I would spend a day in Wuchow to do my necessary shopping.

In the morning I drove to police headquarters for the travel permit. Chief Chee was tricky. He had filled out the document for only two days in order to trap me. We argued as time flew away. Finally, I gave up after recalling our verbal agreement. Between showers I stepped on the starter, and the jeep started to roll up the fifty rough miles to Yunghui. Halfway there a mountain stream in freshet had carried off a bridge. There was nothing to do but wait a day until the stream got over its rampage and settled down to where a jeep could drive through the water.

Everything was going wrong. The Communists in Yunghui had recently stopped a movie Father McDonald was showing to the neighbors. I could not really blame him for refusing a favor to them now. Next day I went shopping like a truant who knows the teacher's stick is waiting for him to come back.

Tired and muddy from laboring the jeep through the stream and shores covered with silt that challenged my right to pass for several hours, I got home. Two policemen were waiting for me at the mission.

"Who is this man with you?" they asked officiously.

"Father X from Virtue Village six miles west of here." This Chinese priest was to become a hunted man later, so I'll call him Father X.

"Has he a travel permit?"

"Yes, of course." They demanded the document, scanned it a moment and were apparently satisfied, then handed it back.

"And you, we sent you for that projector, where is it?"

"Father McDonald did not care to lend it, so it is not here."

They lit into me, saying that I had deliberately failed in carrying out their orders, disobeyed by overstaying my travel permit, was stubborn, disrespectful and imperialistic. A tired man is in no mood to be needled, and their tirade touched off a fuse. I lashed back, telling them what I thought of their police state methods, their tyranny, and their slave state where no freedom was left. Such bold words startled them and they hurried off to report me to the Chief of Police.

We had just finished supper when a gang of police banged at the door.

"Come along with us, both of you," one ordered.

Their guns covered us as we were marched down the streets to police headquarters. At the desk sat Chief Chee Yao, with his face screwed up in wrath and ugliness.

First, Chief Chee Yao demanded the travel permit from Father X's trembling hands.

"Not valid; it was not issued from here. Throw him in jail.

Police jumped up at his shout. One of them taking each of his arms, they rushed the timid Chinese priest through the room and pushed him into a cell where there were thirty prisoners panting and sweating in the hot July night. His travel papers were valid, but it seemed they wanted to terrorize him into spy work, as I discovered later.

"You overstayed your travel permit!"

"Yes, but let me explain.. " Here his shouts interrupted me.

Later: "You failed to get the movie projector."

"Yes, let me tell you about it..." Again his loud yelling stopped me.

"And you told the police there is no more freedom in China."

"Yes, and I repeat it."

Down came a storm of invectives against Americans, against me, against foreigners, against missionaries. Every time I started to reason, explain, or answer his jabs, he flooded me out with his screaming.

I was chain-smoking to hold my temper and quiet my nerves. Finally I got tired of the Chief's bullying and bluster, as he jumped into every word I tried to speak. Settling back in a chair, I smoked silently until his tirade blew itself out. Then I sat up and said quietly:

"If you are through now, I shall talk and you listen." He nodded assent. Hardly a sentence was out, however, when he shouted and slapped the table again. I pounded the desk with one hand, shook the other in his face and ordered:

"You shut up until I am through!"

The encircling police stole startled glances at each other. Such "insolence" by this "foreign imperialist" was almost unbelievable they told Father X next day, — but the Chief sat back to listen.

According to Communist routine, any person dragged into the police station is to be browbeaten into admitting guilt, then sign a confession before being released. Chief Chee was not getting anywhere in forcing me to admit guilt, so he tried new accusations.

"Last month you refused to stop your jeep at the bus station for search."

"False, I never refused to stop."

"You not only did not stop, but called out, 'I do not have to stop; Communists do not dare fire at me'."

"Another lie!"

"I'll call the officer from the bus station who heard you."

"Go ahead, I would like to hear his accusation."

The Chief sent for the bus station officer. The half-hour interim was filled by interrogation. This was my first experience under the routine used on offenders, dissenters and people under suspicion. A secretary writes everything down. The queries bring out a man's life history, his views and his friends. Hundreds of silly questions are asked about events long past. Then they are asked again at a later interrogation to try and trip up the victim.

Officer Tee who was brought to accuse me lost his nerve.

"Did Tien-Yee-Ren (Chinese for Tennien) refuse to stop for search?"

"He stopped, but protested against search."

"I may have called him a nuisance if he was troublesome," I interrupted.

"Did he say he did not have to stop because Communists dare not fire at him?"

"Well, someone in the jeep said it. I thought it was Tien-Yee-Ren."

The Chief was furious when this accusation fell flat. He

peremptorily dismissed Officer Tee. When he had gone I commented:

"Officer Tee is from North China; if I had made those remarks they would be in the local dialect, which he couldn't understand anyway."

"He understands the local dialect," lied the Chief.

"Why not call the carpenter and houseboy who were in the jeep with me? They know what was said."

Interrogation went on while he sent to get them out of bed. Chief Chee took them into another room. The testimony of both these men made a lie of Officer Tee's accusation, so the Chief came back to dismiss me until tomorrow. The five grueling hours brought me no nearer admission of guilt nor willingness to sign a confession. Under Mao Tsetung's picture the clock struck twelve. I got up to leave after the Chief's dismissal, then begged:

"Why not put me in the cell and release Father X? He has done nothing."

"Take this man away," Chief Chee ordered. A policeman took me home and stood guard all night in front of the mission.

After breakfast I was brought back for more. Fortified with two packs of cigarettes to soothe the nerves, I faced the storm of threat and accusation of the Chief and other interrogators. Our mental battle of "catch-as-catch-can" went on until the bell rang calling Chief Chee to late afternoon rice. He was wearied out; I was exhausted, but I still refused to admit guilt or sign any confession of crime.

"Go home until I send for you tomorrow." I walked out unescorted and past the prison gate next door, which might be opening for me tomorrow; but he dropped the case, and I had a few months more before I was arrested.

The Communists grew bolder and their claws pressed harder, squeezing the people into submission as time went on. Not long after the last clash with Police Chief Chee I ran into trouble with the military.

Two soldiers came boldly in one day to borrow my jeep trailer. They wanted it to haul bricks for building block houses; but on a recent trip with them the soldiers had insisted on overloading the jeep and trailer, which broke a spring. Consequently I refused their request and started to my room. The bold pair went back to the garage, pulled out the trailer and started off. I watched their action with anger. When they came by the door I dashed out, grabbed one in each hand and shoved them away. Completely stunned, they stared silently as I pushed the trailer back.

"I said no to your request; do not touch that trailer again." With this warning I walked into the house and locked the door. But they did not give up their mission without another maneuver. Caressing their burp guns, they evidently planned to force my consent. The cook came into the house to see me and one of the soldiers pushed his way in the door. He followed all the way to my room and started to shout.

"Please get out!" I tried to figure accounts with the cook, while the loud-voiced demands kept up.

"I am busy now, get out."

His continued browbeating finally got me boiling mad. I slipped my left arm through his right, which neutralized the burp gun, and then I practically carried him to the door. When I released him he backed off, faced me and cocked his gun. The cook jumped in front of me, crying:

"Don't shoot, don't shoot."

I shoved him aside, faced the gun and said:

"I am not afraid of this house breaker; now get out of here!"

"You come down to military headquarters with us," they ordered with pointing guns.

"I will not," and the door slammed in their eyes.

Their footsteps pattered away to report the incident. It was time for me to cool off and think. The military also had a prison.

A tough, bossy sergeant came back with the two soldiers

and hammered the suffering door for entry. The sergeant slapped his gun on the table to frighten me and bellowed like a bull:

"I order you to come to headquarters."

"I would be glad to go if you insist, but now, as you see, my rice is on the table. Please sit down while I go and eat."

I let the bantam sergeant rant about Communist might, Communist bravery, about the glad welcome people gave them, and other uncertain points that he shouted out to convince himself as well as me. Another day I would have disputed every point; now I was silent. When he had emptied his fangs of all their venom maybe I could reason with him.

"Will you read this copy of Mao Tse-tung's decree?"

"I cannot read," confessed the tamed sergeant.

"It states, Communists may not occupy missions or borrow their property without consent of the man in charge."

He admitted this by a nod and a grunt.

"If you push this incident, your young comrades will be in lots of trouble, for Communist soldiers have good discipline and must follow the orders of their leader Mao. This youngster forgot himself, I was harsh and rough with him. Why not both admit our fault and forget the thing?"

This gave him a way out, and the lad with a burp gun leaned to whisper in his ear. My own unpleasant fate was in the balance, and I was praying for a way out. The sergeant got back his commanding poise and thundered:

"Hereafter when you are ordered to come to headquarters you must obey."

"Yes."

"And dealing with us you must be *lao shih*." (This means tame or gentle.)

"Very well."

I meekly listened to his long lecture, then breathed a sigh of relief as the trio marched off. Another near miss had cheated the jail cooties from feasting on my blood.

An aftermath with a smile came a few days later. When I went downtown the lad thrown out of my room ran out to greet me. He put his arm around my shoulder and invited me to their quarters for a cigarette.

"Good friends, aren't we, venerable Tennien?"

"Good friends. *Hsiao shih wang chi liao* — The little affair is forgotten."

Communists are still Chinese and they had lost face as the news was whispered about town. Old Chinese custom follows a winding route to ask any favor — a delightful diplomacy! They primed a businessman to ask my cook to ask me if I would lend the trailer a day. It would give them back face, the merchant explained. I gave it to them with a chuckle. Humor is not quite dead in China when tragedy can end in laughter.

Little altercations continued almost daily. They were like probing attacks to test my resistance. But it was nearly a month before the next big clash. The process of interrogation and threats held me for days this time, but I shall state it briefly.

One afternoon a Communist general who had studied in Russia and Japan came to arrange for jeep transportation to Wuchow. He offered to pay travel expenses, so I agreed to take him next morning.

Later that afternoon in August, Father Justin Kennedy of Long Island, N. Y., came in by motorbike for a visit. The guard at the bus station yelled that his travel permit was invalid. After a session of shouting and kicking the motorbike, he arrested Father Kennedy. I heard the argument and told the guard he and his government were a domineering nuisance. He arrested me also for this criticism and the two of us were marched to the police station to face Chief Chee for interrogation and sentence.

I faced my antagonist of many bouts, Police Chief Chee Yao. Chee was a personable fellow — pleasant enough off duty when suspicious Communists were not within ear shot to spy on him. Tall for a Chinese, he was five feet ten; handsome, without the Mongolian features of most northerners, muscular and hardened by years of soldiering in Communist campaigns, Chief Chee cut an impressive figure. The young Chee worked in a foreign embassy in Peking where he picked up a passable knowledge of English. If any Communists were near when he tried out a few sentences on me they warned him in harsh command, — speak Chinese. He could flash a winsome smile when asking some special favor. But the same face could be twisted into frightening utter ugliness, the routine make-up for a Communist functionary on duty. As we drew near he took a sip of strong tea like a metamorphic potion, and looked up with the fearsome monstrous mask of Dr. Jekyl.

He heard the guard's account, then sentenced us to jail in Wuchow. He directed the guard to escort us there in my own jeep the next day.

In the morning the Communist general failed to find me at the mission. He stormed into police headquarters where an officer was questioning Father Kennedy and me.

"What are you doing?" he shouted at the officer.

"Writing up the case against these men before sentencing them to Wuchow."

"Well, stop it! I have arranged for Tien-Yee Ren to take me and my staff to Wuchow."

When the jeep was loaded, Chief Chee ordered the guard and Father Kennedy to crowd in. I complained that the overload would break the jeep springs.

"Take these two men out of here," the General called to the Chief of Police.

Police then stood at attention while I drove off with the General and staff. When I returned to Shumkai a day later Chief Chee was alone in his office.

"I am sorry if I insulted your guard at the bus station."

"Will you and Father Kennedy sign confessions stating

· 26 ·

that? If you will do this, I'll settle the case here, and not send you to the Wuchow jail."

We agreed to sign. It took another day before we could agree to the terminology of confessing guilt. Finally he was satisfied, and the next day he released us from arrest and sent us back to the mission free again. We had cheated the jail once more, but, with severity increasing, we knew it would not be long before our time would come.

I shared the gloom of the people, when new restrictions came along each month. Marriages were held without a feast lest the government put the finger on them as capitalists or at least as having money. On the birth of a manchild, my cook asked me if he could hold a little feast upstairs in my house where wandering soldiers or spies would not see the spread. A handful of his trusted friends came stealing in to celebrate in secret.

The Communists were gradually tightening the noose they held round the necks of the general public. But special measures against Americans also came in stages, along with changes in world events. When United Nations entered the Korea conflict in June and Truman's declaration jolted them, the Communists here got their orders from above. They took away our freedom of movement and watched us as spies. Mission work was halted and the priests could not move out, even for a sick call. I was the only exception in our diocese where thirty some Americans worked, and this was because of the jeep. Every week or two the Communist officials had some urgent need for transportation and they were forced to give me a travel permit to take them. In order to prevent trips to places where I did not wish to travel, I kept vital parts of the motor and carburetor hid. I crossed the wires, spread the distributor points and added a secret ignition switch hidden behind the dash. An expert mechanic, even if he could replace the dismantled parts, would need from hours to days in order to trace down so many things thrown out of kilter.

One day the Communists tried to start the jeep. Officials had pressed hard for a trip to Nanning, 270 miles away, and I did not want to go.

"The jeep is out of order," I tried to convince them.

"We can get it going."

"You may try, but it really needs a lot of time for repairs and I cannot get to it now."

They churned the starter, whirled the crank, juggled the carburetor, juggled the wires, puffed and sweated pushing the jeep up and down the road. Still the belabored motor refused to give out a cough, a sneeze or a puff. They had to give up after hours of fruitless labor. Always after that they were forced to write a travel permit and let me out of confinement to take them.

The next big step in closing down on us came in November, 1950, when the Chinese Communists crossed the Yalu into Korea and joined the war "against Americans."

The middle of December, 1950, our newspaper carried the article from Peking *Peoples' Daily,* the mouthpiece for the Communist Party. "Cadres do not understand clearly and fully the government policy. Some of our cadres have confused the severe suppression of counter-revolutionary activities with the consolidation of the united front, confused the objection to indiscriminate arrests and killings with the severe punishment of arch criminals, confused the suppression with magnanimity with the result that deviation of boundless magnanimity was not corrected in time . . ." The government thereupon ordered new measures to be carried out ruthlessly, and now the wholesale arrests included Americans. Officials took the upbraiding to heart, and a purge on a big scale started with arrests, trials and executions.

Late November, 1950, just before the new instructions came, the police were forced to give me a travel permit to Watlam, in order to repair a jeep spring they had broken. Watlam police seventy miles west had evidently just received the new orders. They pounced on me like a spy caught at large, searched my clothes and my underwear, my shoes and socks. It seemed they were puzzled to find me not yet interned in .my mission and had to ask the Provincial headquarters what to do. As excuse to hold me, they claimed my travel permit was invalid. They searched the jeep all day, took off everything unscrewable for a look-see, even pulled off the tires to feel and peep inside. The jeep was held at headquarters and I was detained at the mission with orders not to move out.

Three weeks went by as I stayed with Father George Gilligan of Brooklyn, New York. He had come to China in 1930. Usually a lively argumentative conversationalist, the house detention since July had left Father Gilligan low in spirits. Things were moving fast now. Communists came one day and took his radio; the English paper from Hong Kong was stopped in the mails; letters, though censored, had been delivered before, but now they stopped. The iron curtain was dropping. Night searches of the house and daily questionings became common.

December days had half run out when police told me to come for the jeep and drive directly back home. (I was glad to get away from the annoying visits of police in Watlam.) But at home the police had also received the new orders and turned to a new chapter with the Chinese invasion of Korea. The Chief of Police informed me that henceforth no travel permit could be given me under any circumstances. Although there was no guard assigned to stay with me, I was ordered to remain at the mission and was told that I would be arrested if I stirred out.

There was no restriction on walking about the yard, and people with courage still called to see me. A few days after my return, a bicycle rider from Watlam brought news that Father Gilligan and his assistant, Father Chang, had been locked away in jail. After five months' imprisonment, Father Gilligan was subjected to public trial and then expelled from China.

Another messenger told us that our bishop and missioners in Wuchow had been led off to jail the night of December 19. Messages and rumors flew in to say that priests and sisters of every nationality were being picked up on false charges or on planted evidence. The big change had gone into effect, and I saw great numbers of people rounded up and marched toward the jail. Later we came to know other reasons for the change. The new regime had been here a year and now the land reforms, which I'll describe later, were starting. The machinery had been readied and they were plowing a vast turnover in the first great stage to inaugurate and plant Communism everywhere. Americans felt special measures of the Communists' resentment, for the United States was leading in halting their aggression. But religion was their prime target since it was a counter force which must be either bent to submission or crushed. And so their measures struck at every missioner, both Chinese and foreign.

Terror tactics were further intensified now, and traps were laid to catch us in some misdemeanor. Police came day and night with demands and searches trying to prod us to anger. Plainclothes men dropped around to engage us in tempting chatter that might bring out some criticism of the government. They asked around to find someone willing to accuse me but found no one.

Now I was certain I would be arrested, and it became only a matter of time. Christmas was sad, for the recent terroristic measures had frightened the people and only about a hundred braved the Communist anger to come in for Mass. And New Year was dark, for a friend who had attended a government meeting sent word that the mission was to be taken over, and I was to be held under house arrest in one room with guards to watch me. This would be in about two weeks, he said. The remaining days were like time in the death cell.

CHAPTER III

Arrest

SATURDAY MORNING, January 20, 1951, was a dark day, cold and misty. I finished breakfast and sat for a while talking to the cook boy as he picked up the dishes. It was strangely quiet. Almost every day for the last half month the group that had been organized for the land reforms, and villagers nearby had been noisily buzzing by the mission.

Suddenly a rumble of yells filled the quiet. An armed mob of several hundred people came running toward the mission over the knoll from nearby Kom village. They had been forming there in ambush, and on a signal stampeded (like Indians around a covered wagon) to surround the mission. The simple villagers had been fed the propaganda I was later to read in their books in jail — that all Americans were trained to kill. One of the Christians heard a villager say afterward, they thought that I would have hidden machine guns to shoot down a mob of them before I gave up.

They surrounded the mission and covered it with guns

from every direction. The land reform group men, long seasoned by Communist indoctrination, were leading the mob. These reformers rushed towards the mission door, pounded it with their guns and shouted, "Open up."

I threw down my napkin, put out my cigarette and then walked over to slide the door bolt. I was frankly scared and puzzled by this surprise attack.

As the door opened they rushed in and thrust Luger pistols at me from every angle. They pushed me out the door with their guns and felt me over for hidden arms. My cook intervened, "Don't push him around like that; he is not a criminal." For his pains he was pushed along with me. We were lined up outside the mission near the highway. The mission help and families were brought to join our ranks. Next the two Chinese Sisters were led out, and last of all some Catholic masons and a carpenter we had building a kitchen were lined up with us.

Strolling up and down the road was a policeman, one of the force that was supposed "to protect the foreigner and his property," as their earlier posters claimed. In their typical devious manner of acting, the police force and officials of the county had used the village as a cat's paw. The villagers, led by land reformers, came in high hope of loot, as we heard them say. If there were any unfortunate accidents or incidents, the police and other officials would disclaim all knowledge and responsibility. But if the take over was accomplished smoothly by the armed villagers then the police would step in.

It was a fixed job, and the policeman strolling there was just an observer. I tried to signal him to come nearer so I could claim police protection, but he ignored me and walked farther away.

We stood for hours in the mist and cold wind while the land reform group and village leaders with them ransacked the house, church, convent and servants' quarters. They said they must search for guns, radio sending sets and other

· 32 ·

contraband. There was glee and chuckling when they found three new packs of cards. Gambling instruments were not allowed in the New China they said, so the cards must be confiscated. They pocketed the cards without giving me a receipt. "Those cards will never be cast in a bonfire," I thought.

The head of the land reform group came over to us and delivered one of the packaged lectures from the propaganda book. It was the usual, — American common people are good, many of them are already Communists. But the American capitalists, and leaders such as Truman and MacArthur, hold them in slavery. Now imperialist America is our enemy, invading our fatherland. During the land reforms of the next six months or so, we cannot permit you to teach religion for you are American. Today we are to close and seal the mission and you are to cease all activity during land reform. The church we shall not seal for we need to use that as a meeting hall.

The searchers finished their task toward noon. Since they found nothing more wicked or startling than playing cards, all the mission personnel were questioned about where I had "the guns." The inquiries met with no success. Finally they ordered the mission help and me to pick up some clothes and personal effects; all of us were to be crowded into the Sisters' convent. The cook and his wife, the catechist and his family, a carpenter and several masons shouldered their duffel and were all herded along with me to the convent. As we went out the searchers locked every door and picked up all the keys from the priest's house and servants' quarters. Official papers were pasted over every door declaring the closure of the mission. The land reform leader called his helpers and the village mob and went off.

We moved into the convent, a house of three rooms and attic. We could all breathe easier even in crowded quarters, for we knew something of what was up. And now the first act was over.

The greatest disappointment to us all was that we were not allowed to go into the church to get vestments and the things required for Mass. The Sisters, as wise as they are simple, told us that their key to the church had not been surrendered. The mob and the land reform group had all gone for afternoon rice. I told the Sisters that I would watch by the road and signal if anyone was approaching. They slipped in and locked the door behind them while they gathered things needed from the altar. When they rattled the door, I signaled that no one was passing near and they carried the Mass equipment to the convent. It was our good fortune and blessing to have Mass each morning.

After straightening out the confusion of duffel, I was settled in a corner of the slant-roof attic. The carpenter and masons were parked with me in the one big room. The mission help and families took the Sisters' spare room.

Covering the slant-roof attic were tiles, laid loosely. The wintery wind sweeping through the crevices under loose tiles made the attic as cold as it was outside under the stars. When it rained the tiles sponged up water, and our clothes stayed wet and soggy all day long. This prison in January was not unlike a dungeon.

On the ground floor charcoal braziers were set up and we cooked the first meal that evening. We rolled up in quilts on the floor and went to sleep while the sabbath turned to Sunday.

Next morning Assistant Chief of Police P'ang went with the land reform men to Kom village and demanded the keys, peremptorily stating that their task had ended. The farmers saw they had been cheated out of the expected loot, and a heated argument followed. They finally gave up the keys to the men's wing only. As a concession to the people, police told them they could have the use of the chapel for their meetings. They would also be given the rice grain the mission had stored, for distribution to their poorer families. On Satday Kom village farmers took over the church and put up posters announcing it was to be their school. They claimed the jeep and mission goods were their loot prize and started hauling things away.

This was Sunday, the morning after the seizure. The Assistant Chief of Police came with twelve police guards. They broke the seal on the men's wing and stationed their guards "to keep the villagers from further looting and protect the foreigner," they said. Actually they came to isolate me and keep me under house arrest and guard.

The Farmers' Chairman from Kom village was called to police headquarters and was forced to give all the keys and to return the lamps, kerosene and other things they had hauled away from the mission on the day of closing. We felt more secure with the armed guards to keep the mob from arson and looting.

The news of yesterday's events flashed across the countryside. But, even so, the Catholics began to show up for Sunday Mass. Most of them left as they saw the church doors closed and armed police standing around. About twenty of the faithful made their way to the convent for Mass. The guards let them in, but they were told that hereafter they must stay away.

Monday, the second day after the seizure, Police Chief Chee Yao visited us. He told the help and the Sisters they must make preparations to go away, for I was to be isolated and kept under house arrest and guard during the land reform months. Maybe he thought I would be scared out by the happenings of the last few days. Certainly he hoped I would. First he asked if I was going to leave China. I said, "I can't without orders." He urged me to write my superiors and ask if they were not going to call us out of China. Asked if he had any orders from higher echelons to throw us out, he answered no. I told him we were here for the spiritual welfare of the people and unless ordered out by the government or our ecclesiastical superiors we would not leave.

After all, it was not desirable for them to have me here

as an observer whose thoughts and voice they could not control. I took the Chief of Police to task then and there for desecrating the church and putting it to the profane use of a meeting hall. It was evident that he wished I'd pick up and leave. With me out of the way, they could grab and carry off things from the mission without protests, taunts and accusations from me.

Chief Chee could not very well talk to the mission help, the way we were all jumbled together, so he told them to come down to the police station that afternoon. He seemed to believe he could thrust a wedge between me and the mission family, and turn the help against me.

His theme in the lecture to the help was: America is the imperialistic invading enemy of China. You are Chinese and must not continue to work for the American priest. A travel permit will be issued, and all of you must leave and return home within a few days. To justify closure of the mission in their eyes, he told them that America had confiscated the property of Chinese in America and was expelling them from American shores. The Chief then told them American troops were badly defeated in Korea and only four divisions were now left to destroy. In Europe, he continued, France and Italy were on the verge of turning Communist. Only America opposed this movement of the people and because America is wealthy it will take time to defeat her. Hence, the help were told they must march along with the Communist movement. There is a new order, or society, in China now and you must have the new mentality only. He ordered them not to repeat his conversation to me. The help returned and faithfully recounted all that was told them.

A week and two days of our cubby hole existence had passed, when police from headquarters led by the Assistant Chief barged in to state that everybody except the priest must get out within two hours. The Sisters were handed travel permits to return to their Motherhouse in Pakhoi.

They gathered up wet clothes just washed and hurriedly packed. The workmen were also handed travel permits and ordered home. There were few buses running, so the Sisters and workmen had to sit waiting in the bus station for two days. From now on I was to be held in solitary confinement. I could not go out to the bus station a hundred yards away nor could they come back and pick up forgotten articles.

In a little while they were gone. I walked through the littered house, staring at the broom, the water buckets and shoulder pole, the charcoal brazier and pots and pans. The pacing of the guards outside the door was the only sound invading my solitude. The guard would buy the raw food I ordered, but after that I was on my own.

I picked up the broom and started cleaning up and straightening out the confusion left by the quick departure of the mission help. Perhaps the police and government officials thought that by making things difficult I would ask to leave.

It came time to eat so I got together the tea kettle, frying pan and small kettles. There was no baking since our stove was only a charcoal brazier. The charcoal stove was a little potbellied affair, fashioned from clay, then baked. I had once cooked for a summer camp, but I had never cooked rice, so that was my first downfall. One must cover the rice with double its volume of water. The rice swells as it boils, soaks up the water and then a slow heat steams it dry. But I had poured in only a little water and went about other work. When I next looked, smoke from the charred rice was fanning out around the cover. There was nothing to do but throw it out and try again. The second try brought success, and I had a pot of nice mealy rice.

Next came the vegetables and pork. It was a few days before I got the knack of seasoning and flavors, but soon I could please an epicure. I had a tin of flour, but there was no way to bake bread. However, fried cakes would make a desirable variation from rice so I decided on fried cakes for one of the two daily meals. Here in China, just as back on the farm in Vermont, I had home-cured half a dozen slabs of bacon every winter. There was still on hand plenty of R. & G. coffee bought from army surplus after the war. Hence, the morning meal of fried cakes, with bacon to take in the fingers and tickle the palate, and coffee to wash away the morning scowl made the house arrest and isolation less trying. It was too good to last.

Cooking can become a creative art. But the kitchen sink with its piles of post meal dishes, pots and pans is the heart-breaking task where I did bitter penance. Wash day over a scrubbing board was far less agonizing, or hauling water from the valley stream below.

Three days went by and Thursday, February 1, came. Tomorrow would be the First Friday. A group of Catholic women came to the field beside the mission and started digging roots for firewood. When the guard walked around the back wing of the mission for evening meal, they slipped nearer to the open window where I stood.

They asked if there was some way for them to receive Holy Communion the next day. I quickly heard their confessions and told them to return tomorrow morning and dig roots again. At Mass I consecrated the extra hosts and placed them in a small tin ointment box. Next morning about a hundred feet away from the open window they were again swinging picks into the brush roots. I went about the chore of cooking breakfast. In a short while the guard walked around the mission for breakfast with the other guards. I beckoned one of the women to come to the window. Quickly handing over the ointment box with the Sacred Hosts, I gave word for them to take communion themselves there in the field. They knelt on the carpet of pasture grass among the clusters of brush and received the Host.

The Christians were bringing me cigarettes, eggs, vegetables and food. For the first few days the guards let them hand the gifts through the window, but evidently on orders they forbade them to continue. Whatever food was to be purchased would have to be done by them, and they had orders to restrict my purchases to a bare minimum.

Garden season here in South China is during the winter, and the garden was like hidden treasure. With the guards' permission I could step out to the garden and gather vegetables needed. Carrots, turnips, cabbage, tomatoes, lettuce and greens flourished. My cook whom they had sent home stole in every few days with meat, salt, lard, etc. But the guards threatened him with jail if he came again, so that source was stopped. My persecutors were tightening up all the time.

Men from the police now had the mission keys and started taking things from the mission. They always use the word "borrow." It is a prettier word than "steal." Their reasoning is that Communism is the people's government and soldiers and police are servants of the people. The people therefore must co-operate by lending, and pressure is used when people decline or hesitate to lend.

First they drove off in my jeep I had bought from the Foreign Liquidation Commission. Next day they came for the drum of gasoline I held in reserve. (After America stopped shipments of gasoline in September, the price had jumped to $3 U.S. per gallon.) Police Chief Chee stood around while others opened the gas drum. I could not complacently look on, so I called from the window, "First you take my jeep and now you steal all my gasoline. Is this observing international law?" I was not born a diplomat! Chief Chee came nearer with a menacing frown, and said, "I'm only borrowing the jeep to keep in safe custody during land-reform months." Then he shouted, "Communists keep international laws to the letter."

After that when they came to carry off stuff from the mission they instructed the guard to keep me away from the window so I could not be a witness. (But the upstairs window gave me almost as clear a view.) Later they took several rolls of electric wiring, and a dozen bulbs, three empty kerosene drums, tools, spare parts for the jeep, a new tire, camera, films, some of the canned goods and medicines that they needed from the dispensary. However, they took only small amounts of the total, and after all one must allow for human weakness. The things were a big temptation to these "have-not" borrowers.

One day after Police Chief Chee took out some canned food, the guard, a pleasant youngster from the country, asked me if they had sought my permission. I told him no, that it is not right to steal. "Yes, but they have the power and guns in their hands and can do as they like." Then he asked a startling question, "When do you think a world war will come to get rid of this government?"

About ten days after my house arrest, the crowd from Kom village that had helped in the taking over of the mission came in led by a policeman. He opened the storeroom over the garage and told the people to take out the rice grain. This was evidently the village bonus for their work in closing the mission. I heard later that the grain would be used for relief among the village poor. I had bought the grain at November harvest time when the price was low and planned on having the grain for mission expenses during the winter months.

The villagers got thirty piculs (about sixty bushels) for their bonus and seventy piculs were brought to police head-quarters. I was left none at all. Perhaps they were going to try starving me out. At a meeting of the police later, they remarked that all my goods were "frozen," but I could apply to police headquarters for enough funds to eat. I had been put off twice when I asked (but maybe they would loosen their purse strings later).

Chief Chee's idea of keeping the jeep in safe custody was

to drive it around the drill ground several days to learn how to drive. He thought then that he was a proficient driver. He overloaded the jeep with people and started for Wuchow fifty miles away. Halfway there he lost control, ran off the road and tipped over. Everybody was bruised and scratched. The windshield, bumper, radiator, lights were smashed and the front axle broken. I was not surprised, as I had figured that the way they treat machines, it would not be running a week. After some weeks out for repairs they had the jeep running again, but it was not long after that the news reached me in jail that they had ruined the transmission case when it ran low on oil.

Their trips were limited by the high price of gasoline. In the past when they had urgent trips to Wuchow they pressed me until I would take them. They always claimed they were allowed to pay only what buses charged per passenger. I had to furnish the balance of cost. Often they walked off without even giving the amount of bus fare. Now the Chief of Police had to buy gas at $3 U.S. per gallon, so they could not travel much.

We had a great deal of altercation over their seizure of the church and putting it to profane use. I protested to the police that both international law and the laws of Communist China forbade them to take over and occupy churches. They knew they were in the wrong but the Kom village group already had taken possession. The Magistrate reluctantly let them continue to use it. To put them out after their assistance in seizure of the mission would be a loss of face for them and prestige for the imperialist American priest. They were permitted to keep the keys and use the church for meetings, court trials, etc. in carrying out the land-reforms for the village.

I was held under house arrest in the convent, isolated and kept under guard to prevent any possible interference in their land-reform program, so I was given to understand.

The sketch of the mission shows my house prison. The mission is built in the form of a cross. One arm of the cross is the convent, the other arm is the priest's house, the top of the cross is the men's study hall, while the long upright of the cross is the church. Detained in the convent wing under guard, I could look from the upstairs window directly into the church. The land-reform meetings, the trials, the beatings and speeches could be seen and heard in the chapel below. Even when the conversation was low, it came to where I sat through the vents near the roof from the body of the church. This gave me a ringside seat for events taking place in the chapel, where I could take notes unobserved.

The time of my house imprisonment was running into weeks and I had made no move to leave China. I received the Chinese newspaper daily and read of the exit or exile of foreign missionaries from China. In all the big centers the Christians were being called together and told of the government policy — that there would be freedom of belief, but the church in China must be self-supporting, self-governed and self-propagated. The foreign missioner would no longer be permitted to work in China.

When the rally was held here in Shumkai to announce the new religious policy, the authorities called together some of the leading Catholics from surrounding villages. The meeting was held in the church where the new policy was announced to them. They could not come near or talk to me, but from my window I could see them giving signs of recognition. Some made the sign of the cross, others gave a smile or a quick wave of the hand toward my window.

With all this news in the papers of the end of foreign missioners day in China, I still made no move to quit the country. Chatting with the guard, I told him I had notified the United Nations of the seizure of the property, goods and jeep. I knew this would be relayed to the Police Chief. In order not to expose people who helped me get a letter through secretly, the details must be left unexplained.

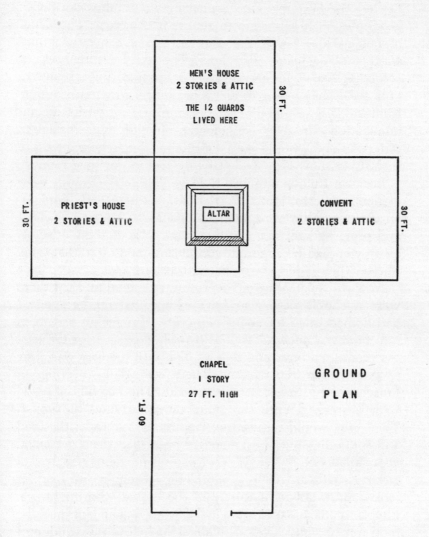

MEN'S HOUSE
2 STORIES & ATTIC

THE 12 GUARDS
LIVED HERE

30 FT.

PRIEST'S HOUSE
2 STORIES & ATTIC

30 FT.

ALTAR

CONVENT
2 STORIES & ATTIC

30 FT.

CHAPEL
1 STORY
27 FT. HIGH

60 FT.

GROUND

PLAN

· 43 ·

The authorities were irked to know I had broken through their iron curtain and had informed the United Nations. During the next few days someone came daily from police headquarters to urge me to return to America. The Chief of Police came twice, the Assistant Chief came twice and another officer came once later. They said a travel permit could be issued for me to go if I applied. But (I had to give the same answer to all) I could not go without orders from the Bishop — and he had been in jail cut off from communications for over two months now. If they wished to order me out I would go, I told them. But they wanted the records to show that we left freely and at our own request.

Because I made no move to leave China, the guards were evidently told to tighten restrictions, making it very unpleasant for me. They were told they could no longer buy meat and provisions for me, and they were to keep the Christians away who had been permitted to bring food up to that time. Maybe they could starve me into asking out.

Now started a game of wits to smuggle food in. First there were a couple of beggar boys who called for leftovers. I had helped them for about two years. Hunger pushed them into taking chances as well as it pushed me. I kept the leftover food in a bowl and they waited until the way was clear to sneak up to the window. There were daily meetings in the chapel by the Kom village folks. The beggars mingled with the crowd until the guard moved around the house. Then they would skip to the window. I gave them the food and some money to buy more for me. I had them get meat, vegetables, rice and eggs. Next day, in their beggars' basket covered with an old torn cloth, they brought me food. It looked quite all right to any of the crowd who might see. I took in the basket through the window and dumped the food out of sight. Then in plain sight before the window, I dumped leftover food into the basket. I also slipped in money and gave my order for food in a low voice. The beggar kids sauntered out through the crowds. This went on for weeks, and they were only discovered with my food the week I was taken to jail.

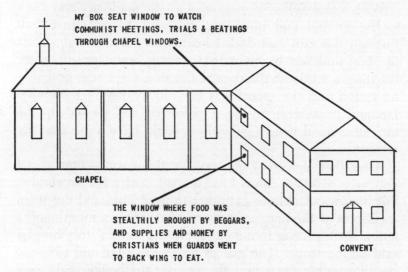

MY BOX SEAT WINDOW TO WATCH
COMMUNIST MEETINGS, TRIALS & BEATINGS
THROUGH CHAPEL WINDOWS.

CHAPEL

THE WINDOW WHERE FOOD WAS
STEALTHILY BROUGHT BY BEGGARS,
AND SUPPLIES AND MONEY BY
CHRISTIANS WHEN GUARDS WENT
TO BACK WING TO EAT.

CONVENT

But I had another source of food also. In going through the mission house, the police had not locked the doors that led from the upper porch into the house. Father X had been my assistant for eight months until terrorism had forced him to escape. In one of the rooms Father X had left an extra set of keys to the house and storeroom. If I could get them, I could loot my own canned-food supply.

I watched for a chance. The guards usually went to bed before midnight when they were sure I was asleep. On a dark rainy night I slipped over to the priest's house with ropes and a sack. I climbed the grilled window on the first floor, then threw a rope over the upper porch railing. With a loop for one step I could reach the porch railing and pull myself up over. The keys were still in the drawer — a prayer of thanks! I opened the storeroom and with my flashlight, darkened by a black cloth except for a small crevice, I raided the canned goods I had stored there. Each board that creaked sounded like a burglar alarm and I would listen a while before going on.

With a sack full of provisions, I finally made my way back to the ground and put down the sack to rest. Just then through the rain and dark I heard the guard cough. I left the bag and ran barefoot back to my house prison. After listening a while at the door, I decided there was probably no cough and the guard was very likely sleeping soundly. I edged back with my heart pounding and picked up the sack of canned goods. Now they would have a job starving me out.

After that the great mystery for them was — how was I getting food? They knew I had a good garden for vegetables, but how was I able to get other things? They did not learn the secret of the beggars' two-way basket for a month and a half and they never found out about the second-story burglar raid on my stores. The guards watched closer and closer to see that nothing was brought me. But the beggar kids were smart and kept watch for the moment the guard walked around out of sight.

The corner window lives in my recollections as an anchorite's cell light or as the turnstile used in Carmel convents to pass in provisions. I had given Holy Communion out through the window on a first Friday. The Christians had smuggled food and money to me through that window many times. The beggars got their food and passed me mine through the all important window. It was around the corner from the front where the guard stood. And when he walked away still farther around the opposite corner people stole up to the window. Sometimes I would not get to see or talk to the person, but found money, a letter or food-stuff just inside on the floor.

About dusk each evening the guards used to let me walk just outside the door while they looked on. In March, 1951, about ten thousand Communist troops were to pass, called up, I was told, as reinforcements in Korea. During those days I was not permitted outside at all. After some days, when they seemed to have all passed, the guard let me outside for some fresh air. The tough little sergeant appeared and bawled out both the guard and me. He got so mad he hit me on the chest with his fist. He only weighed about a hundred pounds and realized I could hardly feel the blow. This angered him all the more and, shaking his Luger, he said he would shoot me. I faced him, saying, "Go ahead." So then he pushed me in through the door and ordered the guards to be more strict with me.

I was a thorn in their sides. Evidently they would have liked to put me in jail, but for the records they needed to have some justifying reasons for their actions. So far I hadn't given them any.

My time was up, but during the two months of house arrest I had a box seat to watch the land reforms and the public trials. These events were held in the church, less than a hundred feet, where I could look on.

CHAPTER IV

Land Reforms

THE TERM "land-reform program" does not describe adequately what goes on in this stage of communization. It is really the first wholesale step for indoctrinating and communizing the populace in a complete new way of outlook, life and thought. Preparations for it had been going on in a thorough and painstaking way for a year now. The Communist army had marched through in conquest thirteen months before, and the new Communist government had been in control almost a year when the land reforms were started. Immediately after their arrival, the Communists took from their records names of Communist sympathizers, guerillas who fought for them against the Nationalists and their agents who had been working undercover. All these people were sent to take the indoctrination course forthwith.

It was startling to see this massive organization come out in the open. Even some of the teachers in our Sacred

Heart School in Wuchow were a part of the Communist underground. Several of the religion teachers for the mission of Watlam had been duped into joining the Communist party while at the university and now came into the open. In the past, one Catholic schoolteacher, more discerning than the ordinary, told the pastor he had received an offer of financial aid if he would teach Communism on the sly. He turned it down, so he was now on the black list.

The Communist government had scarcely taken over control before they accepted young people from every village and put them through the indoctrination course of six weeks. All schoolteachers were required to come immediately for the indoctrination drill course, and after finishing they were to return and put the students through the drill course. Students once trained had to spend much time touring the villages on propaganda trips, preaching the new Communist doctrine to country folk. School textbooks were replaced by pro-Communist books, already prepared, on history, civics and social science. Everyone taken in as an official or government worker was first given the indoctrination course to *Kai nao chin* — reshape his thoughts.

From each village a farmers' chairman was picked from one of the poor families and sent for the indoctrination course. The poor were to be the support for despoiling the rich, so that the have-nots and unlettered were chosen for key positions.

The farmers' chairman picked and recommended boys in their teens from destitute families to be trained as soldiers. Boys from thirteen to twenty who had nothing at home were brought out for military training. They were to be the enforcement arm when land reforms should be inaugurated. Besides these soldiers, a farmers' militia was raised in each village. The farmers' militia were not issued regular uniforms — only rifles and cartridges. They were issued the old rifles that had been taken away from the village people or surrendered by guerillas.

During the year before, the Communists had used all means — fright, threat, force and torture — to get every gun away from the people and into their own hands. The people must be made helpless as lambs to forestall any resistance to the communization ahead. Soldiers gradually cleared out the guerillas in the mountains, one group after another.

This tireless activity and organization went on day and night for the whole year in preparation for land reform and mass communization of the citizens. Those who have contended that the Chinese were not Communists, but were only land reformers, simply did not know the facts. Anyone who saw the program pushed through, and has been associated with the Chinese Communists for very long cannot but be convinced that they are fanatic Communists driving through every Communist aim and practice. Before seeing the program carried out, I could not believe the Chinese character capable of the relentless and inflexible drive toward Communist aims, or of the clocklike mechanism that is everywhere evident.

Now the year of preparation was over, and the time had come for the land reform to be initiated. The last three or four hundred people trained for land reforms came back from their indoctrination course in Wuchow. With them were several hundred Communists from the North who had administered land division and reforms in North China. With their experience they were to be team directors to work with the trained local people.

A massive crowd of people were ordered out to welcome the land-reform group's entry to Shumkai. They lined the road, waved banners, sang and cheered as the convoy of buses arrived. This had happened in January about a week before my house arrest and the closing of the mission.

Next day the land-reform groups were assigned to the villages. Their task would keep them there from six to eight weeks. The land reforms, as we learned later, were only incidental, only the occasion for pressing the populace into the Communist way of life.

They had sufficient indoctrinated personnel to undertake the program in two whole districts (about sixty villages) at the same time. The reformers lived and ate in the villages where they worked, but slept in outside villages or in different parts of the same village each night. This was to escape any attempt at revenge from people objecting to land division.

To insure the success of the land reforms, anyone with influence or power was picked up and brought in to jail. Several hundred of the young soldiers now trained were assigned to each of the four districts in Shumkai county. They were used together with the farmers' militia of each village to round up all possible objectors to land division or Communism. All persons with any amount of property or wealth were arrested; persons who had been with the former Nationalist Kuomintang government were also seized. The city jails, the county jails and local country jails were soon filled to overflowing. In the jails these people were to be given the indoctrination course, which was supposed to eradicate the old viewpoint and reorientate their minds to the new Communist mentality—the Party Line. Those persons the Communists thought prejudiced and difficult to change were liquidated.

Except for official business, no travel permits were issued for people to move while land reform was going on in the district. Farmers' militia guarded all roads and paths day and night, lest people should run away or move some of their goods into hiding. Everybody, even young children, was told to demand to see the travel permits and examine the baggage of anyone moving. I saw youngsters swarm around a man passing the mission on a bicycle. He had to show them his official travel permit and let them go through his baggage.

Business came to a standstill when so few of the country people could come in for shopping. Buses ran only for the few official persons allowed to travel, so that the mail got in only occasionally while the land reforms were being carried through.

In the villages where the land-reform program is on, the people must attend the meeting under threat of fine or other punishment. The citizens are quickly organized into different societies—the men's society, married women's society, young men's society, young women's society, labor society, etc. They all have their separate meetings and assigned programs. As a result, the people are at meetings all day and half the night. Those who are bolder are heard grumbling—under this regime it is meetings, meetings, meetings!

A few days after the program was inaugurated in the village a stone's throw away, they took over the mission and held their meetings in the chapel. It was there that I saw the program carried out before my eyes while I was under house arrest and guard.

Their meetings dealt with land reform, but they were primarily for the regular indoctrination course for the village folk. There was a song director to teach the Communist songs, there were political workers who lectured daily on Communism, there were party workers who taught how to hold the "criticism, self-criticism" meetings, and they themselves directed the self-criticism meetings. Then there were constant talks against imperialist America, instructions on how to spy and report on fellow citizens — even on relatives or one's parents, or anyone who spoke or acted in any way contrary to the Communist government. Later on I was given this same indoctrination course in prison.

The general assembly meetings of all groups were usually held in the evening from seven to eleven. A kettle drum and cymbals were the toxin calling the people together. While waiting, the young folks danced the Communist swing timed by the kettle drum and cymbals. Their dance is much like the old square dances in vogue among American country folk fifty years ago.

When the crowd is gathered, choral singing of Communist songs goes on for at least half an hour. The assembly is divided into the men's, the women's, the youth and the children's groups for competitive singing. Each group has its cheerleader, and cheers pep up the crowd between songs. The meetings starting off this way sound much like a college football rally the night before a big game. They practice their songs and cheers hours on end, so the singing and cheers are well done. This communal singing and cheering is supposed to lift the spirits of everybody now marching under the new Communist regime "to prosperity and happiness." It is needed to veneer the reality that China is about the poorest country in the world. (The Communists are always taken aback when I tell them, in discussions, that Communism is accepted only by the poorest and most backward nations of the world.)

At the general assembly meetings in chapel, each person was asked to declare exactly how much land he owned. The land-reform group had the old government tax records, but many people had graded waste land or garden land into rice paddies. They had not registered the new made fields as rice paddies to avoid the higher taxes. Now these (*hei t'ien*) "fields kept in the dark" were to be accounted for and back taxed in the "settling of accounts."

When a person finished declaring all his holdings, everyone present was ordered to tell of any other holdings this person might be concealing. The land-reform group was out daily between meetings, checking and measuring declared land holdings, asking the neighbors, the friends and the enemies of the person under consideration, the exact extent of his wealth.

In about three weeks' time, the investigating, measuring and checking of each family's wealth was finished. All families of the village were discussed and classified at the general assembly meetings in chapel. Families were placed in one of the following categories: (1) landlords, the wealthy who did not till their own fields but rented them out on a fifty-fifty basis and lived off the field income without doing the labor themselves; (2) wealthy farmers who worked land of their own, but also had extra land they rented out to be worked by others. Land wealth is measured by the amount of seed rice a farmer sows. A farmer sowing over sixty pounds of seed rice was rated as "wealthy farmer," and part of his land was to be confiscated and divided. Sixty pounds of seed produce on the average twelve hundred pounds of rice grain twice a year. This twenty-four hundred pounds of rice grain is worth about thirty-five dollars in U.S. money, and here it makes food for two people living skimpily. In the third category were middle-class farmers — who sowed less than sixty pounds of seed grain and did the labor themselves; and in the fourth, poor farmers who lived by share cropping the fields of others and who owned little or no land of their own.

At the meetings held in our mission chapel, each family's wealth was discussed for about a half hour before final classification. The number of mouths to feed was considered. Then facts were charged that would change the wealth rating. The man had a small business, a home factory, a shop, a brick kiln, or he had sufficient income to keep a concubine, etc. When the discussion was over, the family was voted into a certain classification. All were present for discussion except the landlords. These were taken off to jail at the start of the program and hence were not present for the preliminary discussion. They were to be brought back later for special discussion, and the "judgment of the people" in taking away their land.

After numerous meetings, every family was classified in one of these four categories, and their names and wealth classification were posted outside on the church wall. It filled one side of the church.

The next step was to bring the wealthy landlords back from jail for the "people's judgment" in taking away their land and holding them to an accounting (*ts'ing suen*) for their wrongs. The people had to be readied for this, so rehearsals were held beforehand. All the wrongs or injustices that the crowd could dig up were listed. One of the land-reform directors would read out an accusation or call upon a person to restate it. Then he would ask the mob, "Is that right, is that just, what should be the punishment? etc." Remember this was all rehearsal to train the populace on what to answer and to work them up to the proper pitch of frenzy or anger or even mob violence.

Posters were put up at the door and around the church announcing that the people's court was to be held. The crowd was trained in the responses, the songs and the cheers.

Land to be divided included the endowment lands left for schools and temples, the properties of wealthy "landlords" and part of the land of "wealthy farmers." But the landlords were the only class that faced bitter odium and revenge.

They had two prospects ahead. If they had always been considerate and charitable and there were no charges against them, they were to have their land confiscated to be divided among the have-nots. The benign landlords would be assigned a small residue of their land to keep them from starving, but they must till this themselves.

If the landowners had been (*oo pa*) tyrants or unjust, the people's court was to condemn them. At the people's court they would have to face one or more of the following sentences: death penalty with confiscation of everything they owned, a public beating and a prison term. Restitution for injustices was to be made first from their properties in case they were to be shot.

On the first morning people's court was convened in the chapel, a noisome crowd gathered and sang Communist songs and cheered while waiting for the landlords to be brought up from jail. The landlords came in sight down the road, and the crowd went with drums and cymbals to meet them. It took on the appearance of a circus parade. Behind the landlords marched the police with guns pointing at the victims' backs. The landlords wore cone-shaped dunce caps with their names and their odious crime "landlord" printed on each cap. Their hands were roped tight behind their backs, to make them more criminal-like. The procession slowly wended into chapel to the accompaniment of pounding drums, clapping cymbals and a hurly-burly of shouts and cheers.

People's court was called to order. The accusers had been well rehearsed and the alleged crimes had been listed. All that remained was to work the crowd into the proper state of frenzy and hatred, and then, after the accusations were repeated, call on the people to fix the punishment. The landlords were not permitted to say a word in their defense.

The session started, and after long speeches on democracy, the will of the people, the judgment of the people, etc., the accusers threw their darts. What surprised me was that women did most of the accusing. They yelled and screamed out like alley cats, naming the crimes of the landlords. One would charge, "He demanded exhorbitant interest on a loan and when I could not pay he took my fields"; another would shout, "He robbed all irrigation water," or "He cheated in weights," or "He fixed the court by bribery against me." The women talked so fast and wildly that I could not follow many of their accusations.

The four landlords were under fire all day long, and then came the people's judgement. The leader would ask the assembly after each accusation, "Is that just?" And the mob would shout, "No." "Should he be punished?" Shouts answered, "Yes." "Should he be whipped?" — "Yes" came the answer.

That morning I saw one of the land-reform group take a board from my garden fence and shape it into a paddle. As

· 56 ·

I saw later, this was used for beating the landlords sentenced to whipping. The accusers and persons who suffered wrongs were then ordered to beat the condemned. They took turns beating him, sometimes on the head, sometimes on the buttocks. That afternoon I saw them leading the battered and beaten victims of public whipping back to jail. I heard one woman say as she walked away while the beating was going on, "I can't look at such actions."

One of the four landlords was sentenced by the people to be shot. But I heard the people say his case must be reviewed by the court officials down at the Yamen. The people's decision was upheld and he was to be shot with several others from nearby villages.

I watched the crowd during the people's court trials. Many, of course, loathed such inhuman measures, but they were helpless. The mob ruled, and if someone suggested that a landlord be shot it was impossible to get up and defend the victim. One would be open to the accusation of defending an odious tyrant of a landlord. In this "democratic process," a proposal to shoot the accused was put to the people for a voice vote. No one dared to shout in the accused's defense. Anyway, his sentence had been fixed beforehand, so any protest was useless. I looked on from my window and I am sure many in the crowd looked on with a bitter pain of shame that men could be so like beasts.

The final scene of the people's court was enacted with the executions the following morning. A procession of several hundred villagers with a group of soldiers formed about 10 A.M. Crowds joined from several other nearby villages where landlords had been sentenced to die. The executions were to be staged together so a bigger celebration could be held. The young people were dressed in "glad rags" and their faces were painted. Some of them walked on stilts, milling around the road in front of the mission waiting for things to start.

The four condemned men were marched up from the jail

with hands tied behind them. They looked like wrecks after the beatings they had received during the last few days. Drums beat the tempo for singing while the macabre procession started moving along in the Communist swing dance. Youngsters took it like circus day, darting in and out of the procession. But I wondered what was in the hearts of the grownups who had to join this crazy parade of song and dance to see men shot.

The parade accompanying the four condemned moved slowly toward a village a little more than a quarter-mile from chapel. I could still see the crowd, but could not distinguish what was being said. Songs and speeches and Communist cheers followed until late in the afternoon. The four condemned were lined up near a cemetery mountain and were then shot. The parade again went past singing and dancing, then broke up for evening rice. Two of the men just shot were well known to me. They were businessmen who burned brick and lime, and also sold lumber. Their profits were put in fields. What injustices, tyranny or cheating they did, I do not know, of course. Now, their families were stripped of everything and would have to try to live by coolie work. Rumor had it that the sons of the executed landlords were also to be shot, but I seriously doubted such measures would be taken.

The meetings went on in the chapel, and land division continued. (The fields of the landlords, a part of the fields of "wealthy farmers," endowed school and temple lands were to make up the total to be divided.) Each landless poor person was allotted fields for ten pounds of seed rice, which should net him four hundred pounds of rice grain per year. This would make for a definite and considerable alleviation of the poor. The land reforms were carried out with relentless drive, vigor and thoroughness. There seemed to be valiant effort to make an equitable distribution of the fields and goods confiscated from the landlords and other sources mentioned above. But they were not Robin Hood benefactors. Their motive was not love of the poor but rather an attempt to consolidate power and win the poor to their side against the people of wealth and power.

One thing must be kept in mind in order to understand their actions. If a man has wealth and goods, these belong to everyone (Communism), and to take them from the wealthy is not theft in their system — it is for equitable distribution to all. Several Christians have told me that Communists inspecting or passing through their village have picked up the catechism to look through it. Invariably they take issue with the commandment "Thou shalt not steal." They preach there is no such thing as private property. It belongs to all in common.

After the execution or jail sentence of the landlords came the confiscation of all their wealth (their fields had already been taken over). I listened to their meetings in chapel before they went out for legalized looting. The crowd was harangued on the justice of their seizure action and the wickedness of the landlord. They were brought to a pitch that would stop at nothing by the speeches and singing, by shouting slogans and cheers.

The people then lined up by the road outside the chapel. Armed soldiers went to direct and protect the shakedown. The people had baskets, shoulder poles and ropes to carry the loot from the landlord's home. It was orderly and not a free-for-all. And I am told that, on the whole, the spoils were fairly divided among the poor.

I watched them strip the home of the landlord just across the valley of rice fields. Rice grain was loaded into baskets and a line of carriers cheerily jaunted by the mission with it. Furniture and clothes, lumber and firewood were lugged by. Chickens were carried in baskets, but pigs were driven ploddingly along. Flower pots, kitchenware and pottery made it look like moving day. All day long they worked, and finally the place was cleaned out. How it was divided I cannot say, for this was done in the center of Kom village where I could not see.

The police and government offices seemed to get first pick at the wealthy homes. Down the road three miles was the house of a wealthy landlord. The police who had taken my jeep and trailer away taxied by all one day with furniture, porcelain vases and the better furnishings of the house. The poor never saw the division of this stuff.

I have written briefly of the so-called "land-reform" program as it was carried out at Shumkai before my eyes. Many phases of the program I have kept for later chapters. (Why they left me where I could listen in or see it all for months, is still a puzzle.)

The full meaning of their land-reform program was brought out in their speeches, and in their Chinese newspapers I read each day. Here is a brief summary on the scope of land reform translated from a newspaper article — the explanation in brackets is mine:

"The land-reform program is to be carried out in seven stages:

1. Bandit Suppression (the disarming and liquidation of guerillas and calling in every gun held by civilians);
2. Removal of influential figures (former government officials, and citizens of wealth, education and leadership to be taken to jail where most of them disappear);
3. Refund of land rents which landlords collected from tenants in past years (landlords were tortured until they paid with interest the land rents collected throughout their lifetime);
4. Differentiations of classes (classification of each family into landlords, well-to-do, middle class and poor families);
5. Confiscation of land owned by landlords;
6. Allocation of lands to tillers;
7. Review of the program."

The last point bears explanation. About six months after the program was completed, a land-reform group spent a few weeks in the village again. Their purpose was to see if the former landlords were kept on the starvation ration assigned, ask spies if the landlords had called out any hidden wealth, inquire if the people were carrying out the policy of despising and persecuting them. The land-reform group made certain the program was going on — that meetings were held, Communist songs were sung, Communist societies were functioning; that schools were studying the books assigned, singing the songs and spying on their parents and others. A thousand questions had to be answered by all, and any shadow of "deviation" brought great numbers back to jail, while terrorism struck deeper into the populace.

What the Communists did not publish are the further steps. Their system is organized for each step and follows a time schedule. Land reform, first of all, is a bait to attract the masses of poor peasants to welcome Communism. The wealthy are despoiled and their property is distributed to the very poor, who are the masses. Only at a later stage, when they are hooked, do the poor realize that land division is a hoax that leaves them worse off than they were before.

Middle-class farmers were to come in for treatment later when they would lose ownership of their land. As control was tightened, this was often announced during speeches at land-reform meetings. People were told that the government would later get to the merchants and city people with their socialization program. One of the speakers explained to a mass meeting, "All classes and all people must be brought to socialism first. Later we move into pure Communism. Even Russia, our great model, is still a Socialistic State gradually moving into Communism."

CHAPTER V

Achievements

I HAD SEEN the Communist regime in operation for well over a year at that time. Abrupt and tremendous changes had taken place. It was time to sit back and appraise them, for changes do not always mean progress, nor are changes always for the better. The house prison detention gave me leisure, and one day I started to write in the diary under the heading of Communist Accomplishments Up to Now. One must admit in fairness that they have done much for the benefit of China. But their accomplishments must be carefully weighed and measured, to determine both the loss and gain from the deal.

First they have brought discipline and order. Educated Chinese themselves have long admitted their people were the worst disciplined and the poorest organized nation in the world. Exactitude is something they have had little reverence for. Their artisans miss perfection in their craft because they are satisfied with *ch'a pu toh* (not far off). Boats and trains have run on a schedule that is behind time, some-times hours, and sometimes days; yet in their minds it was *ch'a pu toh* and mattered little. The school days and classes in all the country schools were run on a hit-or-miss, mostly miss, schedule. And the discipline of the children in the homes was so lax that one might say, with little harm to truth, there is no discipline.

Hence, I believed the easygoing, individualistic, freedom-loving masses of China would absorb and emasculate Com-munism. China seemed too big, unwieldly and disorganized to be molded and marched into the ranks of Communism.

Before the advent of Communism in this area, I met priests from North China in Hong Kong, who had lived several years in the Communist-dominated areas. I held that China could not be regimented into the Communist system, but their contention was quite definitely the opposite. You will see, was their comment, the Communists will organize and tie up every thing and every person to follow their dis-cipline. Now, after living under their rule for well over a year, I am much more inclined to concede that our confreres from the North were right. The populace is being disciplined, by force and punishments, of course, to do things on time, and to strictly obey the laws, order and instructions. This ex-acting discipline is so much against the Chinese temperament that only time, measured by decades, will tell if they can be changed fundamentally.

This ancient and massive nation has absorbed so many races, "isms" and systems, like the flower that closes over and devours insects that try to feed on it, that I hope China may, in the long run, absorb Communism. The system is foreign to man's nature, foreign-born and forever foreign to China, a nation that has absorbed so many foreign invasions. History has a way of repeating itself, and I still look for China to devour this latest "ism," given time enough.

The first thing to impress me was the discipline of the soldiers. I saw over a hundred thousand of them pursuing the Nationalists in the final campaign. Although flushed with victory (though easily earned or bought most of the time) and confidence, they were by far the finest and best disciplined troops I have seen in China.

In twenty years I had seen very few Chinese soldiers at drill who marched in step. But these Communist soldiers at drill were different. At drill their march was in step, they did double-quick, present arms, setup exercises and the rest, which would delight even a German army sergeant.

When they were marching by the mission, a Nationalist plane appeared overhead. The bugler blew out a call and everyone vanished into the grass by the roadside. With ferns and branches in their hats, it was hard to spot them even a hundred yards away. The plane went out of sight, the bugle sounded again and they were instantly in rank and again on the march.

The road in front of the mission is a flat stretch between hills, and is just along the edge of the town. Each battalion was usually signaled to sit here for a short rest. None would admit being tired, though they looked worn out. During most of the rest period one of their lecturers harangued them with propaganda. The Communist army keeps its men so occupied that they have little opportunity for griping or planning any treachery against the government. Singing, lectures, study, races and games fill all their free time, and the political commissars with the army are forever searching for any dissatisfaction or opposition.

The soldiers I saw marching through here were Lin Piao's troops, generally conceded to be the best in China. Each evening for ten days several thousand, arriving at dusk or later, were billeted in nearby villages. I heard of only one case of rape.

A few of Lin Piao's troops asked to stay at the mission, which I knew was against their regulations. When I insisted that they keep the regulations their government had promulgated, they ceased their pressure and politely went on to where they were supposed to stay. A couple of times they threatened to force their stay upon us. But when I said if they did, I was reporting it to Lin Piao they went away. Their discipline was impressively good.

I have heard the soldiers talk about and praise foreigners for their efficiency, organization and punctuality. They often carry their imitation to silly extremes and make a fetish out of time limit for getting things done. I saw an army truck engine with bearings burned pulled apart. Though they had no spare bearings, the officer fixed a limit of two hours to get the truck repaired and moving. Repair was impossible, so the soldier mechanics put the machine together and probably ruined the engine up the road a ways. Though they often carry what they believe to be efficiency too far, they do get things done with a speed and exactness China has never seen before.

The discipline of the police and soldiers of the local garrison was also impressive. Before dawn they start their drill. For the rest of the day they have indoctrination lectures, meetings, singing or games to fill their time. Two of the police were brought in under arrest while I was in jail and irons were put on their hands and feet. The assistant chief of police was caught in fraudulent use of funds not long before. He was disciplined after public accusation, degraded and sent out as a common guard to the prison labor camp in the mountains. The severe discipline and drastic punishment make officials observe honesty through fear. When I was under house arrest in February, one of the police guards at the mission asked to borrow money to buy tobacco. I consented. But after talking a while, he gave back the money. He said he was afraid some of the police would notice he had smokes and would report his getting money from me. This would mean a stretch in jail, he told me.

The people everywhere are under the same iron discipline. There, too, it is a discipline implemented by ruthless punishment and hence is carried out through fear. But if it lasts long enough, it might become habit-forming and routine, for the philosopher wisely says: *La vie, c'est une habitude continuelle.* Right now the discipline is apparently making a new kind of people out of the Chinese.

Their rules and orders are very often unreasonable, but the Communists are tyrranical and imperious in demanding that they be carried out. As one man remarked, "There is no reasoning with them; if they tell you to tear down your house, you had better do it. If you delay, they will force you to do it and punish you besides." This attitude and spirit is far different from the spirit of the Chinese up to now. They were famed for their reasonableness, their willingness to talk and make concessions. Call it a police state, a people regimented by terror, or an oppressed nation, as you wish, but they are forcing unbelievable discipline and system upon this unwieldly mass of humanity, hated though it be.

Also there has been elimination of graft. Before the present regime, it was the common and accepted practice for every official to take squeeze. The officials received low salaries with the presumption that they would get the rest on the side from tips and bribes. This squeeze system contaminated people in every walk of life, and unless one paid squeeze, it was almost impossible to get anything done. We were caught in the web ourselves, and to buy land, or get deeds registered, we had to throw in a certain amount of squeeze. On the trains, the boats and the buses one paid squeeze into private hands or favors were refused.

Under the Communist regime this has been cut to a minimum. Again this is accomplished by an over-vigilant surveillance, by a system which tries to enlist every individual as a spy if he remains in good standing, and by ruthless punishment of those caught. Law observance and honesty are motivated by the cowering fear that hangs over everyone. But for the present at least, it is most effective in eliminating graft.

The government officials from top to bottom, the police,

the soldiers and government workers must get a receipt for every cent that is spent. When the Magistrate or Chief of Police went in the jeep with me to Wuchow and helped pay for gas, I had to give each a receipt for what he paid. When they took the sampan to ferry into Wuchow, they again demanded a receipt from the boatmen as proof of expenditures. This requires lots of detail work in accounting, but they check with the receipt on every cent that is spent, and this cuts down the opportunity to squeeze. And woe betide the ones caught cutting corners in their system.

One of the government truck drivers who came occasionally to borrow tools told me he was jailed for picking up people on the road and accepting a fare. "No more," he said, as he was telling about it.

The land-reform officials were holding a meeting in the church in February. I heard a commotion and shouting, then one of the officials was dragged out and down to the jail. On inquiry, I was told that he had accepted squeeze from one of the farmers who wanted special treatment. The two police then with us wearing irons had accepted tips for favors, so I was told. They were learning the hard way that "crime does not pay."

A good number of the country district-head officials called *hsiang chiangs* were now serving in our jail. Under the old regime, or at the beginning of the Communist rule, they took "squeeze" in handling cases of disputes. One I know quite well here told me he was sentenced to three years. Three years should put a control governor on his avarice when he gets out.

The Communists brag to the country people that under the new regime the citizens do not need to lock their doors at night. With every other person spying for them, they are not far wrong.

How long will this righteousness through fear last? Talking with a professional man now forced to work for the government or be shot, I got his views. Corruption, he told me, is already finding its way into the government offices. Up to now the Communists have had ceaseless adversity to sober them and keep them straight in their struggle for conquest. Now that victory has arrived and put many of them in a position for easy money, many are giving in to the temptation. The Communists are now in the first fervor of their religious zeal. This will wear off in time, especially without an uphill fight to cleanse them. Great numbers of those now in authority came from destitute families. They have good food now; with the all-embracing taxes they are clothed well, and many have money passing through their hands. In time this will soften them, then corrupt them, this official believes. He holds that it will take from ten to fifteen years of rule, and then they will be entirely corrupt and will fall. A materialistic regime gives no high motives for virtue. Guns and terror can control men's conduct for a while, but virtue that is not from the heart and conscience will disappear as soon as fear relaxes.

Pagan China with its traditions for squeeze is a difficult soil for Communism to grow in and prosper. Those who have traveled or lived much around the world will not question the fact that Shanghai holds first prize for rackets, racketeers and corruption. When the Communists were closing in on Shanghai, one of the tycoons in wicked traffic remarked over his glass:

"We corrupted the Manchus, we corrupted the foreigners when they came to Shanghai, we corrupted the Nationalists and we corrupted the Japanese who sojourned here. And in time we shall also corrupt the Communists."

The many corruption cases now recorded in the Communist newspapers, and the campaigns and the speeches by officials against corruption lead one to believe that the tycoon was right.

The land reform may also be called an achievement. Dividing large holdings amongst the landless or poor is a good and desirable end. In principle, it is not difficult to agree with the Communists that this is good and should be a definite accomplishment. But the injustices, cruelty, force and robbery in bringing it about, no one with any morals or conscience can condone. There must needs be a few words on how land often gets into the hands of wealthy landlords.

In China there are almost no investments in stocks and bonds, nor in industry, for the country has no big industries and no shares to place on the market. Up until a score of years ago there was no central government money. Each province or the local banks issued paper money, and frequently failure to redeem the script ruined confidence in holding paper money. The Nationalist or Central Government got economic control of the country and has issued paper currency during the last twenty some years. But they were dogged by exhausting wars and ennervated by graft and poor organization. And so the currency suffered increasing inflation as the years went on.

All this left no source of investment or safe holding of wealth, and so people with funds invested in rice or other grain fields. They let them out for tilling, and half the produce was collected by the owner of the land. In time the rich became richer and the poor became poorer, and with the passing of many years a considerable portion of China's productive fields became tied up in the hands of the wealthy.

The share croppers who had to lose half the crop to landowners could not get ahead. Other abuses crept in, and in some districts the tillers of the soil had to make other gifts to the landowner. Big landowners often became like feudal lords who could take away the tiller's right to work the land for any reason whatsoever.

For instance, here in the countryside a few years ago several poor villages wanted to become Catholic. The landlord who owned the big share of the land tilled by the villagers threatened to take away their privilege of tilling his land if they became Catholic. He knew the Church would help the poor fight injustices, and, with the Church taking part, his tyrannous hand would be held. This landlord, Mr. Lin Kooi Shang, along with many of his relatives, was recently purged by the firing squad. His lands, like the properties of landlords everywhere, were divided up amongst the poor. Starving members of his family came to the mission for help and, of course, were assisted in the charity of Christ.

The methods the Communists used in their land reforms were drastic and dictatorial and ignored a person's right to personal property, as well as all rights. It was simply confiscation, barbaric and brutal, without any compensation or consideration for anyone except themselves and their own ends.

Although I did not see any instances of the practice right in Shumkai, the deeds to the land in many districts were destroyed or burned. An official demanded the deeds to a mission sixty miles from us. He tore them up, saying, "Now the place belongs to the people." That night the local guard shot the official when he returned to quarters. The guard said he failed to recognize him.

Another evil practice of the rich was to lend rice toward the end of the season when people had eaten up their supply. Then at the next harvest the people had to repay two bushels for every bushel borrowed. However, this is not so bad as it seems, for the price in times of scarcity when they borrow is more than double the price at harvest time. Still, it gives the rich landlord a chance to store up big supplies and hold until the dearth, when he can sell at high prices. This practice was wiped out with the elimination of landlords.

The poor have apparently benefited by land division, but economic reactions of the program on business life have in fact reduced income so the poor are worse off than before. The middle class suffer from the same economic reactions and lowered standards of living. They live in constant fear of what is to come, where only the poor are somewhat safe from exploitation.

What the backwash of it all will be only time will tell. But priests from North China where Communism has been in power for a good number of years have this to say: The poor and the beggars are worse off now for there are no rich to give help or lend to them. In spite of the Utopian claims of the Communists, the poor we shall always have with us, as the gospel avers.

Since the land reform took place, people from the country villages everywhere have told me that the year 1951 has brought the greatest suffering and hunger to the countryside they had ever seen. There was no haven, no source to call upon for help! Guards let me go down to the valley stream each day to get water, so I had a chance to walk through the fields near the mission and talk to the farmers. Asking how they were faring under the new regime, even though they have received the pittance of land given out in the land division, I always got the same answer. They told me their hands were tied, there was no business and no work for them to bolster their income, and all said things were much better under the old regime. When I repeated this information which I had learned from the people, to the officials they answered, "Of course in the beginning there is this suffering, but everything soon will be organized, and in a year or two there will be great prosperity for everyone."

Another evil practice, and one of the most upsetting factors in economic life, had been the wild interest rate charged on money. Twenty per cent yearly interest was considered low in normal times, and when inflation rocked the country during the world war 20 per cent per month was gladly paid. In one month's time paper money lost enough value so that goods bought and held a month's time could be sold at a price high enough to pay 20 per cent interest and net a good profit besides. But all this wrecks economy, industry and stability. The new regime has done away with these crazy interest rates, and China is far better off in this respect.

Nationalism is another development under Communism. China up to now has been famed for its loyalty to the family and lethargy and indifference to nationalism and patriotism. This was due in no small part to lack of schools and communications. But these barriers are all being overcome now by intensive, profuse and widespread propaganda.

It must be admitted that the Communists with their police-state rule have given the Chinese an *esprit de corps* in national outlook and feeling. There is a unity of purpose now, and the Chinese march as a nation toward the ends presented by Communist propaganda. This may be only skin deep, as often happens when nationalistic spirit is not spontaneous but regimented. A few months after the Communists had taken over, a group of people in a nearby village wanted to study in preparation for becoming Catholic. They asked the farmers' chairman, who is now boss of the village. He told them no, and gave his reason in about these words: "We are now one party and massed together for one aim, and the Church is outside this."

A group of high-school students who were filled with the Communist propaganda talked with me one day. One asked in surprise, "Are you still trying to teach and spread your religion here?" According to what they hear, missionaries are representing imperialistic, warmongering nations who use missioners for aggression and, therefore, have nothing but evil to spread. Religion is not tied up with national aims and can have no part with them, they say.

The propaganda is having its effects, and youngsters up to fifteen, or even some of them up to twenty, will be converted completely to the Party Line and intensive nationalism. Given a generation of time behind the "bamboo curtain" to develop nationalism, the Communists will no doubt build a race of fanatics, convinced that their mission is to liberate the rest of the enslaved world from imperialism and capitalism to enjoy a paradise of "freedom" like theirs. Their power, enthusiasm and zeal should not be underestimated nor ignored if our way of life is to survive. On their side, they are like Communists everywhere, denied outside knowledge of other countries. They also make the mistake of overrating their own strength and badly underestimating the strength of opposition countries.

Zeal for work is a trait the Communists have forced on everyone, and this accomplishment is hardly less than inspiring. The Communists have come to power here not only through determination and relentless drive toward their goal; a good part of their success and accomplishment is due to their zeal for work. They cherish a messianic belief in themselves as saviors of the world, and their fanatic faith inspires them to work like all missionaries should.

They have a definite aim — world conquest. They have an organization and program to attain that end, so there is no groping or uncertainty. Their means are ruthless, brutal and uncompromising. And with the conviction of their holy mission and zeal to carry it through, they are not easy to stop and not easy to deal with or deflect from their purpose. These characteristics, of course, should not be overvalued, for regimented Germany and Japan could have been described in almost the same words a few years back. However, I want to put down a few examples of their zeal which have come under my observation.

In their campaign I saw soldiers march all night as well as most of the day. Soon after they took over here, I was in a country village that is on the way to guerilla territory. At 1 A.M. we heard the pack mules and soldiers clanking over the gravel, going to attack the guerillas. Soldiers go prowling all night long through the villages when searching for people.

I have gone to the Magistrate's office at nine o'clock in the evening and found everybody still at work. The police office is the same. One night the Chief and staff had me up for questioning until after midnight, yet they were all out for drill before dawn next morning.

The land-reform officials and workers for the village near the mission held meetings and worked in the church every night until eleven o'clock. Before dawn they were back hitting the drums and bells to assemble the people again. This schedule went on day and night for over two months until they finished the job and moved to another village.

Some of the officials and technicians of the Nationalist government who were considered indispensable were kept on. A few of them are Catholics who stole in to see me when I was under house arrest. They say they have to work all day and half the night, and get paid far less than they got under the old regime. They try to resign and go back and work their fields, but are firmly told to stay on the job, otherwise their heads will go down. (This expression means there heads will be put on the chopping block.)

This terrific drive for work is a revolution in itself. China's happy-go-lucky citizens, who toiled so leisurely in the past, are going through a face-lifting operation. How successful or lasting the new pace will be one cannot guess. However, their drive and work is rapidly rounding up the entire nation's people to march along under the dictates of Communism faster than I ever dreamed possible. Their numberless meetings, parades and songs give the appearance — forced though it be — of gaiety and joy in their work. It could well deceive anyone who did not have access to the heart and voice of the people who are being herded along in the noisy ranks of Communism. So many people talking to me remark with a helpless shrug of the shoulders, "They are in power (it is their world, is the Chinese expression), and we have to live and eat. Hence, we have to fall in line, appear to be happy and praise Communism."

The most remarkable of all the Communist achievements

is the suppression of opium. Their method was drastic and cruel, but it got results.

After they had been in power a few months, the order came out that the use of opium was to end. They fixed a time limit of several weeks for addicts to surrender or destroy their opium pipes and opium. Dens must be closed within the time limit and merchants must get rid of all dope supplies before the set date. Addicts were told they could voluntarily come to jail to break the habit. The sudden cure without medical supervision is a dangerous shock to the system. One man I knew well took the "voluntary cure" about two months. After his release he went to work mining wolfram. The second day at work he fell dead.

When the time of grace was up, officials, spies and private citizens were ordered to search out addicts still using opium or any of the instruments of dope. Great numbers taken to jail demonstrated that the Communists meant business. Dope users who had hidden a supply or secretly bought from some friend were soon discovered in this New China, where no secret is safe. The fines and punishment were drastic. Those caught were sent to be cured or die in jail. This struck fear into the hearts of addicts, and fright broke habits which people thought could not be broken.

A barber I knew stopped voluntarily. He put on weight and supported his family for the first time in years. Many die breaking the habit, and later I was to see a victim, on forced cure, die in the prison cell where I was kept.

One cannot condone a method which treats men like animals, but the results are indeed praiseworthy. Every large village in China had a number of opium smokers. The neighboring province of Kweiyang is famed for its fields of opium poppies, and the product is cheap. Missioners there told me it was not an uncommon practice for mothers to feed opium to their babies. It kept them quiet while the mothers worked. All who have seen this widespread curse in China must give a word of praise to those who have suppressed the evil — or reduced it to a minimum at least.

CHAPTER VI

Communist Economy

ALTHOUGH most of this chapter was written near the end of my period of house arrest and stay in China, it is moved up to complement and give a better understanding of the land-reform program and its aftermath.

I am not an economist, but only a spectator at the game watching the men carry the ball toward a goal. I have given considerable thought to fundamental things like supply and demand, balancing the budget, the logic of taxation, stabilization of currency and so on. Hence, I can enjoy the game without pretending to know much about it. This is perhaps just as well, for trends and events have often made monkeys out of predictions by the economic experts.

To begin with: China is a poor nation. She has the lowest living standard of any country in the world, excepting possibly India. Laborers building houses, making roads, burning bricks, or doing any other common labor, get ten pounds of rice a day. This equals fifteen cents in U.S. currency. Half a laborer's wages must be used for his coarse food of rice and vegetables.

Farmers and their families, except during the heavy work of planting and harvesting, live on rice gruel at the cost of three or four cents a day U.S. currency. The Communist land reform, seeking to give everybody the same amount of land, has allotted enough land for nine pounds of seed grain to each person. This would theoretically give each individual a harvest of less than six hundred pounds of grain a year; in two crops. This gross income of six hundred pounds is worth nine dollars American money. Try to imagine a person living on that for a yearly income. This is the gross in China's new Communist paradise, before the government chops off a big chunk for taxes.

In all the regions of China that I know of where land reforms have been completed, the per capita allotment of land has not exceeded the amount of land for ten pounds of rice grain. That is all the land there is in this heavily populated nation. The Communists have put on a laudable drive for tilling the hillsides, the plateaus, the roadsides and other wild plots not yet brought under cultivation.

The land in this country must feed four times as many mouths as the land in U.S., and it is conservative to say that all China's millions do not consume as much food as the hundred forty million people in America. The hills are deforested, except in uninhabited regions, the land eroded and the earth exhausted. It is not the "Good Earth," it is the tired earth, worked to death and nourished only by human dung and urine, and the ashes from grass they burn on the hills. They sweat over a shovel, or a plodding ox turns this loess chunk by chunk, plot by plot, to squeeze out new grains of rice for China's millions.

When flood and drought and pest do not strike, the people can eke out enough to keep body and soul together. The fourth horseman has been released with the coming of the

Communist government, and that is taxation.

The Communist army marched in on the heels of the Nationalists in December, 1949. The Nationalist soldiers filled their sacks from the government granaries before leaving, but they left a supply for the schools and the salaries of officials. When the Communist army arrived, they, too, had to provision, and they scraped the bins clean.

Following the army came the government administration a month later, and they found the taxes taken up in grain had all been carried off by the armies. After two weeks of feverish work, the new government came out with the most devastating tax assessment these people had ever seen. The people were allowed no questioning, no delay and no adjustment of the amount.

Here is our own personal case. The church is built on land that was formerly rice fields. These fields were recorded with the government as two and a half mo — one third of an acre. The fields, if they could be cultivated, would produce seven hundred pounds of rice grain at a harvest.

After this first Communist assessment in January, 1950, a slip was delivered to say that I was to pay a thousand pounds of rice grain and five hundred pounds of firewood; taxes for *six months* on the fields where the mission is now built.

Surely there is a mistake, I thought, and sent a man to the government offices to ask them to look into it. Next day a tax collector came with two soldiers at his side carrying guns, to give me my answer.

"You will deliver the full amount on your slip at the government storehouse within two days," he stated, in a "do-it-or-else" voice. I delivered rather than see what "else" this new government had in store for me.

In their arbitrary assessment, people of means were burdened out of all proportion. I happened to know Wong Pee Chun quite well, the wealthiest man in one of the nearby villages. He owned land to the value of about five thousand dollars U.S. Always generous in times of famine and need, he held a place of affection in the hearts of the village folk. But he was a landlord.

They soaked Mr. Wong Pee Chun thirty thousand pounds of rice grain in that first round of taxes. When he pleaded his land would not produce that much in a year, they answered, "You have gold hidden away; get it and buy the grain for taxes." In the land reforms that came later, Mr. Wong was stripped of his land, his home and all his goods. Reduced to begging, he came to the mission a couple of nights for help.

The poorer farmers were only taxed half their harvest in that first round. But that meant half the food supply they had stored and counted on to feed them until July. The tax was a deep scoop into the rice bowl of people who live close to starvation anyway, and 1950 was to bring the saddest and hungriest winter they had ever seen.

Communists try to hide the grief and gloom of these people who are being sapped of their lifeblood. A day was appointed for each village to deliver their taxes. Armed Communist soldiers on hand to direct the display called upon a group to bring out drums and cymbals. Then the people carrying their baskets of tax grain on shoulder poles lined up in procession. Firecrackers were set off to give an appearance of gaiety, and the noisy parade was marched away to the government granaries, where they poured out the tax grain.

Propaganda speeches, newspapers and posters declared the people were so happy with the new Communist government, they came spontaneously with drums and singing to pay their taxes. Reading this, perhaps you will say, "I do not believe such a farce could take place." I would not believe it, except that I saw it with my own eyes. People who pay taxes with joy are unnatural, even the Communists should know that.

Before many weeks had passed, the village farming

folk had eaten up all the rice remaining to them. The winter of 1950 will long be remembered as the first under Communism, and for marking the worst famine that ever swept this district.

Father Lynch in the next mission to ours lived on the edge of a large farming village. He told me that in the morning he saw groups of ten or fifteen families start for the hills to dig roots. Nobody in the village had any rice left to eat, they told Father Lynch. There is a mountain tree that has a starchy tuber root, tasteless but edible. However, it has a mild poison, and if too much is eaten, the legs swell and the body bloats, sometimes causing death. The hungry people kept alive several months by eating this tuber root and pulling leaves from tree branches to boil up with the roots. When the pigs of the village were finished, dogs, cats and rats were cooked and eaten in the struggle to live.

The July harvest gave them rice to eat again, and taxes levied in July were less devastating. From now on the land taxes were to be only 200 per cent higher than the former Nationalist government levied. The Communists tried to equalize the burden by taking 50 per cent of the crop of the better-off farmers, 30 per cent of the middle-class farmers' crop and 15 per cent of the harvest of the very poor. This tends to bring everyone to equal poverty. In Chinese the words Communist Party and Poverty Party are pronounced almost alike. One often hears the cheated country folk speak of it in derision as the Poverty Party.

It soon became evident why the Communists had to impose their devastating tax program. The standing army of regulars ran to several million men. As soon as the Communists took over, they called for local enlistments in every district, and they got them, for the army is comparatively well clothed, fed and taken care of. But their civil service and political organization far surpasses the military and runs to an astounding figure.

For an example, take this county of Shumkai. Before the Communists came, there was a police force of thirty, one of the police told me, and the soldiers kept on duty numbered around a hundred. Afterward we had a Communist police force of over a hundred, and a military force of well over a thousand. Their political functionaries and civil servants, all on government payroll, are scattered in every village.

Several thousand of them are called in here from time to time for meetings. I asked one of their minor officials called in how many civil and political servants there were on the government meal ticket in Shumkai. Close to ten thousand, he told me. If this is true, the Communists employ ten times as many as the old National government.

This goes to explain their ruinous tax program, which is draining the lifeblood from the people and drying up the sources of revenue. It is an elementary principle that a government can tax people only up to a certain point. Beyond that point the law of diminishing returns sets in with a vengeance. People need hope and incentive in the struggle for livelihood. These are destroyed if taxes are excessive and the production or business that gives tax revenue is soon killed.

I remember reading about the Communists take-over in Hungary. They ordered a tremendous increase of the output from the oil wells. Engineers told them if a well is pumped too fast and not given periods of rest, it is likely to blow into gas and stop the flow of oil. Ignoring the caution of experienced engineers, they got their "increased production" but at the cost of destroying sources. Tax revenue is very much like an oil well. A sensible assessment brings a flow into government coffers. An excessive drain is bound to dry up the sources.

In China the Communists have chosen to ignore this elementary principle, overloading every possible source, even down to the smallest trickle. And they see that taxes are enforced and collected. Youngsters with Communist encouragement and blessing prowl through the markets and village paths, demanding to see the tax receipts for a pound of salt or meat a person may be carrying home. The youngster reporting an untaxed morsel is rewarded with the goods. The person caught is fined or jailed.

When the Communists first came, the bus and truck traffic looked like a lucrative source, but their handling of it is a good example of their tax folly. They slapped on taxes nearly four times what the Nationalists charged. The tax, along with the many other Communist steps that killed business, just made it impossible for the buses to run. Before long there were almost no buses running, and after a couple of months the road taxes for buses were reduced more than half. This pump priming did a bit to start things moving again, but it was lancing an abcess when the entire system had tax poisoning and called for drastic surgery.

The buses still have their woes with the annoying taxes. For example, a bus prepares to leave Wuchow for Watlam. The driver has to wait his turn for the inspector to get to him. He has to show a tax paid slip for every item of goods, and each item is then inspected before loading. He pays a road tax to the bus stationmaster. Next he has to go back to another office and pay a tax on each passenger fare. Twice each year he has to pay registration fees on the bus. Before starting he must pay a tax for the two ferries and a tax on the new bridge recently put in.

He starts for Watlam and after fifty miles gets to Shumkai. Everything must be unloaded and tax and other papers inspected by the police at the bus station. Later, however, they began to pick a bus only now and then to unload. If he was lucky, a driver got through inspection at Shumkai in two hours. Each passenger's travel papers are inspected and personal baggage searched. If the passenger is the least bit bold in holding out for his rights, the police say, "Let's go to the police station and settle this." The bus goes on and the passenger is detained from one day to several weeks at the jail. I have often watched the unfortunate passengers and the bus driver being put through the mill at the bus station next to the mission.

If the police inspectors found the bus had taken on pigs, chickens or other goods between inspection points, and hence had no tax paid receipts, they threw the goods off and fined the driver. One driver walked over to where I was standing, muttered a string of oaths and said, "There is no more freedom in this country; look at this stack of tax slips; how can anyone do business?" If the police had heard him, he would have had to cease business immediately.

When the bus got to Paklau seventy miles further on, perhaps there would be another unloading, inspection and search. As a result, the 140-mile trip, that used to be made in a day, took two or three days. Under the past regime, thirty to forty loaded buses went through Shumkai every day. The average was now five, and many days there was not even one.

Several of the missioners had jeeps, so we came under their various and multiple charges. A person does not mind an outlay if he gets value for his money, and we were all willing to pay higher taxes if they improved the roads. But after nearly two years of Communist regime the roads had deteriorated and were worse than in the old days.

I see little hope for China's advancement toward prosperity while the army, the political and civil servants eat into the revenues like termites. The government cannot go on applying new taxes like leeches to an anaemic, poverty-ridden people, without bringing weakness and ruin to the people and government. Yet the government faces a serious dilemma. In order to survive with this regime of force, which is contrary to the laws of individual freedom and the natural aspirations of man, the government must wage an endless war against the people. If they cut down the hordes in government employ, they are weakening the numbers needed to hold the people in line. If they keep them, the burden of taxes threatens to wreck the country. They are riding a tiger, hard to get off, hard to stay on. We cannot condone their destructive taxes, but it is well to understand the government's predicament.

China is a backward country, at least fifty years behind the nations of an advanced economy which China is dealing with and trying to ape. Farms here do not mean large tracts of land as we know them in America. Here a farm means a few garden plots a fraction of an acre in size. The plots are worked by hand or oxen in the most primitive style. Machine farming to give efficient production is almost entirely absent. Since most of the farmers can neither read nor write, scientific advances in farming cannot be expected. The work goes on in much the same fashion as it did with their forefathers a thousand years back. Consequently, the land and its farmers — and most of the population are farmers — afford a hard-up, cupboard-bare source for taxation.

Except for Shanghai, a few cities along the coast and a moderate number in Manchuria, there are no big industries to furnish tax revenue or aid prosperity. Heavy industries like the steel, automobile, airplane and shipbuilding industries are not found in China. Natural resources, when properly exploited, are mammoth sources of income and tax revenue. Many important resources are lacking in China, and they have hardly scratched the surface in developing what they have. There is a wealth of coal along the Yangtze River, which could be used for power and industry, and a plentiful supply of coal in Manchuria. But the mining methods that I have seen are outdated and reminiscent of the horse-and-buggy days of the last century. Oil, so essential for the wheels of modern industry, has been found only in one small region of China's northwest.

The nation's sizable exports of bristles, dried eggs, silks, tea and wood oil have been stopped by the war. All this leaves the government sources of revenue so low they have resorted to taxing the land and small businesses and industries to the limit and beyond. The nation has been classed with the Big Four and the Big Five these recent years. China is entitled to this in respect to size and population, but certainly not in wealth and power or living standards.

Mind you, I am not lauding the industrial or machine age with the multiple problems and woes it brings. Nor am I holding it up as a standard of contentment or happiness. The machine age is with us, and since we cannot set the clocks back, our responsibility is to deal with and make the best of it.

All nations who have not yet reached it are fiercely striving for industrialization. In this race China has been left almost at the starting post. This will help understand the state of the nation, her problems and her manner of dealing with them. Maybe expedience, rather than wisdom, is guiding her acts and measures, but I hope the bit of background I have sketched will help in giving a more impartial and objective view of what threatens to be suicidal taxation.

A new source of government taxation was announced not long before I left China. It was called the "Three Anti" campaign. During 1951 they had drives to buy tanks, drives to buy planes, and drives for the Korea war effort. At meetings in the church I heard them announce what was assessed each village as the drives opened. Collectors, accompanied by armed guards, went to each family for the amount assessed. The Chinese Communists claim these "voluntary contributions" for the heavy-arms drive netted them five trillion (or $250,000,000 in U.S. currency). With the start of 1952 the "Three Anti" movement was initiated.

The "Three Anti" movement or campaign was to bring income from new sources. It was labeled antigraft, antiwaste and antibureaucratism. Informers and spies everywhere helped the government point out offenders. Accusation meetings imposed fines on accused people in every part of China. The huge fines collected added to government income the first three months of 1952.

It must have been lucrative, for a "Five Anti" movement was instituted. These were listed as "tax evasion, bribery, fraud, theft of state property, theft of state economic secrets." This "Five Anti" campaign was aimed principally at the urban middle class. Land reform and the "Three Anti" movement had already tapped and drained the landlords and country middle classes.

This "Five Anti" movement, carried on from March to June, 1952, seems to have broken the will and perhaps the economic back of the urban middle classes. Mass suicides reported from every big city indicate the thoroughness of this "Five Anti" movement. Businessmen were forced to confess their alleged transgressions against the state as members of the decadent capitalistic class. Accusation meetings forced them to pay up when other pressure failed.

It was a highly successful drive. The *Far Eastern Economic Review,* published in Hong Kong, states, in the May 15, 1952, issue, that in the "Five Anti" movement it was estimated that China had collected more than $200,000,000 U.S. currency. This was quite a windfall that came in less than three months' time.

Stabilization of a country's currency is a sign of the economic health and well-being of the people. Democratic countries follow the practice of issuing a certain amount of paper currency against gold or other metals of intrinsic value, which it holds in the treasury. Any other good resources or income a government has may also back its paper currency with firmness and the confidence of the people. Confidence in the currency is shaken when countries run close to bankruptcy in times of national emergency like war,

Shouldering their children and their belongings, the people fled to the hills at the approach of the Communist army.

This child's father, our leading teacher and organizer, declined
to join the Underground and became a marked man. By now he
may have been liquidated by the "army of liberation."

Father John McLaughlin prepares lunch by the roadside. He survived when Nationalists burned fifteen truck-loads of ammunition 300 feet from his house.

Seven members of Mary Wong's family were tagged as "land-lords" and were liquidated in the purges the new regime carried out from 1950-1952.

Mary Wong's grandfather served overseas in World War I and has seen war come to his own land since that time. Now he is in a Communist prison, but without a charcoal brazier to warm his hands.

Crossed wires, a hidden rotor and other tricks deactivated the jeep. Communists, unable to get in driving condition for a year, accused the author of sabotage.

Explaining the "shadow likeness machine." Communists later seized the camera in order to snap the "smiling faces of the liberated peoples."

Lee Wei Sz, the Shumkai Magistrate under the National government, was in the early group to be "disposed of" as Mao Tse-
tung directed.

Yu Chu-yin, who led his
clan into the Church, says
farewell. We met again in
jail. Condemned to slave
labor three months later,
he is probably now dead.

Mao Tse-tung ordered the churches closed. The pastors are exiled or in jail, and the churches have become Communist assembly halls. This is the chapel at Blue Cloud, six miles from Shumkai.

and inflation starts. Democratic governments can use numerous artificial means to check inflation to a certain extent. The authoritarian police states use ruthless force, punishment and fear to hold back inflation.

But the normal, natural and easy way to have a stabilized currency is by balancing the budget. When a government keeps its expenses somewhere near its income or ability to pay, the currency stays firm at full value. When a government goes overboard in spending and incurs debts far beyond its income, currency inflates to its natural level — to what the national mind thinks is the government's ability to redeem.

Other factors enter when inflation begins, such as printing press money used to cover for lack of income. This is Ponzi finance, and you and I and the man in the street know it will not work; that kind of remedy weakens the sick patient and hurries him on toward the final catastrophe.

In the war years I was having dinner with an admiral of the Chinese navy. He remarked that if he had a press to print currency, he could build a battleship. The poor man did not realize that the law of balancing income and expense has a way of catching up to, and trapping its violators.

When I was in Chunking during the last war, I saw a great deal of Ted Acheson, our Treasury man there on Lend-Lease. Ted told me that one day T. V. Soong asked him, "How can we stop this inflation?"

Ted spread his red mustache with a big smile and answered, "I can give you the remedy, but you will not follow it. Send half your army back home and cut down the other government expenses so that there is a hope of balancing the budget, and your inflation will stop."

When all is said and done, that is the simple remedy for economic health — a balanced budget.

The Communists burst into control of all China with tremendous expenditures and meager income. Inflation set in to push down the value of their printing-press currency. They coped with it in different ways; some orthodox, some otherwise.

Their financial difficulties were not brought on by wasteful extravagance, but primarily by the top-heavy political, civil and military personnel. They came up the hard way and were trained to stretch a dollar. Nurtured in penury, they command admiration for their haggling over costs of everything they buy and the way they are held to account for each expenditure. The only place I did not admire their parsimony was when I was in jail and they kept us half starved. The Communist soldiers and government borrowed or requisitioned everything possible from the people, going on the principle that they were the people's army and government.

No it is not waste, it is simply that their hordes of personnel swallowing up government funds was too much top sail tipping the boat dangerously — the boat that carried so little ballast of income. Their methods of cutting inflation and attempting to bring the boat back to an even keel are an interesting study.

The Communist army, marching victoriously into new territory, had pockets full of printing-press currency, which they forced the people to accept. People who had been taken in so often by worthless paper currency were reluctant to use it. For many months all local prices had been quoted in pounds of rice grain, and trading was done by barter, with rice grain as the exchange medium. Although this was clumsy, it was carried on after the arrival of the Communists, for people had no confidence in the new paper currency, which was valued at $35,000.00 for one American dollar.

Measures had to be taken to stop the falling value of their printing-press money, and to force the people to use it. When the Communists arrived, prices in the larger cities of

South China were quoted in Hong Kong currency or silver coins minted twenty years ago, and lately brought out of hiding.

Soon after the Communists were installed they set a date, and after that the use of Hong Kong currency was unlawful and it was confiscated wherever found. Next went the silver coins, and later even the coppers were declared illegal. A time limit was given to turn in these currencies to the government banks in exchange for their printing-press currency, and after the set date use of coins or foreign currency was illegal. They put teeth in their orders by sending numbers of spies around the markets and shops to arrest people using foreign currency or metal coins.

Finally they put a stop to the use of rice-grain barter in place of what somebody fittingly dubbed "the Mickey Mouse currency." Orders were put out that grain must be brought to the government barter center to exchange for paper currency, and only this currency could be used in the market trading.

The police, plainclothes men and soldiers paced the streets of the market with eagle eyes, and anyone seen using rice grain for purchases was arrested, fined and jailed. With their usual inconsistency, the government demanded that taxes must be paid in rice grain. A year and eight months later, from the time I originally wrote the notes for this chapter in my diary, people were still paying their taxes in rice grain.

Their scheme of hauling in Hong Kong currency and silver and rice gave a shadow of backing to the paper currency they were scattering around, and inflation was retarded. Forced to deal in this currency, the place was now being flooded with it. People were afraid to hold the paper and were spending freely.

Kids were gambling with five hundred dollar bills, coolies paid three thousand dollars for a pack of cigarettes, workmen got fifteen to twenty thousand dollars a day. One of the missioners, noticing a farmer with a fist full of ten-thousand-dollar bills, facetiously remarked, "The Communist paradise has now become a land of millionaires."

As the Communist program despoiled the rich of their land and wealth, and taxed the life from business and trade and farming produce, the despairing people spent the uncertain currency more wildly. And this, of course, gave a shove to inflation tendencies. A farmer said to me, "No one saves these days, for the government will take it away if we save. If we make any money now, we put it on the table and eat it up."

In order to scoop in the flood of currency that was threatening a worse inflation, the government came out with a Victory Bond issue. A district was assigned to collect so much. Each village in the district was in turn assigned its amount to collect. Village meetings were held and attendance was compulsory.

I listened to the neighboring villagers meeting here in the church. Each person was told how much he was expected to purchase. If a person tried to dispute the amount assessed, he was quickly silenced by shouting and scolding as armed militia gathered around him. Armed militia are always brought around for "contributions" to flood and famine relief, or to borrow things from people who show unwillingness to lend. I smiled, listening to the speeches about spontaneous contributions to the Bond drive for a greater China.

Draining back this expendable currency for bonds helped check inflation to a small degree. But the thing primarily responsible for a halt to inflation was that the Communist actions had brought all private business and trade to a standstill. When that happens there is little call for currency.

Money, like any other commodity, varies in value with the demand for its use. When there is no business and no demand for currency to buy goods, the money market is "easy." Lacking demand for its use, the money value holds steady and inflation automatically stops. Depression always brings about currency deflation when the business of a nation is killed.

Killing all business and trade is a drastic remedy, and effects a cure that is worse than the disease. I do not believe the Communists were stupid enough to kill business deliberately at this time as a remedy for inflation. Business is their big source of revenue, and as the saying goes, nobody wants to kill Santa Claus. It was indirectly that they caused business stagnation by their inordinate taxation, interference, inspections, regulations and a thousand other annoyances and hindrances.

The war in Korea made new taxation necessary. Russia must be paid in grains for armaments "given" to China. I saw a large convoy of trucks, carrying four tons each, transporting the tax grain to the West River. Boats took it to Canton or Hong Kong to buy war materials. It took the trucks all November and December, 1950, to move this one batch out. This may give some idea of the taxes collected. New taxes were devised all the time, yet they could not keep up with the war costs in Korea.

Officials and schoolteachers were told to hold democratic meetings and offer to give a slice of their salaries to buy armaments. Village meetings were again called and people told to make new contributions to the airplane fund. In 1951, when they seemed to have collected from and taxed every source, they started asking for taxes two years in advance. Although this is an old Chinese custom, it is ruinous to national economy.

The embargo against China had a far greater effect than people outside realize. Soon after shipments were stopped, the buses and trucks had to switch from gas to charcoal for fuel. But gas had to be used to start the motors and help the charcoal gas on the hills. The price went up to 3.50 U.S.

per gallon. Kerosene sold for 3.00 U.S. per gallon. Medicines jumped over 200 per cent.

A drive was started in late 1951 for old paper, for scrap iron and steel and for old machines, and the government paid an exhorbitant price to get them. Cotton had jumped to 2.50 U.S. per pound in September, 1951, when a big shipment from Russia brought down the price. One wonders why the Communists do not realize that their program of interference, taxation and war is breaking down the whole economy of China.

Part Two

Part Two

CHAPTER VII

Sent to Jail

MARCH 20, 1951, marked off two months of house imprisonment, a curious existence that had made the erstwhile missioner a cook, an unwilling dishwasher, a proficient sweeper, a handy seamstress for the wears and tears and a man of know-how at the washtub and scrubbing board. Each day went by with cooking and housework, prayers and reading until the sun was painting long shadows in the afternoon. Then it was time to start the evening meal, so I kindled the brazier and fanned the charcoal to a red glow. With the rice on to boil, I picked up a cleaver-shaped vegetable knife and a basket and went out to the garden.

The guard on duty was a hill-country lad of sixteen with fat cheeks, sleepy eyes and a dull mind. His only schoolbooks had been the plow and the hoe. Candidates for the police were chosen from the poorest families only. Their illiterate, unquestioning minds were ready-made for the job.

The fat boy's name was Comrade Chen. He was as friendly as he was stupid. On cold days he stood around the charcoal cooking brazier or scrounged cigarettes and tobacco while we visited. This afternoon we were chatting at the door as I started for the garden with the vegetable knife in one of my hands and the basket in the other. To josh the boy, I held up my knife and said:

"*Ta sz ni* — Strike you dead," a jocose term used in everyday conversation.

His life in the country watching cows had evidently given him no sense of humor and he looked up, frightened.

"You cannot say that, in the new society," he said.

I thought he was putting on an act, so I laughed and walked into the garden for vegetables. But he hurried to the guards quarters and came to the garden fence with two rifles. The other guard on duty had gone off somewhere for a stroll. Chen assumed an official voice and said:

"Are you a reactionary?"

"Sure I am a reactionary," and with these words, intended as a joke, I condemned myself as a criminal. In the Communist book, anyone not sympathetic to, or critical of, their government is dubbed a reactionary. Great numbers are being shot every day for this crime. Chen lifted one rifle to his shoulder and cried out:

"I shall see if you are afraid to die."

The rifle cracked, and garden dirt flew up ten feet away from me. It was still hard for me to believe that he was not putting on an act, so I plucked away at the peas without even turning my head. If I had realized Comrade Chen was serious, I would not have been so casual. Loaded guns are dangerous in a simpleton's hands. Now he was bewildered at my lack of fright and did not know what to do. The other guard, Comrade Tang, returned from his stroll and Chen rushed off to report the incident to police headquarters. Comrade Tang came over and said to me:

"I tried to tell Chen you were joshing him but he will not

believe it and has gone to report. I was away and saw nothing of the affair."

The police were delighted with the news. All their efforts to find someone willing to accuse me of something so they could lock me in jail had been in vain. (The last few weeks news was seeping in that missioners not yet in jail were being picked up on false charges and planted evidence.) Now they had a case for arrest without planting guns, bullets or opium in my house, and they pounced upon it.

When my rice was cooked and the vegetables boiling a half hour later, a whole squadron of police came rushing up and threw a cordon around my house prison. The cocky sergeant was in charge. He called me to the door and asked solemnly:

"Did you say, 'Strike you dead;' while holding a vegetable knife in your hand?"

"Yes, I said it joking with the guard."

"Enough! He admits his crime; take him down to headquarters" ordered the little sergeant.

With my meal still cooking on the fire, they marched me down the road, a rifle pointed at my back and police on either side holding guns. They had rounded up the would-be murderer and counter-revolutionary, the sergeant made it appear. At headquarters I had to squat on my heels, as all criminals they haul in had to do, while they reported.

The Police Chief was not around so the secretary Liu, who is a local man, took me in hand. After only a few minutes' questioning, since it was his mealtime, he made out a jail ticket. He handed it to a policeman and told him to escort me to the new jail. He said to me:

"I'm going to detain you in jail three days to let you reflect on all your offenses against the government. Then you will write a document of confession and amendment. If it is not satisfactory, you'll stay in jail longer."

I was disposed of for the evening so he could go back to his meal. The prisoners had eaten when I got there, so I would get no meal that night. This was the beginning of my reducing diet.

Liu's three-day sentence did not sound bad. But he had not talked with the Chief of Police, whom I had called to task several times, nor to the little shouting sergeant.

I afterward learned that there was a police conference the night of my seizure, when they evidently decided they had jumped the gun. They had put me in jail for attempted murder with no witness to the crime, and they knew it was impossible to get an admission of crime from me. It was only simpleton Chen's word against mine. Now they resorted to a snare that would catch me in confession before witnesses, so that their propaganda mill and newspapers could make a monstrous case of admitted guilt for the people.

Next morning Secretary Liu called me out of jail to his office. After a short period of interrogation he accused me:

"Comrade Tang says he was a witness to your attack upon the guard Comrade Chen."

"False! Comrade Tang was away for a walk. He told me yesterday he saw nothing of the affair. Why not call him and let me hear the charge you claim he made?"

Secretary Liu was caught, so now he proceeded to the real business of the summons.

"We want to settle this and get you out of jail" he lied. "Would you go up to the mission and show me what you said and did?"

After all, there was no choice, so I agreed to go. Cheated of a meal last night and called out of the cell before breakfast, I was hungry. A cigarette might ease the gnawing, but he would not let me get a pack from the road stand as we passed. Arriving at the mission, I saw the surprise they had prepared and was put on guard against their ruse.

Chief of Police Chee Yao, an army officer, government officials and a dozen armed police were in audience to witness the affair. With sweet, cajoling words they asked me to re-enact the scene of yesterday afternoon with the guard, Comrade Chen. He had been properly coached.

We stood at the door and chatted, and, at the words "Strike you dead," Chen started to run around the house.

"Chase him, lift up the knife and chase him" came their shouts.

They coached me on what my part should be, then tried the act over again. When I refused the cue again, one of the officers tried kicking me into chasing the guard. Next they gathered closer and pointed a dozen guns at me yelling:

"Chase him, hold up that knife and chase him."

Screaming at the failure of their game, they pulled back triggers on their revolvers, slid cartridges into their rifles and gave me what they threatened would be my last chance. When I refused to budge, Chief Chee's face went purple with anger; the vessels bulged with blood and he bellowed:

"Take him back to jail."

Just inside the prison main door the warden and a helper searched me. After emptying my pockets of penknife, money and keys, they took my wrist watch. My funds totaled less than three dollars U.S. Each prisoner is allowed to keep up to thirty cents for personal purchases, so the warden returned that amount to me. They also lifted my Ronson lighter, for the prisoners are not allowed to smoke.

Then I was led off to a cell where about twenty other inmates started to question me. They asked how long I was sent up for. I told them, "Secretary Liu said three days, but I believe nothing a Communist tells me."

"Oh, no, if a government man said three days, it will be three days," they said, as they were supposed to say.

"We'll wait and see. I may be wrong this time," I replied.

The jail had formerly been a Confucian temple. Last year, after the Communist government got control, all the jails began to overflow, and the temple had been converted to a prison and divided into twelve cells. Double decks were put in as the numbers increased. After a month in one of the two remaining single-deck cells, we had an upper platform put in and our numbers went from twenty to forty. Some of the cells had sixty inmates crowded into them.

The temple-made-jail was of conventional temple style. Buildings were built around a rectangular court open to the sky. These large buildings were blocked off into cells eighteen feet deep and thirteen feet wide. An undersized door and two small windows opened onto the court, but heavy wooden bars blocked out half the light and air.

A narrow aisle down the middle divided the cell, leaving a five-and-a-half-foot platform on either side for sleeping. My feet hung out in the aisle at night because the bunks were not designed for six-footers. The platform for bunks was a foot above the dirt floor. Underneath was an inviting rat run for playful rodents. We stored our empty rice bowls there, and at night we could hear the rats nosing and tumbling over the bowls. Sometimes we saw their beady eyes in the daytime as they hunted for stray grains of rice. Their carousing on the loose tiles overhead each night made a jingle like cowbells. Some of the inmates contended they must be cats to make so much noise. Someone chirped in: "They sound to me more like water buffaloes."

This platform, with rats on the roof above and under the boards below running, squeaking and fighting, was where we slept at night and sat for classes during the day. Each prisoner had a foot-and-a-half space on the staging for his apartment. When sleeping on my side, I could not double up my knees without bumping the prisoners on either side. The local folk are about half my size, so were not troubled by the narrow quarters.

The first night I lay down hungry. I had no covering, so a prisoner shared a dirty quilt with me for a week until the warden went to the mission and brought a blanket for me. There was the gnaw gnaw, crunch crunch of fingernails scratching from the prisoners on both sides of me. I joined the exercise before long, and next morning learned that these interloping bedfellows tickling us were body lice.

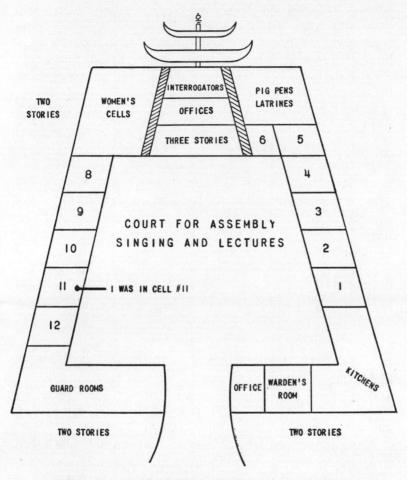

TWO STORIES

WOMEN'S CELLS

INTERROGATORS

OFFICES

THREE STORIES

PIG PENS LATRINES

6

5

8

9

10

11 ● ——→ I WAS IN CELL #11

12

COURT FOR ASSEMBLY SINGING AND LECTURES

4

3

2

1

GUARD ROOMS

TWO STORIES

OFFICE

WARDEN'S ROOM

KITCHENS

TWO STORIES

NEW JAIL MADE FROM CONFUCIAN TEMPLE

During free time each day, everybody stripped off clothes and underwear and hunted out the body lice. Most of them were found nestling inside the underwear. The first two days, since I had just come in, I did not join the embarrassing hunt. But when it felt as though the crawling things would walk away with me, I too stripped down and started to hunt. I plucked from my clothes and killed thirty-eight cooties that day. The prisoners showed me how to end the life cycle of a louse. One closes in on the louse with the two thumbs and presses it to death between the thumb nails. The kill is signaled by a snap, and generally a blotch of blood spreads over the nail.

The prisoner on my left was a university man. He claimed a newborn louse mates and lays eggs when three days old. Then it becomes a mother-in-law and a grandmother within a week. It may be hard to verify his assertions about the sex life of a louse, but it needs no Kinsey report to know they increase and multiply with incredible speed.

In our daily classes the theme "increase production" was harped upon daily, so one of the prisoners stopped the hunt, held up his thumb nail with a fat louse just killed and asked:

"Does America have such production?"

The prisoner was reprimanded by the cell chief for improper speech.

As I sat on the boards stripped to the waist, hunting lice inside my undershirt, the prisoners gathered round to stare and ask questions.

"Do all Americans have hair on their chest?" one asked.

After a pause another hillbilly came up with the question, "Do American women have hair on their chest, too?"

Most Chinese have only a few whiskers on the chin and lip to pass for a beard. They looked at the forest growth all over my face which had sprung up during the two months as a house prisoner, and the hillbilly asked:

"Do the women in America also have beards?"

I laughed at this, and most of the prisoners joined in, leaving the question unanswered.

When the summer heat came, everyone in the sweltering cell stripped down to his shorts. Flies were not too numerous because the kitchen and latrine were near the cells across the court. The cell was quite dark, and with the break of dawn mosquitoes swarmed in like an invading army. At night they attacked us like dive bombers. I wore my clothes and socks and preferred to sweat rather than be eaten by mosquitoes. I spread a handkerchief over my head and face as a shield against them. After a time I got tired out each evening and fell asleep in spite of their attacks.

We sat in our shorts when the heat made our cell into a steam bath. I wore a crucifix hanging from a silver chain around my neck. This was an object of constant interest to people looking at me or visiting with me. One of the prisoners asked to let him wear it awhile, probably thinking it was some special charm. It brought many questions about the crucifix and the Catholic religion. One of the guards suggested that I throw it away, because the day of religion and God was gone.

When some of the officials got curious about the crucifix, I told them that the Founder of our religion was falsely accused, arrested and jailed. So why should I complain against a like honor. This always angered them, and they often replied I should not say I was falsely arrested.

My morning and evening prayer also caused much inquiry from my cell mates. The guard's bugle blew about fifteen minutes before our rising bell in the morning. I got up with the bugle, knelt on the boards in the dim, gray dawn and made my orisons to God. The guard often looked in, but never scolded me. In the evening when all-quiet was signaled, I knelt again, as darkness closed down the day and lulled the world to sleep, while I whispered vesper prayers. The wings of prayer lifted me for a few moments above prison walls to the realm of peace and calm. The prisoners questioned me wonderingly about prayer and the God I prayed to. They fingered over the rosary beads and crucifix, asking for an explanation. And in sweltering weather when we were stripped down to underwear they saw the callouses on my knees, and questions on prayer and religion came up again and again for conversation.

The first morning after a night under a dirty quilt I got up itching with lice and asked, "What about a wash and what are the chances of taking a bath here?" The fellow next to me said, "Don't talk about it. I've been here seven months without a bath." Then he went on to say, "During the hot summer months when prisoners are consigned to labor gangs outside, they may take a bath once a week in the river." This explained the sickening stench of sweaty bodies I noticed when I came into the cell. And the itch and skin diseases so many of the prisoners have is, of course, brought on by lack of a wash. When the warden and helpers came in to search a cell for contraband, they wore a gauze pad over their mouth and nose.

Before each meal a bucket of water was delivered to the cell. Each prisoner got a tin cupful of cold water to wash his rice bowl and chopsticks. One could dip a handkerchief in the water cup, then rub it over the face. A few of the prisoners used to take a cat wash this way. We could also save a little of the precious water to wash our teeth. Sometimes a prisoner would collect the water after the bowls were washed and use it to wash out his underwear or shirt. One day as we washed the rice bowls a downpour started. I asked the guard to let me catch the rain water pouring off the roof. He consented, and I pushed the bucket out and got enough water to wash out my underwear once.

When the warden went to the mission to get a blanket for me, he also brought a bar of soap, a toothbrush and what he thought was tooth paste. Everybody borrowed the precious bar of ivory soap to get one good wash, so it disappeared quickly.

A few days after my consignment to the jail the warden passed our cell door. I told him the lice were a nasty problem (and that in American prisons the warden is held responsible for health and cleanliness). "What can be done about it?" he asked me. I told him I had a small drum of D.D.T. at the mission he could use if he wished. He sent men for it immediately, and next day prisoners in each cell were asked to contribute money for kerosene, to mix the D.D.T. He called me to his office to ask how it should be mixed and used. I made bold to ask for a cigarette, thinking I had him in my debt. He did not want to consent to this, but the Assistant Chief of Police was in the office and ordered him to give me a smoke. It tasted good after several days' abstinence.

The cells were sprayed and this cut down the undercover population so much that the warden promised to spray once a week if prisoners contributed kerosene. In about three weeks the lice were so few that lice-hunting hour was eliminated. Only when prisoners came in as transfers from other jails were we annoyed to find they had brought them again. After each spraying we had a relief from the mosquitoes and flies for a few days too.

In announcing the D.D.T., the warden told the assembled prisoners simply that the prison now had D.D.T. Not a word of credit to the mission for donating it.

Each prisoner's daily food was limited to the amount of nine hundred dollars Communist currency, or three cents U.S. This is not a special hunger diet for prisoners only. Poor farmers and poor people spend about that amount for their daily fare.

The three cents per day bought one pound of rice and three ounces of vegetables. For the morning meal five ounces of rice were weighed out for each prisoner and cooked into rice gruel. It gave two large bowls of gruel or porridge, of about the same consistency as watery oatmeal. But without any salt it tasted pretty flat. Several times I asked the warden for permission to buy salt, but it was never granted. We were prisoners, and they often let us know they could not be bothered with our wants and needs.

The two bowls of gruel and two spoonfuls of beans or like vegetables were brought to us about nine o'clock. It had to tide us over until the afternoon meal at four. For the afternoon meal eleven ounces of rice were thrown into the pot for each prisoner and cooked into steamed or dry rice. The amount of salted vegetables was the same as with morning meal — two tablespoonfuls.

I remarked to the prisoners, as food was being measured out for each one, "This is the way we feed cattle back home on our farm: a measure full of this grain, a measure of that and a bushel of silage for each cow."

When Communist prisoners have served their terms, they are presented with a bill for their food and firewood. The prisoners' family or friends have to bring in money or rice to pay the board bill before the prisoner can be released. Only the very poor are exempt. These are fed from the rice grain confiscated from the landlords.

Although they had taken over five tons of my rice grain, they presented me with a bill when preparing to release me from prison. My answer was that the government had taken all my rice so the warden would have to ask the government for my board. He released me with directions to get it from the government and pay it into the prison.

The division of food in each cell is amusing. A homemade balance weight has notches cut along the baton to mark each ounce. The rice bowl at the other end is filled to balance, then is dumped into the prisoner's bowl. Rice is brought from the kitchen in a large basket with a slip marking the weight, so many ounces to be given to each prisoner. One small bowl of rice is weighed out first. It is the bonus for the two prisoners whose turn it is that day to weigh and divide the rice, wash the vegetable bowl and sweep the floor. If there is a bowl of rice left over after weighing out each prisoner's portion, it is auctioned off to the highest bidder.

The vegetables for the meal are brought in one large bowl. Each prisoner has a small bowl and these are lined up for equal division. These hungry men watch with hawk eyes to see that they get every bean and every grain of rice due them. The vegetables given to us had about as much variety as the rice. The variation runs from white beans to yellow beans to brown beans to black beans. About once in ten days a green vegetable was given us.

Until a man is forced to live on a pound of rice and 3 ounces of vegetables a day, he cannot appreciate how precious each kernel of rice is and how good a grain of salt tastes. Every last kernel is garnered from the bowl, and rice is rubbed around the bottom of the vegetable bowl to soak up every drop of grease or grain of salt. If any grains of rice fall on the bed boards, they are picked up and eaten.

From noon until the four o'clock evening meal I suffered with gnawing hunger and trembled with weakness. Perhaps the Chinese do not mind so much, for they average about half my weight and perhaps need less food. But every prisoner was vocal in talking about his hunger.

One day prisoners who knew the art were called out to butcher a prison pig. There was jubilant chatter in every cell as we watched the butchering through the bars. That night each prisoner got two ounces of pork, and there was more appreciation and joy over it than the politicos back home have over the Jackson Day dinner. I had been in jail about a month, and this was the first morsel of meat given us.

About ten days after this one meal with pork, our vegetable bowl arrived with two small morsels of pork for each prisoner. One fellow near me remarked, "One of the pigs must have died of cholera." When a hog goes off feed with cholera, the people here normally butcher it right away and sell the meat. The guess of my cell mate was correct. A few minutes later we saw the remaining side of a small butchered hog lying in a basket in the yard. It was bluish in color, and immediately I lost my appetite for the pork just brought us to eat. The prisoner beside me noticed I did not touch my share of meat, so he asked if he could have it. I held out the bowl for him to pick out the cholera meat with his chopsticks.

Instead of water to quench the thirst, we were given rice-wash water. Before cooking the rice, it is washed in cold water. This washes out the rice dust and dirt and is usually fed to the pigs by country people. But here at the prison the rice-wash water was heated to a boil, then brought to each cell for us to drink twice a day. We christened it our coffee, soup or milk at different times. Outside of prison we would have called it by its proper name, swill.

The toilet was a platform in back of the pigpen, so the same pit stored the refuse from pigs and prisoners. The walk between pens of some thirty odd pigs led to the toilet platform. Two rows of boxlike stalls, ten in a row, back to back, were the "rest rooms." The stalls were built up one foot from the floor. The center board in each stall where a prisoner "rests" is cut out for the drop into the pit below.

Prisoners were released twenty at a time in the morning and in the evening for toilet calls. When the turn came to our cell, the door was opened until the number of twenty passed out. They lined up outside, counted off, then were told to run for the toilet. In about three minutes, the guard yells hurry, which means time is up. He blows a police whistle, and the group is supposed to run back to the yard for the count, then into the cell. The whole operation took about five minutes per group. But there were nearly five hundred inmates here, so they had to rush.

The prison ration of rice only, without meat, grease or vegetable roughage, was a problem for bowel traffic. I could not operate in this subway rush hour speed of five minutes, twice a day, for toilet. For nine days I went to the box stalls without any success. All this fertilizer is used to "increase production" for the new China. Toilet refuse is saved and spread on the fields to fertilize the crops.

My fingers and toes were numb from the poisons, and hammer blows went through my head with each throb of my pulse. I had asked the warden to get a laxative from the Public Health Center several times, but he kept putting me off. I was really worried and decided something must be done.

I had a tube full of Gillette brushless shaving cream, the one the warden brought from the mission thinking it was tooth paste. This contained soap and oil and should start the traffic moving inside me. On the ninth day of no success in the box stall toilet, I injected half a tube of the shaving cream into the bowels. This solved the traffic jam.

For a urinal a wooden bucket was placed outside the barred door and a bamboo spout run between the bars into the cell. The stench it gave off in warm weather was indescribable. Even though the Chinese live with urinal buckets in their homes to furnish fertilizer, they were sickened by the stench here. This stench mingled with the smell of sweat and unwashed bodies. I heard one prisoner say the first three days getting used to the smell was terrible. The smell from a tannery or rendering plant is less offensive.

My first month in jail, March 20 to April 20, we painfully managed to get along on the ration of one pound of rice per day. But as spring passed on, the stores of last autumn's rice ran low and the price of rice grain soared. The limited funds allotted for each prisoner then cut the food in half. From then on, we were given four ounces of rice made into gruel twice each day. If hunger gnawed at the insides on a pound of rice each day, the poor stomach became a growling, echoing, empty cavern on half a pound. My belt tightened each week, and each day I went to bed and got up hungry. When released from prison, I weighed 158 pounds. Before going to jail I had weighed 195.

One of the prisoners had a cup of rice gruel left over one

day. He placed it near the window and the sun turned it sour. He offered it to me, and I gulped it down to stop the hunger gnawing. This sour gruel started a violent dysentery, with a call to action about every hour. Since prisoners are released only twice a day for toilet, the inmates in each cell buy an earthen pot to use for emergencies. The situation is not so embarrassing at night, but picture a man using a pot in daylight with a crowded cell of prisoners around. Twice a day at toilet time I took the pot to empty into the pit.

The dysentery continued for over three weeks and brought on blood and mucous colitis. The tearing pains in my intestines often doubled me up. Finally I began to run a slight fever and have night sweats. This worried me because of the T.B. twenty years before.

When police secretary Liu called me up for questioning one day during this illness, I staggered out and talked in a weak, husky voice. They were concerned about my illness. The warden asked the cell chief if there was danger that I would die. The cell chief said he didn't think so, I was pretty tough. But prisoners frequently did die of sickness and lack of care in the prison.

Shortly after I had arrived in the prison cell, I heard a low moan as a sick prisoner in the corner let out each painful breath. He was an old fellow quite emaciated by weeks of fever, and he lay with his head covered, panting and moaning. Around his wrists were iron bracelets, and chains hung from the anklets binding his feet. When he coughed or turned, the chains clanged and jingled. It was only with labored effort that he could sit up at mealtime and eat a little gruel, but he was getting weaker and weaker as each day passed. Formerly he was an opium smoker, I was told, and opium smokers were being jailed under the new regime. But he wore the irons because he was supposed to have been a guerilla, or have been in league with them, at least.

Each day or two the cell chief wrote a note to inform the warden of the man's condition and recommended sending him to the Public Health Center. Nothing was done about it. One of the cell mates was a herb doctor, so he took the man's pulse to diagnose the sickness, then wrote a prescription. But the old man had no money, and, as the prisoners hopelessly shrugged their shoulders, I asked if I could buy the medicine for the patient. This offer by the American just arrived in jail made them lift their eyebrows.

Next morning when the prisoners were discussing what should be done, I offered to carry the sick man down to the Public Health Center if the warden would permit him to go. This offer caused the cell mates, who had been so indifferent to the patient's suffering, to search their hearts. Through pride and shame, they could not let me do this. One of them spoke up:

"It isn't right for twenty of us Chinese here to sit back and let a foreigner carry one of our sick people through the streets. We'll do it if the warden grants permission." But permission was refused. "Too bothersome!"

I helped the man sit up to eat and let him lean on my arm to go to the bars for the urinal. When he could no longer walk to the toilet for weakness, I got the guard's permission to carry him. He was emaciated and light, so I took him in one arm like a child and carried him with his chains rattling to the toilet.

Charity moves the heart of everyone, pagan or Christian. At discussion of faults hour that day, several prisoners accused themselves of lack of mercy. They decided to assign two of the inmates, if they would volunteer, to look after the patient's needs. This was arranged, but when the sick man wanted to sit up or be waited on otherwise, he beckoned for me to help him. I had helped him when the others seemed not to care and so he still looked to me.

Two weeks after my entry into jail the old man approached the end. I felt his pulse late one afternoon and told the others he would most likely die before morning. The cell chief wrote an urgent message for the warden, repeating

· 111 ·

what I had told the group. Meanwhile, I bent over the old man and told him he was about to die. He shook his head with understanding. Then I asked him if he wanted to go to heaven and be happy with God after death. He answered, "I want." As briefly as possible, I explained God the Father and Creator, God the Son and Redeemer and God the Holy Spirit who lives in us and gives us all the graces of Christ's redemption. Next I told him about Ma-lee-a, the Mother of Christ. The prisoners sat in respectful silence listening to our words.

One of the prisoners had saved a small cup of water to wash his teeth that night, so I asked him for the water. As I poured the water over the sick man's shaved head, I repeated the words giving him citizenship in the kingdom of heaven: "*Ego te baptizo in nomine patris et filii et spiritus sancti.*" Then I taught the dying man a little prayer to repeat up to the end, "Jesus save me."

In a little while the assistant warden came with two labor squad prisoners. They had a pole between them and a door hung by triangle ropes to make a stretcher.

The bars were opened, and I took the dying man in my arms and carried him to the improvised stretcher. I told him to continue repeating through the night at the Health Center, "Jesus save me." As he lay on the board stretcher, the warden came out. He saw death on the man's face, so he unlocked the irons from his wrists and ankles before they carried him away. Word came back through the labor gang that the patient died that night.

During the next couple of days two of the prisoners who had borrowed doctrine books to read from Catholic friends, asked me if they could be baptized here in prison. I put them off until we would be out of jail. The same week two others told me they would like to take instruction when we were free again. This leads one to believe that the materialism they were giving us every day in the drill course was not going very deep into the hearts of the prisoners. The demons of the new regime work like mad to tear down idealism, faith and heaven, but with doubtful success.

One cell in the prison was for the women. There were between twenty and thirty of them. Several of them were wives of political prisoners, or wives of guerillas or other offenders. Others were in because of their own offenses. One woman who wore chains clamped to her ankles was said to have murdered her husband. A Catholic woman was among them. Her husband was an official with the Ministry of Public Works under the old government, so the family was always under suspicion.

The most pitiable of the female population in jail were the babies. Four nursing babies were cursed to endure the prison routine. They attended classes, labor and assembly, strapped to their mothers' backs, papoose fashion. When they cried during assembly or singing, the mothers pivoted back and forth to quiet them by this rock-a-bye swing. At the same time the mothers' arms swung around to pat the baby in cadence with the swing. If a baby was hungry, his mother nursed him at the breast while listening to some diatribe about Communism.

CHAPTER VIII

Indoctrination Course

THE INDOCTRINATION COURSE for prisoners is the same as the course for officials and for the general public. As their propaganda and songs declare, the purpose is to change the whole outlook and mind of a person, so that he thinks, speaks, lives and acts only according to the Party Line. This means you are to surrender all independence of thought and let the government and party do the thinking. Your part is only to reflect their thoughts. You are to swallow all the government propaganda and all their declarations in unquestioning faith and block any contrary thoughts from your mind. You are trained and cautioned to stop all talk except what the party directs to be said. Your actions and lives are to be all pro and nothing contra the government and party. As their instructors "reason" and lecture: One cannot criticize the [people's] government, for this is to criticize yourself. The course is supposed to give you a faith that this singleness of party line action will bring prosperity and blessings to everyone.

The iron discipline and frightful punishments used are aimed to sear into your heart a fear that will break your spirit. It almost always does, and I saw prisoners suffering under blows and chains and ropes who, although they hated Communism mortally, sang the praises and glories of the regime.

The Party Line is like a bible for the Communist party, and the people are supposed to trust its infallibility. But the Communists, who trust no one, do not merely trust that the people will accept this Party Line. They have ever-present spies and guns to force it down with fear and terror.

One has to live with, or mingle closely with, Communists for a long time to understand the full meaning of the Party Line. It is not grasped at a glance or even by a cursory study; it must be absorbed slowly as you go along. Communism, though the same everywhere, is a complicated but well-organized system. It is a doctrine and, like religion, must be digested with time and slowly absorbed to be grasped fully. That is why the masses of the people have their indoctrination courses forced upon them, so that its opiate will be needled slowly into their veins day after day and week after week. And the Communists believe then that the people will be sufficiently drugged so they will think, act and talk only in the channels of the Party Line.

What astounds me is the Communist's seeming faith that indoctrination will really convert all the minds and hearts of the people who get it, to their way of thinking. I heard some years ago that the Communists put the Chinese priests in North China through their course, believing this would change their mentality and outlook. The Communists released the priests at the end of the course, thinking they had made solid converts to the new way of life. I could not at the time think so little of the Communist intelligence as to believe it. But now I could see that they believed the course would even change, externally at least, the mentality of a hardheaded American priest, myself!

· 115 ·

In my opinion, however, it is a game of make-believe with them. Unless they are stupid in the extreme, they can see that people are only pretending to follow and praise Communism. They accept the people's external assent, "the surface praise," and hold them in line with threats, tyranny and guns. But they must really know the sentiments deep inside the great majority of people. Only a few fanatics and some of the poor who have profited by Communism are exceptions. This opinion and conclusion is reached after talking to prisoners, and to great masses of the people after they had gone through the indoctrination course that goes along with the land reforms, and after living myself under Communism for two years.

Some details of the course given in prison are different from the courses given outside, and I'll discuss these first. The prison organization dovetails with the indoctrination course, since the majority of the prisoners are detained only for the length of the course. Prisoners who give the appearance of true conversion by the course have a chance for freedom. Those who show little or no progress in "changing their views" are liquidated.

There are three committees whose members are chosen by the prisoners, but are approved or rejected by the warden and Chief of Police. The first is the *Study Committee*. This group has two members in each of the twelve cells, and, from the group of twenty-four men, two or three are picked by the prison authorities to meet and carry out the work. These members choose the Communist songs to be learned and teach them to the prisoners at assembly time. They record and distribute the Communist books and pamphlets to each cell and do the library work of exchanging the books from cell to cell. They also make up the daily topic for discussion by the prisoners and deliver a copy to the different cells. From time to time they write plays along the Party Line for prisoners to put on. They also write out posters of anti-imperialistic and pro-Communist slogans, and post them up all over the place.

Production Committee. This Committee is made up in the same way, by two members from each cell. Two of them are picked for the outside work. They are in charge of the outside labor squads, the prison workers for the kitchen and the caretakers for the pigs and chickens. They also direct prisoners who cultivate idle lands nearby. Carpenters and mason prisoners are assigned work in the prison and come under the production committee. This committee is important, for "increase production" is the constant cry. Everywhere around the hills and valleys prisoners are putting fallow and wild land under cultivation.

The Communists have learned from Russia, and, consequently, after indoctrination the long-term prisoners are farmed out to prison labor camps. Three hundred of our prisoners were taken to Tai Ping, fifteen miles away, where they mined wolfram. People tell me that the wolfram, a precious war material, all goes to Russia. Another company of our prisoners was taken out to quarry stone and burn lime in a district two miles to the south. A third group was at a mountain village burning charcoal. Cheap lime and charcoal from these prison camps are sold in the market. Road gangs and agricultural gangs were taken out each morning, but returned to the prison at night.

Shortly after I was taken from prison back to house arrest in June, 1951, a new government directive was published in the newspaper: "All counter-revolutionaries who can either be sentenced to death or dealt with otherwise should not be executed, but should be *disposed* of [italics mine] by means of imprisonment with hard labor." This would explain the lengthening lines of slave labor gangs I saw led by the mission. One told me his death sentence was changed to life imprisonment, which was the practice for those who labored well, in their "reform by labor."

The Economic Committee was in charge of the buying of food, livestock, kerosene, lumber and other supplies needed in the prison.

The cell chief, to whom I have often referred, has an important role. The warden appoints a prisoner in each cell to be the representative for the other prisoners and the go-between for the prisoners and the prison officials. He assigns the prisoners to their places in the cell, settles disputes and presides at meetings and elections for the cell. Our cell chief was formerly local secretary for the fallen Kuomintang party.

The daily prison schedule kept the prisoners fairly well occupied all day long, but the nights I found wearying instead of restful. No light was given to any cell, and as soon as dark fell prisoners had to go to bed and keep silence. At the mission it was my habit to read or study until eleven or twelve o'clock, so sleepless, silent hours in prison were a task to fill.

When I came in, there was only a cursory search of my pockets, and they failed to find the rosary beads deep down in a pocket corner. Perhaps they would have left them with me, for they gave back my fountain pen when I begged to keep it. Without it, I could not have recorded this story while still in prison. When the warden went to the mission for blankets and a few other articles, I asked him to bring my breviary. He answered brusquely, "This is not the place for prayer."

My beads were a happy companion that helped fill up the sleepless night hours, and during the day I used them when lectures were insipid or an insult to God.

I was brought to the prison in Holy Week, Tuesday, March 20. This gave me an association and a kind of share in the events of the days just ahead. I was rather elated at being falsely accused and arrested just at this time.

I could travel in thought to a corner of Gethsemane, follow the mob to the homes of Annas and Caiphas and up the incline to the Pretorium of Pilate; I could join the crowd up the narrow cobbled alleys of Jerusalem to the Sacred Hill. This year I was favored to feel and fill up the things that are wanting, as St. Paul says.

The prisoners' schedule (school schedule, they call it, for we were willy-nilly students of Communism in this forced indoctrination course) was as follows:

6:00-7:30	Group Singing of Communist songs.
8:00-9:00	Study of Communist books or lecture in the prison court on fair days.
9:00-9:30	Morning meal of rice gruel.
10:00-12:00	Discussion of the topic assigned for the day.
12:00-1:00	Group singing of Communist songs.
1:00-2:00	Reading and explanation of books assigned.
2:00-3:00	Self-criticism class.
4:00	Afternoon rice.
5:00-6:30	Assembly singing.
6:30	Roll call; silence and sleep with nightfall.

Singing is an integral and important part of Communist life. There are songs composed for every phase of activity, but the majority of them are on the theme of Communist aims and propaganda, and people everywhere in the country sing them. This helps to make the people aware of their aims, propaganda and news. The singing complements their slogans and teaching. The farmers sing more of the land and land-reform songs; the coolies emphasize the labor songs; and soldiers give prominence to the martial and military songs. But most of the songs are sung by everybody and known by all.

Soldiers sing while marching or when they stop to rest. School children sing a great part of their day. Prisoners sing four hours a day. In all the indoctrination courses for the candidates for government positions, singing takes up three to four hours daily. Government officials sing at every meeting. The people in villages and towns also chant the Communist songs as an integral part of every meeting.

We started singing in our prison with the rising bell. Though feeling groggy, ugly and sleepy, you join in your husky morning voice to the song intoned by the leader. With no water to wash your face and freshen up, you croak like a frog while folding up the blankets.

Singing in the indoctrination courses accomplishes several aims. First it occupies the free time with pro-Communist doctrine, time which might otherwise be used to criticize the government. It gives a martial air and feeling of elation to the people marching toward the Communist aims, and it helps to channel the minds of the people into the Party Line. It also helps them forget the misery brought in with the new regime. Because the songs are propaganda, new ones are sent all over the country to be used with each new trend or change in government propaganda. Songs with the theme "destroy the landlords and take their lands" are sung during land-reform months. "Take Hainan, take Formosa; Destroy bandit Chiang Kai-shek" were the most used songs around the end of fighting where we were in South China.

In place of the notes and bars, they use the numbers 1-8 with dots over the numbers that run into a higher octave, and lines below if the notes run lower. Each person when he is taught the song copies it himself, which saves this penny-pinching, impoverished government.

The singing is taught with the same discipline, drive and organization as other parts of the Communist movement. As a result, their singing everywhere is impressive and excellent. It echoes through the city streets, from hills around the country villages and from the mountains skirting the rice-field valleys. A child or two is often seen walking through the fields or along the road singing a Communist song and swinging an arm to beat the cadence. Singing is good psychology to help promote the movement, and evidences the thorough, far-reaching organization of Communism.

I give here a free translation of some of the songs, to give an idea of theme and doctrine.

The Party Line

The Party Line, the Party Line, we must have the Party
  Line;
For New China's People, the Party Line, the Party Line
  has come;
An absolute must is the Party Line.
The whole world must also follow the Party Line.
Imperialists' policy is aggression.
The great Soviet's policy is peace and trust in peace.
Tear to shreds as vain and false,
All contrary thoughts (to the Party Line).
In this world there is no other road but the Party Line, the
  Party Line.
We must have the Chinese Communist Party,
We must have still more the Socialism principles, the Party
  Line.

Stalin then is victory, Mao Tse-tung is victory,
They have fixed on the Party Line, the Party Line.
Discipline self to follow the Party Line through all hardship,
The Party Line is victory sure.

Annihilate imperialism and have the entire world
Follow the Party Line, the Party Line.
Turn to the Party Line and the great Stalin,
Turn to the great Mao Tse-tung and the peace front.
Our strength is like a mountain
And we'll preserve for long the world's peace.

Song to Mao Tse-tung

Just as the sun shines and lights the world
China has the Communist Party, like the sun for light.
Mao Tse-tung is like father and mother,

· 121 ·

He sets the aim for the people,
He suffers hardship throughout the busy day and night.
With Mao Tse-tung China has hope,
With Mao Tse-tung China has hope.
The people are changed over [to Communism], now each
is his own master.
In the liberated areas it is like heaven, every family has good
living,
Their joy is vast as the ocean and they sing songs,
They sing of Mao Tse-tung; they sing of the Communist
Party.
They sing of the liberated areas, the people's happy places.
They sing of the liberated areas, the people's happy places.

One has to smile at Communism using heaven as a
metaphor.
The following song is a staccato march and is as fiery as
Le Marseillaise. Soldiers sing and march to its verve.

Follow Mao Tse-tung
Follow, follow Mao Tse-tung; Follow, follow Mao Tse-tung.
What we demand for the people is independence.
They cannot be America's slaves.
What we demand is livelihood and freedom.
Our lives must not be considered as dung.
Follow, follow Mao Tse-tung; follow, follow Mao Tse-tung.
He is the protector of the fatherland.
He is the leader of the liberated peoples.
Follow, follow Mao Tse-tung; five hundred million people,
Ten hundred million hands.

Lift high your mailed fists,
Strike dead the traitors, strike dead those beasts who devour
men.
We demand their blood to repay for our flesh,
Over twenty years [struggle] in a sea of blood

and deep hatred. We can hold in no longer!
Follow, follow Mao Tse-tung,
Destroy the traitorous bandits [i.e. the Nationalists],
Set up the New China, independent and peaceful,
The people's blessed light which is now before us.

[Youth] Follow Communism
You are a lighthouse tower, lighting the ocean before us,
You are the pilot grasping the helm to direct the ship,
China's Communist youth — you are then the pivot,
You point the way, we will follow you forever.

There are many war songs sung since the Chinese went
into Korea. The theme is generally the same, "Strike down
the American wolf," so I'll give only one of the shorter songs
in translation.

Chinese Volunteers' War Song
With martial order and spirits high,
March across the Yalu River,
Preserve peace and protect the fatherland,
This means protecting our families and our countryside.
Good Chinese boys and girls
With one heart and firmly united
Resist America, assist Korea,
Defeat the savage-hearted American wolf.

I'll give the titles to other songs we had to sing regularly.
The titles will give some idea of the contents.
1. Spring Planting (An urge to open new lands and increase production.)
2. Help Korea; Advance! Advance! (Another war song.)
3. White Haired Lady (Praising Communism.)
4. The Skies in the Liberated Areas (Clear skies, happy people working and singing songs.)

5. China needs the Communist Party (For progress and happiness.)
6. United Is Our Strength (A call to union for aims, work and fighting all enemies.)
7. Land-Reform Song (A long song with the land-reform doctrine, sung during reforms.)
8. Labor Created Man, Labor Created the World
9. Red May Labor Song
10. We are Young People's Society of Democracy
11. Democracies of the World Unite (A call to Communist "democracies" to unite and defeat American imperialists in Korea.)
12. Without Communism There Is No New China (This is one of the most popular songs.)
13. Eastern Sky Is Red (Red skies and red flowers are metaphors often called upon to show the spread of Communism.)
14. Oppose Rearming Japan (This song is to inform the people that America is rearming Japan, and that China can never agree to it.)

Like all the prisoners, I copied songs from the board when they were assigned us to be learned. This notebook had the notes and Chinese characters. The police found it in the first search of my baggage when leaving China. They snatched it away, warning that I must not take it out. Fortunately the translations made in jail were smuggled out ahead of me.

The indoctrination course gives much weight to learning and singing the songs. One fellow in our cell was remiss about this task. The authorities noted his lack of interest and hung bracelets and chains on his wrists and ankles to wear for a month.

Several times the prison authorities asked the cell chief if I was really learning the Communist songs. They were happily surprised to know I had learned them and was singing regularly with the prisoners. I enjoyed the singing even though the words of the songs often seemed silly and useless. But for me, as for most of the prisoners, it was singing with the lips to pass the time, not with the heart.

The song leader in our cell was a sickly, temperamental lad. When he was ill disposed, I used to direct and lead the songs in the cell. On fair days we assembled the five hundred prisoners in the court outside for singing. After songs by all, one cell is called on for a song. They finish and invite another cell group to take the baton in a kind of competitive spirit.

Our cell was called twice. But the song leader was sick, and both times he gave the pitch too high or too low. We got through in a jumble of disharmony. Called the third time, he refused to get up and shook his towel-wrapped head. I stepped up to give the pitch and lead the next song. The whole gang of prisoners in the yard broke into applause at seeing the foreigner come up to lead the songs. I was the only foreigner in this county, and my presence in jail for the forced indoctrination course made me an object of curiosity and special attention. Applause is reserved for the Communist officials and the warden. At the end of the song our cell was called to sing two encores.

By this time the warden, who must have heard the applause in his room, appeared on the scene. He angrily ordered everybody back to cell. First he called our cell chief, then the Study Committee Chairman on the carpet. He called them down without mercy for allowing me, an enemy American, to lead songs. He knew I held Communism in low esteem, and so leading their songs was a subtle way of making them ridiculous.

Next morning at general assembly his words laced the prisoners for their applause, and he went into a tirade against America. I sat there amused and elated, for he did not haul me out front. Though not intentionally (you could not convince them it was not intentional), I had thrown a monkey wrench into their machine of anti-American propaganda. It was like a stiletto jabbed into their sides, seeing the crowd of supposedly indoctrinated prisoners cheering and applauding an American.

The hour from eight to nine is for study of one of the Communist books or pamphlets. The book is passed from one prisoner who can read to the next, and each takes a half-period of reading aloud. The reader or the cell chief is supposed to comment and explain the difficult passages for those who are unlettered.

Besides the books read aloud, other Communist magazines, books and pamphlets are stacked in each cell for free time reading. I read on the average of three of their booklets a week for amusement and time filling. In them America is constantly reviled, castigated and cursed. The Church and religion are ridiculed, slandered, scoffed at and made fun of. For those who have listened to and read Russian or Nazi propaganda before Germany's defeat, China's propaganda has very little new to offer. Marx, Lenin and Stalin are continually lauded and quoted, and Mao Tse-tung is everlastingly praised as the liberator and leader.

A resumé of material in some of the books I read during the course may help you to understand their propaganda.

The Truth about the Voice of America is a lengthy pamphlet that attempts to show all the lies of the "Voice" and repeatedly warns the people not to listen as a patriotic duty. The "Voice" must be having quite an effect, for it is referred to as a danger far, far greater than the atom bomb, because it can wreck the minds and hearts of the people everywhere.

People's Living Standard in Soviet Russia is a translation from a Russian booklet. It is about a hundred pages of glorification of Russia's progress under Communism. The abundance of figures and percentage comparisons makes it dull reading, and the alleged gigantic increases of everything make one doubt its truth.

Introducing the Paper Tiger, Imperialist America. The

tiger fills China's painting and literature and is the boogie used to frighten people, as the big bad wolf is used in American children's books. In this pamphlet and in their newspapers and speeches, America is called the paper tiger — a big bluff. The pamphlet belittles the atomic bomb as a weapon of no use against armies, which can be used only to kill the defenseless civilian populations of large cities. The claim is that Russia would retaliate and drop the atom bomb on New York if America used it against the Chinese.

American soldiers, the propaganda says, are soft, raised on luxuries and cannot take the hardships of fighting. The soldiers are surrendering en masse to the Chinese rather than fight. Many of their books state the Communist Party is strong in America, especially among the working classes. Hence, a great mass of Americans have no will nor wish to fight the workers' countries like Russia or China.

Their propaganda states that Russia's mighty army defeated Japan. Once it started marching, the great Kwantung army of the Japanese surrendered, and Japan itself then surrendered. Russia did not strip Manchuria, they say, this is only a fiction of American propaganda.

Instruction for Youth at the Age of Reason is a booklet for children and has cartoons on every page. It pictures America as a hog that lives on blood, let by war. When business is bad, America starts a war so the capitalists can make money and retain their power. Its cartoons and writings carry a thousand absurd accusations, half-truths and distorted truths.

One of the prisoners was something between a simpleton and a half-wit. He looked over my shoulder while I was reading this book. Uncle Sam was caricatured as a wolf with blood dripping from his teeth. He was standing on his hind legs and a bushy tail hung out of his coat. The half-wit looked and said, "Americans are like that? I did not know they had tails."

Imperialist America's Bloody History of Aggression in

China is a pamphlet that gives America the dubious credit of sharing in every war against China. Here are some of its assertions in resumé!

In 1844 American soldiers helped English soldiers fight the Opium War. In 1857 a U.S.N. admiral placed the American flag on Formosa and declared it independent. In 1874 the U.S. Consul at Fukien went to Japan and urged that U.S. and Japan take Formosa. In 1884, together with Japan, the U.S. attacked Korea. Ten years later the U.S. helped Japan start the Sino-Japanese War. In 1900 America joined the other imperialists in taking Peking, because of the obstinacy of some missioners. In 1904 the U.S. used forty million dollars to help Japan in the war so as to share in the spoils of China's northeast. In 1912 America joined the European powers in exploiting China after declaring the "Open Door" and equal opportunity for all. In 1915 the U.S. wanted to sign the twenty-one demands treaty Japan imposed on China so as to share benefits with Japan. In 1917 Japan and the U.S. signed a secret agreement for the U.S. to support the Japanese position in China and Japan on her part would agree to the "Open Door." In 1925 American interference stopped the Communist revolution in China and set up a government favorable to America. America financed Chiang Kai-shek to side against the revolution and Communism. Relief was used to unload American surplus and make economic slaves of China after the war. Arms were given Chiang Kai-shek and the reactionary government, which cost more blood and lives in the Communist revolutionary army fighting to liberate China.

The above is history written after the Communist fashion.

The prisoners read many of the absurd assertions out to me and asked if they were true. For instance, one book stated that the Du Ponts gave a ball that cost a half-million U. S. dollars. The cigars cost $250.00 per box for these capitalists, while the income of a poor worker in America is only $200 a year. Prisoners listened in amazement when I told them the true income of a laborer and the things owned by a common laborer in America. The income of the average poor farmer in this part of China was about $.05 per day. It is no wonder they gave me a look of doubt when I told them the minimum wage in most American factories is around $.75 per hour.

Some months ago the Chief of Police picked up a *Collier's* I had on the jeep seat. The cover was a picnic dinner, with food piled high and well-dressed people sitting around. He gazed, shook his head back and forth and smiled in somber silence. This silence spoke his thoughts of admiration and envy of American life.

The Communist propaganda booklets contain too many absurdities to list any more. But this morsel is too good for the Dixiecrats to miss. Their books claim that Truman is a member of the party that fought to keep slavery. And he was once a member of the K.K.K. which deprives the Negroes of all human rights. This K.K.K. is armed with military weapons, even machine guns, to carry out their injustices. That Truman is the bête noire and hated oppressor of the poor man fills a good part of their newspapers and books.

The Two Fronts. This book is given over to exposing the so-called aggression of America primarily, though a small share in the sin is attributed to England and France. This imperialistic aggression is then compared (in no complimentary way) with the admirable peace front of Russia. All the conferences, the meetings, the societies, the propaganda and efforts Russia has given for peace are recorded. Chinese Communists claim part in the peace front, though they have been warring ceaselessly for twenty-five years, and their invasion of Korea is in pursuit of peace, they say.

The Period of Mao Tse-tung's Youth is a life story of the man. He had a beastly father whom he fought, but an angelic mother. His virtues and goodness are praised so that it reads like the life of a saint, and the story lifts him to a place just this side of idolatry.

History of the Evolution of Society and *Progress of Society*. These books on the development and evolution of society are purely materialistic. The Comrade explaining the beginning of the world expounded thus: "Teachers of religion use the myth that God created the world, in order to deceive the people." These and other Communist books and magazines explain the origin of the world and species by evolution, eliminating the idea of God even as the governing power behind evolution.

Several times a week at the outdoor assembly, a speaker took over in place of the singing or book explanation. The warden, the interrogators or a political functionary took the rostrum. Their talks were based on the Party Line, what it means, how to believe and follow it. They extolled Russia, their Communist friend, and the might and size of China. Soon China would be the same paradise as Russia. She would have her own factories for steel, machines and airplanes and no longer would depend upon foreign nations for anything. This and more airy promises were given to people of China, now under the banner of Communism.

Sometimes the lecturer, after explaining the matter of the book he read, called upon one of the better educated prisoners to elucidate and comment. A few mornings before, he had lectured from the book *History of the Evolution of Society*. He called on Wong Peng Chung, for many years principal of the Wuchow High School, though his home was here in Shumkai. Wong was classed as an educated reactionary, for many of his folks were members of the ousted Nationalist government. When he returned home for midyear holiday just over two months before, the men waiting to meet him were not the ones he expected. They invited him to the jail to spend the holidays instead of at home.

Wong was making a bid for his life. Before expounding on the subject matter of the book, he lauded the Communist party, the new society it gives the people, with honesty, justice and freedom. Then he proceeded to explain evolution from the ape, the gradual change in posture, bones and organs. He claimed that science has proved for us the evolution of man from the ape. He gave as a horrible example of American imperialism the American University that discharged a teacher because he taught evolution. I smiled at his generalizations that "science says" or "all scientists believe this." However, he was safe from any questions or heckling.

But his flattery for the new government did not pay off. He lost his bid for life, and next week was led home and shot.

Each day the cell members are assigned a topic for discussion hour. The topic usually deals with the matter explained in the morning lecture outside. At this assembly the prisoners are lined up military fashion, then squat or sit on the ground for over an hour. Perhaps this is not so hard on the local gentry who are accustomed to sit on their haunches. But my knees and legs tingled with numbness and ached all the time during this squatting.

More trying than the squatting was the seven or eight hours of class in the cell. We were not allowed to recline or even lean back against the wall. During the hours listening to the reading or the discussions, or singing, everyone sat monkey fashion with arms locked around the knees. This is painful and wearying as the day wears on. I thought I might get bed sores where horse riding sometimes raises saddle sores. But after a while the skin toughened and threatened to grow callouses.

The lecturer at general assembly outside faces his squatting audience and reads in a dull flat voice. So far during my time in jail, the book lectured from on most days was *The Progress and Development of Society.*

After the lecture hour outside came the class of discussion hour, in the cell. Each prisoner in turn gave his ideas on the subject assigned for the day, and one had the duties of a secretary to condense the discussion and send in for the Study Committee to examine. They read this condensation, made comments, then stamped it and sent it back to the cell. Of course, the prisoners dared say nothing contrary to what the book or lecturer outside had said.

Here is a partial list of the topics assigned us for discussion.

1. What means did the Soviets use to unite the aboriginal tribes at the North Pole (Siberia)?

2. What means did the capitalist countries use to encroach upon the aboriginal tribes? The answers given in the book and lecture were: Soviet benevolence and peaceful ways benefited and advanced the aboriginals. Capitalists used trade, missionaries and economic aggression to usurp the rights of the aboriginal tribes and prepare them for invasion and subjection.

3. What was the condition of life for country farming people in Imperialist Russia? The answer, of course, was that life in Imperialist Russia was like slavery — now it is paradise.

4. How did slavery start? Capitalists and avaricious men, together with conquering generals, took prisoners and made slaves out of them, is the answer.

5. What are the means used by the Imperialists in their aggression? Tyranny, deceit, double dealing, economic weapons, missionaries and spies, is the answer given in their books and lectures.

6. Explain how Rome in the golden age was especially noted for her cruelty toward slaves.

7. Under what forms did feudalism take advantage of the poor people? It was imperialistic, tyrannical, and cheated the people out of the fruits of their labor, is the answer.

8. Explain evolution and how man comes from the ape.
9. What do you think of the American university that discharged a professor for teaching evolution?

This last discussion topic was given us the day after Professor Wong's speech on evolution and his accusation of the American university. The proper Communist answer for us to give was that Imperialist America thus showed her tyranny, her suppression of free speech and her perversion of science. I listened to the parrot answers until it came my turn. Then I explained that science does not say evolution is a fact, but that some scientists believe it and hold it as a theory. But the majority of scientists treat it as a theory only. I continued: Perhaps God in His plan did use evolution, and at a certain stage of development in the dumb animal gave intelligence and free will, that is, a soul, to certain species. This would be quite acceptable if proved. It would even show the great glory of the Architect who foresaw and gave such powers to life. Then I went on to give all the arguments against evolution.

This departure from the prepared answer of the lecturer startled the cell mates. The one who was recording did not dare write down my views to be sent in to the Study Committee. I did not insist, for it would only have made trouble for all of them.

But the day we were given topic number five in the list above, I gave them all the guns. Outside we had to listen without comment, but in the cell when they repeated the assertions that America was using missionaries to promote their aggression I let them have it with both barrels. I told them it was nothing but lies and slander and rot, and I asked the recording secretary to write down my words and send them in for the prison officials. He did not dare write down the strong words I was passing out. To answer their lies I said I'd been in China twenty-two years in religious and charity work for the welfare of the Chinese people. The American government had not furnished a cent for this work. The U.S. government had cautioned me many times during these years to leave in times of danger.

They had also made a public assertion that in 1948 I had picked up a magistrate from a wrecked auto, and brought him and the five other injured to a hospital in my jeep. This was done because the Nationalist magistrates then in power were the running dogs of the Americans. I was angered and again told the secretary to write what I was saying, "The present Communist magistrate and the Chief of Police and Communist officers have asked me to take them places in my jeep many times. Are they all running dogs of America? Then I told them I had picked up the wounded from the wreck because several buses with their own people refused to stop and help. It was nightfall, and the bus drivers feared bandits might rob the passengers there in the mountains. But an American stopped and spent half the night getting the wounded placed in a hospital. The prisoners in the cell felt ashamed of themselves and their people when this was thrown at them. But they dared not write down what I had said, and after cooling off I did not insist, so as to avoid trouble and punishment for the whole cell of prisoners.

There is a daily class in self-criticism, and Communists everywhere consider this most important. Their self-criticism is much the same as the confession of faults practiced by many religious societies and seminaries of the Catholic Church. Some think that Stalin learned the practice when he was a seminarian for the Russian Church, and that he made it a part of the Communist practice. But this is guess work.

However, we do know Stalin's views on self-criticism. They were translated in the Chinese papers toward the end of March, 1950. I quote his words, translated from the Chinese newspaper:

"Comrades, I deem self-criticism as essential to us as the air we breathe, or the water we drink. I am convinced that without self-criticism we cannot progress, we cannot lay bare our abscesses, nor erase away our shortcomings . . . since a single party holds the reins of leadership in this proletariat dictatorship, that is the Communist party, and since the Communist party does not share, nor can it share the functions of government with any other political party, it follows that if we wish to make progress, we ourselves must, of necessity, play the role of pointing out and correcting mistakes . . ." The Chinese papers noted that they were translating Stalin's speech to members of the Bolshevik party, April 15, 1928.

The top-ranking party members also hold that the dynamic force and drive of Communism is derived in a great part from this criticism by others and by self.

Here is the way it worked in our cell. At the self-criticism hour the prisoners would sit in a row around the cell. Each person in turn was on the carpet, so to speak. He was supposed to recite any shortcomings and faults committed since the criticism hour of the day before. Then, in order to get "help in improving his conduct," he asks the others to reveal and discuss the faults they see in him. The person under discussion cannot say a word in self-defense or excuse, but must show pleasure in having his shortcomings pointed out to him.

It is surprising to listen to your shortcomings and infractions, your disposition and foibles discussed with such accuracy. Someone is sure to tell you if you are inconsiderate and selfish, sloppy in sitting up straight during class, dirty in spitting, greedy, avaricious, proud, and any other faults or infractions. They also bring out much good they see in you, which you might think is passing unnoticed. When carried out with sincerity and if the results are used to correct one's faults, this self-criticism is a great spiritual benefit. It is a practice taken from spiritual life. But it is too often used like the devil quoting Scripture, by the Communists in their system of make-believe.

Self-criticism is practiced by every bureau of the government and party, and by the farmers' meetings in the villages, by the schools, colleges and societies. To quote again from Stalin's speech: "Criticism and self-criticism should be organized in such a way that it may supervise those for whom it is intended in a lively, admonitory and spiritual fashion. And should the leaders — even those who hold the very highest rank of authority and prestige — wish to continue enjoying the confidence of the party and the working class, they must carefully take to heart the opinions of such popular criticism."

About once a week we had criticism hour at general assembly in the court. The warden or his assistant would pick someone for a flagrant breaking of the rules. The culprit had to stand before five hundred prisoners and tell about his transgression, then prisoners in assembly were called on to tell anything else wrong with the victim.

Sometimes a prisoner was called on to tell why he was here. After his recital, other prisoners got up to tell anything the victim had left out or hidden. Many of the accusers were making a bid for their own freedom by disclosing everything they knew. This is another means the Communists use to pry out facts and guilt.

Criticism — self-criticism class, as was held in every jail, is the common practice for every group meeting throughout China. Accusation meetings are a punishment. They are called before large groups for serious offenders or critics of the regime. Everybody present is urged to expose all the crimes or wrongs of the person held before the gathering. In the prison, accusation meetings were held in the court before the five hundred assembled prisoners with the accused standing in front of us. Police, soldiers or government bureaus often call up these accusation meetings against one of their members. The mass hysteria that is aroused, and the imagined or exaggerated grievances that are aired make everyone fear the accusation meeting. One day I saw a police guard threaten to call a fellow guard up for accusation before the whole force. He immediately went pale and silent.

The third degree is public trial or "people's court," which is followed by a jail or death sentence. I saw only a few public trials, but many accusation meetings.

One morning a trusty came to say that the authorities had heard remarks coming from this cell, which were contrary to progress in the new thought. We were ordered to hold a self-criticism meeting all day long if necessary, so the guilty person could confess his fault. Evidently a note had been dropped in the box for secret reports. It may have been that the authorities were making a guess to alert the cell chief who had reported nothing of consequence for several days.

Each prisoner in turn had to declare anything improper he had said, and when he finished everyone in the cell was called, one after the other, to add anything he had heard the person say which was improper. One of the cell mates was appointed to write everything down. The self-examination and discussion of faults went on all day.

When it came my turn to confess any recent thoughts, acts or words against the regime which might have put the cell in bad standing, I commented:

"My statements have been critical but open. What I have said in the cell is far less caustic and slashing than what I have repeatedly spoken to the police, the interrogators and other officials. If there is freedom of speech which they boast of so often, I have nothing to confess. If there is no freedom of speech, I stand condemned and let come what may." And when the recorder's brush stopped in the air at these words, I urged him to put them on the record. But he hesitated.

I had finished, so now the cell chief went the rounds asking each cell mate what he had to add about my words or conduct. One spoke up:

"Not long ago I asked student Tennien what he thought of the New China. He answered, 'We are all slaves now, and we live or die at the whim of this New China government.'"

All eyes closed in on me, and whispering comment could be heard: "Ai-ya that must be what they heard from this cell." Things looked dark, and when the turn came for the fifteenth cell mate for comments, he added gloom by saying:

"Only a few days ago I stood by student Tennien's bunk and asked, 'The Communist government good, or not good?' He answered, 'Not good! No freedom now, we are treated as slaves or beasts.' Such words hinder our progress in the new thought." Then he added more coals by saying:

"And last week student Tennien resented my criticism of his friendliness with the running dog Magistrate here before. His words insulted our present Communist officials, and he told me I argued like a little boy below the age of reason."

"True," I added, "these last remarks you all heard a few days ago; I also said there is no freedom now, and I do not wish to take it back."

One after the other, each cell mate disclosed his wrongs and the line was fast coming to the end. No one else confessed any words against the regime, no one else was accused by cell mates of "deviation" from the Party Line. My fate looked blacker and blacker, and when a recess was called one of the prisoners warned me:

"You will probably be tied up and face the assembled prisoners for public trial."

This was the usual outcome when serious crimes were discovered. I had seen a prisoner dragged up for this ordeal the week before. The accused stood with arms tied behind him while the crowd threw accusations. One prisoner playing a card for freedom proposed public beating. Another prisoner trying to prove he was now a good Communist suggested, "Shoot him." A vote was taken then and there for the "judgment of the people." This was a bitter scene

· 138 ·

when all hands went up but mine: *"Ts'iang pi* — shoot to death."

Our recess ended, and self-examination class continued in our cell. Next to the last prisoner to speak was Lee Tien Te (Lee of Celestial Virtue), and his electric statement brought a tense hush over the prisoners:

"I have a serious crime against the government to confess."

Celestial Virtue Lee was a gentle-mannered, soft-spoken, friendly man of forty-five. He had been brought to prison five months before after the farmers' chairman of his village turned in a secret report. He will remain in jail until his confession of crimes includes the accusation in the secret files of the police, they say. Perhaps he befriended the guerillas, maybe he spoke his mind about the Communist system, he might have let his mischievous tongue loose with an offensive rumor. He did not know the accusation filed nor did we.

Now his deep, sad eyes looked at us over brass-rimmed glasses that were tied around his head with a string. The voice hardly above a whisper continued to speak:

"New prisoners came to our cell two days ago. They were given paper and ordered to write a frank and honest account of their crimes. I said to those near me 'Watch out, Chen and Lee sat here beside me last week and were ordered to write their confessions. Next day they were taken out and shot.' "

The cell buzzed at this new revelation. No others added accusation, no others brought out details, for this might give away the scoundrel who reported Lee. Heads crowded around the secretary's speeding brush to see Lee's words go down in writing. The sheet was passed from hand to hand while their heads shook to confirm his doom. Celestial Virtue Lee and I now shared the ignominy and faced the punishment, though I seemed to be forgotten for the moment.

Lee hurried to write a confession phrased with words of

bitter sorrow and contrite promises of amendment, in order to send it in with the secretary's report of proceedings. I refused to write a word. These prisoners with broken spirits stared in surprise. Refusal to write the routine admission of guilt was to taunt the torture of Communism and fellow prisoners now looked at me pityingly.

Our six-hour period of criticism and self-criticism carried us to early afternoon. Now the report with Lee's confession was sent out to prison officials. We waited in the suspense of a man just tried while the jury is locked away fixing his fate. A half hour dragged and each minute seemed like living a full year of life. Another half-hour ticked away, and then it came. The guard from the warden's office approached our cell and called with the solemnity of a sentence:

"Lee Tien Te, come with me to the office."

The torture mill had started to grind. In ten minutes Celestial Virtue Lee came stumbling back to the cell gagging and wheezing, trussed with ropes. The rope torture is applied like this. A guard from behind throws the loop over the prisoner's head. The loop knot falls to the middle of the back with two long ends hanging to the floor. One end is wound around each arm above the elbow, then yanked tight, binding the sufferer's elbows together behind his back. When the tightly wound rope stops circulation in the prisoner's arms, bursting pain makes him writhe in agony. Then each twist or strain pulls the loop around his neck to choke him.

Lee staggered into the cell. His arms and hands had bloated and turned red. Pain like a thousand needles shot through them. He struggled for relief, and the loop dug a deep gorge across his neck. His face went scarlet and his lips turned blue. Gasping for breath, he begged the cell mates to loosen the ropes a little. But no one dared touch the ropes for it would bring the same torture on anyone who interfered.

Lee stood on his bed a few minutes then fell over in a dead faint. Prisoners looked on the purpled face with fright, for they thought Lee was dying. I jumped to draw out the neck loop so he could breathe, then assured the prisoners he had fainted, that was all. They helped fan him and wipe his perspiring face with a damp towel. Soon he opened his eyes and sat up.

Between gasps he managed to tell us he was tied up because the warden said his confession was incomplete. The secret report gave more details. Blocked circulation blew up Lee's hands and face until the pressure of blood seemed ready to burst through the skin. Each heartbeat was an agonizing stab in his arms and face that brought a moan and cry. Lee pleaded with the cell mates to loose his bonds a little. But this would only make it worse all around, so no one volunteered.

When the anguish tore through his flesh and nerves with more than he could stand, Lee broke down and cried like a child. Tears ran down mixed with sweat, and sobs came with choking gasps as the bed boards quaked under him. Nothing in this world seems so sad as a grown man driven to violent sobbing and crying. I wiped the sweat from his face and held a bowl of water to his lips. Some of the other prisoners took courage at this and helped to ease his pain. Toward nightfall, when Lee had been tied up for five hours, the agony increased. His spirit was completely broken, and as the warden walked near our cell Lee called out:

"I will confess in full. I will confess anything if you will loosen these ropes, anything!"

The warden walked off toward his office, and we thought the plea was ignored. Prisoners hazarded guesses:

"Lee's written confession left out a part of what he said." "He also gestured the shooting with his trigger finger." "His written words were not sufficiently colored to show the wickedness of his offense."

Half an hour afterward a guard marched across the court, now in dim twilight, and stopped at our cell door.

"Lee Tien Te, come with me to the warden's office."

We watched for the outcome. The confession of crimes he now made to the warden was evidently satisfactory. In a little while Celestial Virtue Lee was walked wearily back to our cell without the torture ropes. He could not eat, he would not talk, but sat on the boards with a dazed look. His limp, swollen arms hung down at his side, and from time to time he would stare at his numbed fingers and try to wriggle them. Roll call and the "all quiet" command from the guard ended the day, but the prisoners felt the incident was not yet ended. Whispering speculation went on:

"There will be more of this at assembly tomorrow. Probably there will be a public accusation meeting and maybe a people's judgment. Tennien will most likely be tied up and punished for his statements tomorrow."

I did not sleep much that night. While Celestial Virtue Lee moaned and tossed with the passing hours, I wondered how much I could stand when it came my turn. Two prisoners had been caught in some offense a few days before. They were called up before the assembly and forced to punch each other's faces, blow for blow, until they were completely exhausted and beaten up. But Lee's arms were helpless now, so that punishment was unlikely.

Through the quiet night I lay awake preparing what to say if they brought me up for public accusation. My views on their freedom, their justice and their system were thought out. Tomorrow if I could bear it, and I prayed for courage after seeing Lee suffer, I would speak my mind to the assembled prisoners and officials.

Morning assembly bell called us out to the court. There was an air of expectancy and tension in the crowd, for everyone now knew that the American prisoner was in serious trouble. The warden spoke. He dressed down each prisoner reported for little faults or infractions. He dressed down Celestial Virtue Lee, and then came my turn. Instead of tying me up or calling me before the crowd, the warden himself addressed the prisoners. First he berated Americans, then he berated me as a stubborn, imperialist reactionary.

"But can he move?" he asked the assembly.

"No."

"Can he run away?"

"No."

"Is he subject to our laws and punishment?"

"Yes."

Then to everyone's surprise he let the case hang and passed on to someone else. We went back to the cell, and prisoners tried to figure why I had escaped. Some thought it was because I was American. My own guess is that the authorities were afraid of what might happen if I were put through public accusation, since they had not, so far as I knew, put foreign nationals through torture to force them to praise the regime. Every time the Police Chief, the soldiers or the interrogators had questioned me, I answered with frank criticism and bitter denunciation of the Communist government. It would be bad to let me face the assembled prisoners and shout the truth about the government. At singing class not long before the prisoners had broken out with spontaneous cheers and applause. The words of truth they knew I would speak out and would contradict everything the indoctrination course taught. It might even cause a riot amongst the prisoners who had already demonstrated for the American. I believe that is the reason I was passed over without public punishment.

Lee Tien Te had to write out his new confession. But the swollen paralyzed hands would be useless for a week or two. He would have to be fed by a fellow prisoner holding the bowl and chopsticks to his mouth. And so he dictated the new confession. Substantially it was the same with a few added details, but couched in terms that made him a master criminal, and praised the just, merciful and lenient government that deigned to forgive him.

CHAPTER IX

The Interrogators

BECAUSE Communist prisons come under the jurisdiction of the police, there is a large group of officials in the police force called the interrogators. About eight of them had their interrogation rooms and quarters at our prison, for their work is to put prisoners through questioning all day. Others lived at police headquarters across the street, and prisoners were led one after the other to be questioned there. Each prisoner is brought before an interrogator about every ten days, and the session lasts from one to three hours. Usually an interrogator sits alone behind his desk, but often two or more interrogators work together on a prisoner.

The majority of our interrogators were young men who formerly belonged to the Communist underground. They had joined up while studying at the senior high school, and their affiliation was made known and rewarded after the Communists got control. These young men were immediately given the general indoctrination course of two months.

After indoctrination they were given some little training as interrogators and put to work on prisoners. But they were both green and young and easily confused if a person refused to be terrorized. I have had no experience under cross-examination, so an old-time interrogator could have tripped me up or tricked me into admission of crimes, where these youngsters failed.

Morning finds each interrogator in his bare little room with the files on his desk for each prisoner he is to question that day. The file contains the prisoner's account of his crime, which he writes after arrival in jail, and perhaps a number of secret accusations turned in against him.

The interrogators are ready to start work. A guard is sent to the cell doors and calls out the names on his list. Bars are loosened, and the guard escorts prisoners to the different interrogators. Though some prisoners are required to stand, I was always asked to sit on a bench in front of the interrogator. It might be called torture to see the official smoke while the prisoner looks on hungering at the sight of a cigarrette. With Chinese brush and a sheet of paper ready, the interrogator writes down any important statement or question, any confession or admission. The prisoner is asked to sign and thumb print the document when he is dismissed. This goes into the file to build up the case against a prisoner.

Interrogation is of exceptional importance in the Communist system, for it takes the place of court process in free countries. Less than 10 per cent of the cases in our jail were ever turned over to the court. Everyone is presumed guilty, and the task of interrogators is to dig out admissions, evidence and guilt. These pile up with each interrogation, and a few cases are passed to the court where the prisoner is called to hear his sentence. But the usual routine is to arrest people, indoctrinate them for months, interrogate them periodically for information on themselves and others. Then the police with interrogators decide to liquidate or free the prisoners after he has signed a confession for the record.

Just before execution the police told some of the prisoners that they had turned the confessions and evidence over to the people's court in the prisoner's home district. The "judgment of the people" had condemned them to death. After all this "judgment of the people" was an unnecessary maneuver, if it really took place. For the people's courts that I saw in action were well coached and gave the decision required of them. But for some curious reason the Communists want to point to their decisions as a "democratic" process.

The interrogators use every trick to get information. Sometimes they are ingratiating and suave to encourage the prisoner to talk freely. Sometimes they use bluff and cunning, and slap the file pretending they have masses of evidence there.

Their tempting advice is to admit everything, confess everything in order to get an easy sentence or a quick pardon. They use threats, shouts and terrorism; they pile on accusations and magnify the crimes to induce a feeling of guilt in the prisoner. The method is not without success, for cell mates come back saddened or weeping.

One of the priests expelled from China just ahead of me remarked, "After the interrogators work on you a while, they really do bring on a feeling of shame and guilt." Many people have told me the same thing, though I never felt it personally. Maybe it was because I fought them at every sentence and hurled back accusations at the regime.

But no one is liquidated, sentenced or freed from jail without being forced to confess guilt, whether he feels guilt or not. Even people who are innocent write false or exaggerated confessions, for they believe it is the only way to satisfy the Communists and get out of jail.

When I had spent thirteen days in jail, the guard summoned me for interrogation. "Student Tennien, Comrade Lee wants you to come."

Cell mates were worried when I leisurely put on my shirt, kicked off the wooden clogs and changed to shoes. They tried to hurry me. The guard marched me upstairs ahead of him to Interrogator Lee's dark little room. Secret-loving Communists balk at giving their full names or their place of residence, and so my polite request got a short answer:

"May I ask your honorable name?"

"Call me Comrade Lee, that is enough. Sit down," and he motioned me to the square stool in front of his desk.

Slouched down in an armchair with his fingers twined over his belly, Interrogator Lee looked as drowsy as a hibernating bear. A flock of long hair kept falling in a crescent-moon shape to shade one eye and ended under his double chin. The little almond eyes, the bridgeless nose with two large holes turning out, and the fat cheeks gave him a pig-face appearance.

Comrade Lee launched into a speech about the glories of Communist China when a curious incident stopped him. The belt loops on the back of my trousers had worn out and let the belt creep up while I sat on the stool. As I reached around to tuck up the trousers, Comrade Lee thought I was digging out a hidden gun. His face froze in fright, then he jumped to get his gun lying on the bed. I read his thoughts and explained what I was doing. He slouched again in the easy chair and started to grill me.

"Your crime is very very grave, you tried to kill the guard."

"Comrade Lee you are wrong, I did not. Your police tried to frame me with this." Now he twisted the lock of hair behind his ear to stare at me with both eyes.

"You have broken our laws, ignored our regulations and refuse to give proper respect to our government." Then Lee recounted a long list of my so-called crimes, counting them off with the fingers of both hands. I sat quietly amused while he painted a picture of my crimes, both gruesome and horrible, then I took the offensive, asking:

"We are all equal under Communism?" He nodded assent. "And Communist officials are subject to the laws and regulations?" He agreed again.

"Yet they steal from the mission, stop people from the practice of religion, seize the church for a meeting hall . . ." And I drew a picture of their crimes, numbering them on my fingers until I was sure to be away ahead of him.

"Do you mean to say the government cannot borrow your things?"

"A person asks to borrow. When officials arrest you at the point of a gun, hold you under guard, then carry off things, the act comes under another name." I did not use the term, for he would have accused me of calling them robbers. Interrogator Lee now switched to another subject.

"Where have you hidden your valuables? You better tell us for we have searched the Christian villages and found out everything."

"You will not believe me, but I left all goods at the mission."

"Truly?"

"Yes, I figured you would take everything, and there would be a better chance for claims if you took the goods out of the mission."

My questioner squirmed to sit up straight at such an answer. It was evident that Interrogator Lee was confused and did not know what to ask next. I filled in the pause with comments:

"Your police have taken grain away from the mission, and collected from shops where I had a credit deposit. You even called back charity gifts I made to needy people."

"Where is your radio sending set hid?" Lee asked to put me on the defensive.

"Let's not speak laugh words; you know very well I have no sending set."

Comrade Lee failed to get any admissions or frighten me

into a sense of guilt with his questions. Now he resorted to a lecture on Communist China's might. A look of distaste for this propaganda hastened my dismissal. Strangely enough, I was not asked to sign any record of this interrogation, which did Lee little credit.

"You will return to the cell and reflect on the gravity of your crimes, so as to write a good confession in the future," was the interrogator's parting directive.

Our cell had an understanding that each man should come back and recount his experiences with the interrogator. It made an interesting bit of gossip in our pill-box existence. Curious cell mates cluttered around to hear of my first bout with the interrogators. They rejoiced at the outspoken criticism they dared not even whisper. But they cautioned me of the danger I might be courting.

My second interrogation came sixteen days later when I was escorted to Comrade Chen's room.

Chen's face showed no guile, and my first thought was, "What is he doing in Communist company?" I was immediately drawn to like this gentle character with a soft voice, kindly eyes, and a little smile that failed to chase away a look of sadness. His inquisition followed the manner of a friendly chat and exchange of views rather than browbeating and threats. Chen invited me to sit down before his desk, which was as neat and orderly as his person.

"I see from your accent you come from the district to the south, near the Kwangtung border," I remarked, after hearing Chen speak. He looked up in surprise. Then he asked:

"How long have you been in China?"

"Longer than you have, since I came in 1928."

This brought a smile to the face of the youngster who was interrogating the ancient, though Comrade Chen probably did not like to have his home and his age called so definitely.

In Communist China officials are addressed as Comrade. The people are taught to leave off all titles and address each other as *lao*, meaning "venerable."

"What do you think of Communism now, venerable Tennien?"

"The same as before. You have my statements in the file."

"Communism has done much good for the people of China."

"Enforced good, yes, but only free goodness in man is real."

Chen was a man of thought, and instead of writing he tapped his teeth with the bamboo writing brush, looked over his glasses at the ceiling and pondered. Many inconsequential questions followed, and then Chen asked:

"What is your view of the war in Korea?"

"The United Nations has voted Communist China is an aggressor. I agree with the decision of the majority, for we all believe in a democratic process."

"But capitalistic America controls the U.N."

"No, I say democracy controls the U.N."

Interrogator Chen now turned to another moot question: "What do you think about America's interference in Formosa?"

"Personally I think it was a mistake." Chen was happy to write this down until I added, "I do not believe you could have taken Formosa anyway. You were not equipped to do it. And now you have made the greatest blunder of all, interference in Korea."

"Why is it a blunder?"

"You can never win your objective of taking all Korea, and you can bankrupt your country trying."

This argument went on for an hour, and because it ended where we started I shall skip this part of my diary. Comrade Chen explained China's case. It was the same as we heard in the daily propaganda. Imperialist countries are meddling in the Chinese land of Formosa, they have invaded the neighbor country Korea, and bombed Manchuria, in preparation for the invasion of China. When a neighbor's house is on fire, one must help put it out for self-protection. There-

Beggar boys smuggled food through the window when Communists put the author under house arrest and placed him on a
starvation diet.

Driven insane by weeks of interrogation and false accusations, the mission washwoman drowned herself.

The war on religion spared none. Christians were ordered to destroy pagan idols; pagans were told to wreck Christian churches by the masters of hate and revenge.

Hwang Hsi-hao's father, mother and sister, driven insane by two years of prison and torture, took their own lives in May of 1952.

Father Peter Reilly instructs Billie on bringing food to his three
co-workers who were held in jail for over five months.

Father Arthur Dempsey was taken to Communist Police Headquarters for attempting to give absolution to the author, who
was imprisoned in his own church.

When Father Joseph McDonald tore down a picture of Mao Tse-tung from over the altar, he was so severely mauled he was unable to remember the "confession" he gave to the Communists.

Bishop A. Paschang was beaten by Communist mobs. He was tried by the people's court and condemned as an "imperialist, reactionary leader of Catholics."

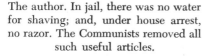

The author. In jail, there was no water for shaving; and, under house arrest, no razor. The Communists removed all such useful articles.

Father George Gilligan, "Truman's special agent," spent five months in jail, was then subjected to a public trial and expelled from China.

A. Bishop Frederick Donaghy: "Spy . . . gun was hidden in his closet."

B. Dr. William Wallace: "Spy chief . . . concealed guns and radio parts."

"American spy ring of four rounded up," announced the Reds on December 19, 1950. Guns and other contraband material had been planted in their personal belongings just before search by the Communists.

C. Father Justin Kennedy: "Spy caught with bullets in his luggage."

D. Sister Rosalia: "Dope peddler . . . opium hidden under her bed."

All the grief, endurance and patience of the faithful are shown
in the face of Mrs. Chung, who came to ask for prayers when her
husband was liquidated.

fore, Chinese volunteers went in to put out the fire before it could destroy their homeland. The reasoning sounds plausible to the masses who are denied any facts, news or contrary viewpoints from the outside. In these conditions false propaganda can easily pass for the truth. But I left no doubts with Comrade Chen about my own opinion. It was a bit surprising to see the interrogation end with no discussion of my so-called crimes. Interrogators are primarily concerned with the effects of indoctrination. They probe hoping to find a change of heart or at least external praise of Communism by the prisoner. After signing the record, I made a suggestion to the affable interrogator Chen.

"You are hoping to indoctrinate the forty Chinese imprisoned in the cell with me. When cell mates ask me about some of the absurd propaganda they hear or read, I tell them the truth, which is contrary to your claims. I am not interested in disrupting your indoctrination course for the other prisoners. If you do not want them to hear my criticism, you should put me in a cell apart."

There were no single cells, but the prison carpenters were ordered to prepare one in the old jail, where I was transferred two weeks later.

My diary was discovered, and this brought me up for another interrogation a few days later. We had to copy the Communist songs, so trusties were permitted to buy notebooks for the prisoners. I got two extra notebooks and jotted down diary notes whenever we had free time. Curious cell mates asked me the meaning of all the English I was writing, and I told them it was a diary. One of them certainly dropped a note in the box for secret reports that told the authorities what I was up to. A guard called through the bars next day:

"Student Tennien, hand me your diary."

The guard walked off with two notebooks of information. Cell mates feared I was in for serious trouble now, and several of them crowded around to ask if I had recorded anything important. They had warned me before that a diary was a dangerous record, to be very careful what I wrote.

Communists pounce on a diary as a prize find, for it is supposed to give personal views and thoughts they cannot get by interrogation. I assured cell mates that I was not worried. Two days went by while the officials tried to decipher my script. Small writing scribbled on my knee for a desk, abbreviations and signs, Latin words and French words, made it a document hard enough for me to read but almost impossible for anyone else. In spaces where details were too dangerous I had notations like "fill in" or "rewrite." The crazy jottings recalled much to me but meant nothing to anyone else. The interrogators gave up the task of trying to decode the books and sent for me.

I was brought before Comrade Lee again, because he had studied five years of English in the high schools. His rapid-fire words, halted by a stutter here and there, asked my views on Communism. These he found unchanged. The build-up was finished, and like a priest on solemn ceremonies he walked over to a side desk to bring out my diary. He held it as a gloating district attorney holds damaging evidence before a judge.

"This is your diary?"

"Yes."

"And you wrote all those things about prison life?"

"Yes."

I knew his talk was bluff and decided to call it.

"You see, the lecturer tells us to take notes, and so the diary records all the things I want to remember about your indoctrination course."

"Is that all?"

"Oh no, the schedule of prison life is interesting, and I have written about the bath, the food, the studies and so on."

"What do these words mean?"

His fingers pointed to abbreviations like "dem. govt." for democratic government, to Latin words and to signs, which made the text unintelligible to him. Comrade Lee looked puzzled and suspicious at the explanation of my self-invented shorthand.

"This is not a code?" he asked.

"It is what you call save-brush writing — a short form to save space and time."

"Suppose you translate this into Chinese."

And for an hour I translated wherever Comrade Lee's finger traced a line. I must admit he picked the ugly passages and the most brutal criticism of Communism, for the topic headings every few pages gave him a steer. He understood enough English to see that I was not shading the translation or softening the blows. Passages like this brought a wince or a scowl: "Once you fall into the clutches of the police for any real or alleged crime, you haven't a chance. The government is always right and the victim is always wrong. People caught in the net soon realize the only way out is to admit guilt and sign a humble confession." This passage he wanted me to explain at greater length. I explained while he listened in astonished silence.

The diary record could well have gone hard with me. But because it was less critical than my repeated statements, it gave them nothing new. Our talk turned to friendly chatter as the session ended. Here was the moment to be audacious, so I asked:

"Now that you know what is in the diary I suppose you will give it back? The notes on your indoctrination teaching mean a great deal to me."

"I must study it further."

Now it looked as if my prison diary were to be lost, but I was not discouraged. The trustee bought me another "songbook," and my pen raced over the lines to write more events of prison life. Three weeks later I was transferred to the old jail under a kindly warden. I asked him if he would get my diary from Interrogator Lee — that Lee had promised to return it after study. He did ask, and to my unending surprise got it back. He was able to hand back my notes through the bars next day. After that my faith in prayer or belief in miracles offers no problem.

The days following this session with Interrogator Lee were hard. Nearly two months in a filthy, stinking, crowded cell, with rice gruel to keep alive had left its mark. My legs were swelling with beriberi, and dysentery was sapping my strength. When we lined up for toilet call, the guard saw me fall out of ranks to retch and heave up the rice gruel. He must have reported my weakened condition, for next morning Comrade Liu, Secretary to the Chief of Police called me for interrogation. Liu saw that I had difficulty walking. Instead of taking me over to headquarters, he led me into a large room where the women prisoners were making cloth shoes.

Comrade Liu is an intelligent lad in his early twenties. The teachings of Communism have so far failed to drag him down to their methods of crudeness and rudeness, and the courtesies and charm of old China still grace his manner. Officials are supposed to be brutal and terroristic in carrying out their duties, but when Liu tries this act he is out of character and fails completely. This morning he greeted me with a cheery smile, then tried the routine gruff queries:

"What is your stand after indoctrination; is it on the side of Communists or the Imperialists?"

"Certainly not with Communists, I prefer freedom."

"Are you for peace or war?"

"We say the prayer for peace every day at Mass, but against aggression war is just." I took some time then to explain Christian ethics of war.

"Your President Truman is a Christian?"

"Yes."

"And your religion has a command — do not kill?" I nodded assent.

"Then Truman is breaking Christian laws in killing our Chinese in Korea?"

"What are your Chinese doing in Korea?"

"They are volunteers."

"They are not; but if they were volunteers for Korea, China has no right to speak for them. Now let us keep to the point I just explained about aggression. The world of nations, except five, have named China the aggressor and therefore subject to punishment until aggression ceases."

The argument was becoming heated, so I looked for a chance to lighten it. Liu slipped off on another angle, saying:

"Your God will judge everyone?"

"Yes, even you and me."

"Then he will judge President Truman for the murders in Korea."

"I see you have read some Catholic doctrine books while studying English with Father Kupfer. Your comrades are liable to accuse you of deviation," I added, with a sly smile to break the tension. Liu's sense of humor showed in a little chuckle,and I continued in a light vein:

"When it comes to God's judgment I would not want to be in Mao Tse-tung's cloth slippers or in Joe Stalin's boots to answer for the murders in Korea."

We bantered about life in America, the English names for Chinese vegetables and a host of other trifles while the audience of women prisoners went back to stitching cloth shoes. When our voices went up, the needles stopped and women prisoners gaped in awe and fear. Liu came back to the Korea affair which rankles in the minds of Chinese Communists. I said:

"I hope the American army is not treating Chinese prisoners like you treat us here."

"How is the treatment here?"

"Fine! Fine!" I shouted sarcastically, imitating the praises other prisoners have to answer. "Sick, and the warden finds it too much trouble to fetch medicine from the mission, too bothersome to let me buy it from the Health Center. In America the prison hogs are fed better than you feed prisoners here."

"Prison hogs fed better than you are!" Liu repeated, and his face looked pained as a titter from the sewing circle reached our ears. They loved to hear a complaint which they dare not speak.

"Venerable Tennien does not like Communism?" Comrade Liu's jesting comment stung. A sick man's temper is short, and I snapped back:

"I like Communism about as much as you like true democracy."

"Tell me why," he suggested, to draw me out. Anger now drove me to prepare a thrust I had been sparing the likable Comrade Liu.

"There are a thousand reasons, but the one I am thinking of now is because Communism is based on the principle of deceit."

"Can you give a specific proof of this?" — the usual reply to any accusation.

"Yes, your broken promises trick the guerillas to surrender, deceive the prisoners into confessing crimes, confuse the merchants to admitting wrongs . . ." Then, after stating many more general principles of trickery and lying, I gave numerous instances of the Communists' deceit when dealing with me personally. And now for the *coup de grâce*.

"Comrade Liu, you yourself said, 'I am committing you to prison for three days to reflect on your crimes and prepare a confession.' That was fifty-seven days ago. Do you need more proof of deceit?"

My interrogator was on the spot before an audience of women prisoners.

"I did not say three days."

"That does it. *Ch'e ta p'au*" — a polite way to say, you lie.

As Liu's boyish cheeks turned red, I felt a qualm of remorse for crowding him. It was a serious breach of old

Chinese etiquette to make him lose face before others, and Comrade Liu was a gentleman. I leaned nearer and spoke in a low voice that would not reach the listeners:

"Please do not think I blame you for breaking your word. I know enough about Communism to realize you are not free once you are caught in the party web. And I can judge character enough to understand you would keep your word if it were possible."

An appreciative smile stole across the face that was trying to frown for his interrogation act, and a nod that was almost imperceptible told me I had pierced the red front. But he was on the stage acting for an audience and for his own protection, suspicion must be dispelled from this unguarded lapse, so he said in a loud voice:

"So you have been sick with dysentery. I shall change you to the old jail where you can buy extra food to build you up. You get your blanket and I can take you now."

This was the last of the routine interrogations I was put through. My two months' formal indoctrination course for *kai nao chin* (mind reform) was now finished. At the old jail where most of the prisoners went on labor assignment each day, we were given only two hours of class. These were used for singing, propaganda and review lectures. Probably I was the only American ever forced to take the regular indoctrination course in a Communist country. Certainly I was the only American priest ever subjected to the course. They give no diplomas, though I passed all the examinations in Communist songs, doctrine theory and other phases of their system.

Their interrogations brought out a fact that seemed to baffle them, that is, I gave no evidence of becoming a convinced Communist. Rather, the opposite was true. They evidently believed they might convert some of us.

Interrogators worked on Father George Gilligan during his five months in a solitary cell in the Watlam prison. They promised him release to carry on his work of teaching religion if he would co-operate and teach Communism at the same time in the Catholic villages. When he refused this freedom, they said they would release him immediately to return to U.S.A. if he would agree to join a certain organization in Washington. This he refused, and they later arranged a "people's trial" to discredit and condemn him, then expelled him from the country.

But I must not have been a promising candidate, for they broached no such proposals to me after indoctrination.

CHAPTER X

Transfer to a Solitary Cell

A SCORE OF LEAVES in my prison diary have thumbnail
vignettes describing fellow-prisoners who were there
at the beginning of my term.

Beside me was Chen Ting Hang, a man of twenty-five
who was pugnacious, loquacious and usually mendacious,
with pronounced views on every question. Fickle and mischievous as a spoiled child, Chen's character made him un-
popular and distrusted. He was trying to play on both sides.
At the daytime classes he was loud in his praises of Communism, during the night, when others were asleep, he told
me how he hated the new regime and asked if there was any
hope of the Nationalists returning.

Chen's family were active members in the Nationalist
party. He was a shrewd gambler and saw the winner coming
in as the Communists advanced. Chen took to the hills and
joined the Red guerillas to help the Communists get control.
If he had not changed sides, he would have been liquidated

by now he told me. But Chen talked too much and twisted himself up in lies. He never told the truth when a lie could substitute. The new rulers put him in jail for indoctrination and mind reform to see what they could do with him. His tricky mind and double talk seemed to fit him well for Communism, but they had to be sure he was not too tricky. Cell mates told me he had two wives, and instead of working, lived by his wits. Interrogators have quite a score against him already, and I have no doubt that the purge will soon leave two widows to mourn his passing.

Student Wang in the next place to Chen was a diamond in the rough, who, to hear him tell it, had lived fifty thrilling years. Wavy muscles and a rough homely face made him look like a Greek wrestler, but he was too good-natured for any fight game. Wang had a storyteller's art which drew the prisoners around him to hear his ribald tales. The stories were vulgar rather than vicious, for easygoing Wang did have a sense of propriety. It was kind of an amusing paradox to see this roughneck hold forth as a defender of the faith. In some time past, he had read our doctrine books to while away the time and often took the stump here in the cell to explain religion.

Wang was brought into our cell at one o'clock in the morning. An overnight guest came to stay at his shop. It was late, so he neglected the regulation to report to police headquarters that he had a guest. At midnight police knocked at the door for one of their frequent counting of noses. Poor Wang was caught and rushed off to jail for his lapse. Less than six months ago he got forty-four days for the same offense. In-again-out-again Wang will get his "brain washed" and his "mind reformed" until he cannot forget Communist regulations next time. The sparkling life story he unraveled had every requisite for a grand book that will never be written. A lost treasure!

Next came a student, Kao, a lad in the middle twenties.

He had long hair, which he refused to cut, and feminine features that needed only lipstick to make the face a woman's. He told me one day, with that dreamy, mooning look in his eyes, "The most beautiful letter I ever got from my wife was after I was sent to prison."

Kao was a close friend of a man picked up not long ago and shot as a Nationalist special agent. His "confession" named Kao as a friend, so Kao was arrested on suspicion. Thirty-six days of indoctrination and frequent sessions with the interrogators seemed to clear him. He was told to write his confession together with a treatise on how to serve the Communist government. This would tell if his mind was now in conformity with the Party Line. The writing, at least, was conformable, so Kao was released.

Lin Kwei Tsan, formerly an officer in the Nationalist army, had the place next to Kao. His bare legs showed ugly scars from wounds he received fighting the Japanese. Captain Lin was a smart, industrious and capable man, with considerable administrative ability and leadership. His *tuan ch'ue* (short places in his character), often pointed out at criticism hour, were impatience and quick temper. His turn at discussion hour revealed a rich knowledge of history and world events. When our cell chief was liquidated a few weeks later, Lin was named to take over his position. Captain Lin used to watch me at prayer with the attitude of a person waiting to speak. One day he recited the Ave Maria, and then confided he had studied at a Christian Brothers school in West China.

When Lin's unit was scattered, he went back to the farm in his native village nearby. The Communists were looking for his superior officer, still unaccounted for. A commonly used trick was tried on Lin. They put him in jail and promised release if he would go out and find the wanted officer. This was an impossible task, so he had been here three months now to see if the jail would change his mind.

Interrogators may have other counts for they press him hard to find out how many Communists he killed or ordered shot.

Then came Student Chen. He was a guerilla of daredevil fame from Vegetable Garden Village. Many of his relatives are Catholic, so Chen knew me quite well.

"It is lucky venerable Tennien did not give us a contribution when our guerilla scout asked him last year, otherwise he might be wearing chains too," Chen remarked one day.

We all knew that Chen did not have a chance. His record of daring thrusts over the past year spelled sure death, now that they had captured him. But their lying promises gave him hope if he frankly confessed his escapades and his associates. He obliged. Disillusionment came a few days later when he was told, "The judgment of the people has sentenced you to death." The prison term for student Chen was just another gala time. I wondered if he did not know or did not care what was ahead, for he entertained us like a vaudeville actor until the last day. The chains ringing from his hands and feet were music accompanying the gay banter, while he paced the aisle and entertained. One of his acts was talking English with me. Somewhere in his travels he had picked up the sound "icity." By hitching "icity" to Chinese nouns, this "English" act furnished fun to the prison audience. I hope the man now has a harp instead of chains for musical accompaniment.

A young fellow called Student Mok, who was twenty-three years old, was the next. He was smart but his smartness was overdone. I sometimes wonder if this good-looking youngster was not an inside man reporting everybody. He had gone over to Party Line talk with vehemence. At criticism hour he had notes to *pei p'ing*, criticize all the others. If his father were there, I am sure he would expose his father's every thought, fault or crime.

Mok was arrested as a rumormonger. Anyone who says he hopes the Nationalists will come back, the guerillas will weaken the Communists or the Americans are winning, is guilty of this crime. In fact, anything expressed contrary to Communist propaganda makes the speaker a criminal rumor-monger who will be arrested if reported. Mok was in jail when I came and was still there when I left, after three months.

In the ranks next to Mok was Liang Ah San. A man with little education, a bald head and pockmarked face, he had been made assistant farmers' chairman of his village by the Communists. Formerly he made his living as a *feng shui* (wind-water) man. These geomancers are called in to pick happy spots for a grave, lucky days to start building a house or starting on a journey. They claim powers to divine luck by the propitious directions of wind and water. Sick people call the wind-water men to find out how they have offended the devils. The family of the sick are told to remove certain nails, change beams or even tear down the house to placate the evil spirits, then the sick person will get well, promises the wind-water man.

Liang had crossed swords with me in the past. Two years before, over a hundred people in his village decided to become Catholic. Liang knew that Christians have no call for wind-water men, so he fought the move with all his might and predicted dire calamities. The people went through with the course and were baptized. When nothing evil arrived, he saved face by saying, "The wind-water powers of the Catholic priest are very strong, that is the reason."

In jail Liang and I were companions in misery and we became fast friends. He told me he was arrested because he knew some people who were guerillas and did not report. As assistant farmers' chairman, the responsibility for crime was greater and the people's court had sentenced him to three years. Though he had persuaded several guerillas to surrender, this counted for nothing.

· 163 ·

"They give no credit for good work, but punish you for bad," he told me.

Liao Chung Yee, a soft-spoken scholarly man nearing sixty bunked next to the geomancer. Gentle and timid, Liao's deep erudition was not in evidence until discussion hour when it came his turn to comment on the lecturer's topic. He could make it easily lucid and understandable in a few moments of explanation. Student Liao had to live at the provincial capital of Kweilin, three hundred miles away, for he had been many years head of the Public Works Department for Kwangsi. He was in Kweilin until the fall of the National government. Then he came home to Stone Quarry Village and found that his wife and children had become Catholic. He looked into the doctrine books himself, he told me. He read and thought, finally reaching the conclusion that he too should become a convert.

In January 1951, with the start of land reforms, Liao was jailed as a landlord. Because he was an official of the former government, he was branded as a political prisoner as well. Because he had brains, he was sure to be liquidated. His home and his lands had been confiscated. He and his wife were here in jail, his children were living in an abandoned shed, scrounging or doing coolie work for something to eat. Many relatives who were also former officials had been shot, so he knew his time was short. One day he confided to me, "In times like these, about the only thing left to give us hope is religion."

A month later he was shot. His wife was left to serve a few months longer in jail, then released to join her children.

Next to Liao was an old man, Student Tang. Time had used seventy-eight years to chisel a filagree of roads and furrows over his face, which gave it an ancient beauty. Skin that was now leathered clung to his limbs like the withered leaves of November that cling to branches far beyond their time. The man sitting silent in his far-off reveries looked like a lacquered skeleton. Then high-pitched words uttered in a lifeless tomblike cackle made you think, "The skeleton talks."

Before each meal Old Tang would offer his vegetable ration for sale — always asking more than it was worth. If some prisoner bought it, he gloated with a miser's glee. I sometimes bought his vegetables to watch the reactions. He would cackle with kind of a stage laughter, fondle the money, count it, pack it away in his money belt. This poor man in his second childhood was happy to go hungry so long as a few pennies were added to his treasure.

Student Tang's brain, now wizened as summer vegetation after the autumn's frost, could not learn the lessons in our indoctrination course. The Communist songs he sang all on one note, somewhere around high "C."

Tang was incarcerated as a landowner. Now stripped of everything, his miser heart must be scalding. Too old to kill when the spark of life was already dim, the Communists were going to let him starve to death. In old Tang, many a prisoner must have pictured his own father in misery and hated the Communists for their disrespect to age.

Liang the opium smoker was next to old Tang. Liang died, and I have already written about him earlier in the book.

Hillbilly Chen, a bantamweight, feuding, fighting type who would fit in the Tennessee hills, was next in line. He was a scrapping half-wit, who fought his way through forty years, but was always in hot water from his uncontrollable temper. The most fined cell mate was Chen. At discussion hour he would sit like a monkey and start digging at the body lice biting him. A fine was imposed for lice hunting outside of the assigned hour. He would then get mad. Another fine! The guard outside heard his angry words sometimes and called him out to kneel a couple of hours in the court outside.

Chen wore chains at this time. Two months before he was on the labor gang in the kitchen, soon due for release. One of the labor gang went crazy and prison authorities sent him home. Chen decided he could play crazy and get out too. But he so overacted the part that his ruse was immediately discovered and he was put in irons and thrown into our cell.

His home is twenty-five miles out in the mountains, a silent place except for the song of winds through tall pines and the laughter of the brook leaping from pool to pool down by his house. Like many mountain men with little land to till, Chen took down the rifle in off season and did a little bandit cruising. Many of his pals took up with the guerillas and Chen's place was supposed to be a guerilla rendezvous. Communists closed in and arrested him for connections with the guerillas. Maybe he did work with them, but if the Communists look only for "homo sapiens" to punish, they should let Chen go free. He could neither read nor write his own name but succeeded in memorizing one answer for every discussion topic: "Communism is good, for it divides the wealth; capitalism is bad, for it scrapes off all the profits from the people's labor and makes them slaves."

Next to hillbilly Chen were two guerillas wearing irons. But they were liquidated four days after I came, so I did not get to know their history.

Two other guerillas came next. Both had surrendered and turned in their guns eight months ago, so they were not put in irons when arrested at the beginning of land reforms.

One of the pair, student Lee, about forty, was a rough-looking type with his four front teeth missing. His boisterous laugh exhibited a yawning cavity and two yellow eye-teeth that looked like fangs in a wolf. The laughter made him look more frightening, and it sounded like the hollow laughter of a lunatic. Lee made his living as a native doctor when the more lucrative occupation of banditry left him free. Native doctors in China rest their fingers on the pulse of each of the patient's wrists for some time, to diagnose the illness. The gesture is humbug of course, but the remedies they prescribe are often effective and excellent. They prescribe a potion made by boiling up certain roots, bark, herbs or flowers, which the patient drinks. Their remedies often cure where foreign drugs fail.

Dr. Lee had no practice now except on cell mates. He had no loot from banditry or guerilla raids since his gun was surrendered and he was now confined to jail, and his past record promised to make his life span short.

Beside Dr. Lee was another ex-guerilla named Chen. This fair-skinned effeminate lad of thirty was a Nationalist soldier for many years. In his soldier life he had experienced about everything the lures of life could offer. When he came home from soldiering, guerilla life tempted him, and now his career will end with jail and liquidation.

Chen and Lee used to hold hands, or sit with an arm around each other. Chen would rest his head on Lee's shoulder and look at him with sheep eyes. One day at criticism hour the cell mate next to me who had two wives blasted and ridiculed the lovers without mercy. After that, we had no more exhibitions of their inordinate sentiments.

Lee left without baggage a few days later, and Chen was alive when I left jail, but soon after, he was sure to join Dr. Lee wherever he was. Chinese herb doctors often live with the patient's family throughout the illness, to watch over and prescribe for the patient. Dr. Lee told me he lived with a Catholic family not long ago. This gave him an opportunity to read doctrine and prayer books, and Dr. Lee told me he had great esteem for the religion. We cannot read men's hearts, but I wonder if Dr. Lee's studies might not give him a ticket to paradise.

Celestial Virtue Lee came next, but I described his crime earlier.

Last in line and next to the cell door was Liao Chih Ch'i — our cell chief. He was named cell chief because of outstanding ability and leadership. With two months more to live,

Liao would reach his fortieth birthday. But his fate was uncertain, he told me one day. Everyone else in the cell felt sure his fate was certain death. After studies in National University, Shanghai, Liao went into politics and held different government positions under the old government. When the Communists came he was Secretary for the Kuomintang Party in Shumkai district, and this put his name on the Communist agenda to be liquidated as a political prisoner.

Liao was a talented storyteller, a brilliant talker, a well-read student and a shrewd politico — but not shrewd enough. He surrendered himself and offered his collaboration to the Communists after they took over. The Communists set the snare for Liao's capture as they set it for all their former enemies. He was assured no harm would come to him, and the Communists even gave him a minor position in the government, so they could keep tabs on him until the proper time. Then with the general roundup a few months later, he was thrown in jail. He was allowed to live eight months in jail while the interrogators pumped him for information on all his associates in the government.

The man tried desperately to live for the sake of his wife and six small children, but he was doomed. Liao sang the Communist praises, confessed his crimes, learned their songs and their doctrine and explained Communism to everyone in the cell. But he felt he was due for liquidation and he wanted to make provision. For hours he discussed religion with me and he could do it intelligently, for he had read not only all the Catholic doctrine books, but had even borrowed the teacher's instruction methods to explain them. When his doubts were solved and his objections answered, Liao gave much thought to death and what comes after. One morning he told me he wanted to become a convert but wondered if there was some way to keep it secret from the Communists.

"They hate religion, and they have so much against me, I do not want to give them another count," he explained to me.

I told him about baptism of desire and taught him a few simple prayers. Not long after, Liao was called out without his baggage. He turned to give me a wave of farewell and a smile through the bars.

"Perhaps this is it," was the message in his gesture. That evening another prisoner came to fill his empty bunk. Next morning trusties called for his baggage to go into the pile until his family called for it. His home and property had been confiscated. When he met the mother of his six children she was a co-ed studying at the university. Now she is carrying bricks to try to keep herself and children alive.

The second month, as prisoners increased, an upper deck was built in our cell and the number went up to forty. On May 14, 1951, Comrade Liu had me up for interrogation and told me I was about to be transferred. Although he said the transfer was because I was sick, it could well have been because I was ruining their hope of indoctrinating the forty other cell mates while I was there. My words were constantly exposing the lies and contradicting the propaganda they were giving out, so I had to be moved.

Comrade Liu waited to escort me to my new cell. I rolled up my blanket, took my rice bowl and chopsticks and said farewell to my companions — forty men in a cell. Only when I started the hundred-yard walk, did I realize how weak the dysentery had left me. The rice-gruel diet lacked vitamins, and my feet were bloated with beriberi. My puffed feet were like risen-bread dough, and when I pressed my finger into the swelling the dent stayed almost an hour. Pressure and bone pain made it agony to stand on them long.

Walking with Comrade Liu toward the old jail, I staggered several times. But just a look at the world outside, and the walk, after two months in a cell, was exhilarating. My feet were tingling and numb, and I was so short of breath I almost bit the air walking along. At the old jail, the bars were open on a solitary cell they had prepared for me. In the corner a couple of doors were spread flat, for a bed. The doors were held off the floor a foot or so by mud bricks. No other furniture was in the cell.

I dropped my blanket on the boards and flopped down for a moment's rest. The long interrogation of Police Secretary Liu, and the walk over had left me exhausted. Outside the cell Liu instructed the warden that I was sick and should be permitted to buy food and medicine. Liu wished me well in regaining my health and left, but he came back every few days to see how I was getting on, and his chats were cheering.

In the court outside, a prisoner was walking in circles, pushing a stick that whirled one flat stone over another to grind wheat. When Liu and the warden walked away, he caught my eye and blessed himself, to signal that he was one of my country Christians.

About fifteen others were in the jail who gave me the high sign when not watched. A Catholic barber was in for association with guerillas, and when he was cutting my hair one day he said:

"Why do you stay in China, Father?"

"I have to stay unless the government throws me out, or the Bishop tells me to leave."

"But the government is urging you to go?"

"Yes."

"Well, get out then. There is no hope of doing religious work now!"

The solitary cell was about ten by ten, which allowed me a bit of walking space from corner to corner. The floor was clay mud, and the walls adobe, with rat holes, nail holes and peg holes scattered over the whitewashed walls. I could almost reach the roof which was covered with local tiles.

But it was comparatively clean. There were no cooties, and if I was to be alone no new prisoners would bring them in. There was a brush broom in the corner, so I could keep the clay floor clean.

In this old jail there were only 235 prisoners, less than half the number held in the new prison. Most of the prisoners were transfers, finishing out the last few months of their sentence. The majority of them go out daily on labor assignment, and since they are about to be released, the discipline is not so tight as at the new jail.

Warden Lee dropped in a short time after my arrival, and sat down to talk with me. He said since I was alone I could smoke during the day, but asked me please not to smoke at night because of the fire hazard. He did not call in cigarettes and matches at night. The thought went quickly through my mind, "This man without the usual distrust and suspicion is an uncommon Communist!" I found out later he was a local man, and a Party Member of recent vintage.

Lee is a soft-spoken, kindly gentleman, and, unlike most Communists, he assumes that the prisoners will be gentlemen. He makes you feel that if you break a rule you are hurting him personally, since he leaves you on your honor to follow the regulations. He dropped around to my single cell a couple of times daily, to ask what food or smokes I wanted to buy. I gave him the money and he went out and bought supplies for me himself. The day was brightened by these chats with Warden Lee.

Night time meant annoyance and trouble. There are more trees, grass and ponds near the old jail, and at nightfall the mosquitoes came out of ambush and stormed the cell like an invading army. We had no nets, so it was a problem to sleep under their attack. When they got tangled in my beard or in my ear, they sounded like buzz bombs.

The red blotches on my hands and feet after the first night made me look like a man with measles, but I had the heavy woolen socks and heavy underwear I wore when arrested last March. At night, I wore the socks, and put one hand in each leg of underwear to keep the mosquitoes from devouring my hands and feet. With pants and shirt tight around me I was prepared for defense. Then I wrapped a towel around my head and face and could get some snatched sleep. Warden Lee kept pressing the police to go to the mission and bring me a mosquito net. It took them ten days before they finally complied.

One night during the first week I was awakened by a rat on the towel over my face. I often stopped writing the diary to watch the rats that rushed along the mud wall under the roof all day long. It looked like a track meet when they got chasing each other. At night my board bed seemed to be a boulevard for them to run down, and when they got noisy I slapped the boards to make them scamper off. After the mosquito net came, I was caged in from the rats and mosquitos.

But, all in all, the old jail was much less insufferable than the crowded cell I was in the first two months. The only classes I attended were singing classes morning and evening. Probably they gave up as a hopeless task, the job of trying to indoctrinate me. I had a great deal of time to work on this diary. Although Interrogator Lee still had my first two notebooks, which he returned after a few weeks, I bought other notebooks and filled two of them at the old jail. I kept Communist books on my lap all the time, and when one of the officials dropped by to talk, all he could see was Communist literature and certain Chinese passages that I had copied out. They wore pleased smiles at my apparent research into Communism. I could even point out where their doctrine was different from what Karl Marx or Lenin advocated, for I did read a lot of their theory when I needed a rest from writing. It must have been a great enigma for them to see a man who had been through their indoctrination, and had read stacks of their propaganda and doctrine books besides, who still did not get the faith, but would argue and condemn Communism as the great deception. Theory and principles have much that is laudable, but their practical Communism is an abomination and contradiction of their principles, I would argue. They called me hardheaded and incorrigible.

Here in the old jail I did not have to suffer hunger pangs; I was permitted to buy extra rice and pork each day. I should have picked up weight, but the dysentery contracted in the new jail came back intermittently to plague me. At the mission I had carbasone and emetine for treating amoebic dysentery, but I was not permitted to get it down here. The extra food I bought and the pacing I did, like a caged tiger, across my little cell did start my swollen legs to shrink.

We were given boiled water for drinking several times a day, so we did not have to suffer parching thirst. Warden Lee told the prisoners working in the yard outside the cell to bring more drinking water whenever I asked. The Catholic grinding wheat took care to bring boiled water often. At the cell door he would say, "God bless you, Father," then if the guard was not close we would chat a few minutes.

The warden at the old jail arranged another luxury. He told the prisoners carrying water to give me a washbasin full twice a day, so I could wash my face and take a sponge bath each day. At the first wash, after two months in the old jail without a bath, the dirt came off in layers. Then when I rubbed with a towel, more dirt came off in little black pin rolls. It took two or three scrubs before I got down to clean flesh again. Now I could run my thumb along the bare skin without digging up little black rolls of dirt. Fortunately I had not developed the itch or other skin irritations so many prisoners had from lack of washing. Some of their sores looked like biblical Job's at his worst stage.

My birthday came along five days after I was transferred to the old jail. I saw some chickens running around that were picked up at the mission when I was arrested. I asked Warden Lee if I could kill one for the birthday feast. He was willing and said he would have it cooked for me, but he had to ask the Chief of Police first. The answer came back no; that it was waste, and one person couldn't eat a whole chicken. I wish he had been on a starvation diet for two months.

On labor assignment prisoners could smoke, so each morning prisoners going out from the neighboring cells would ask for the cigarette ends left from the day before. I always saved them and in addition put a few cigarettes out for them to lift as they passed the window. I knew what a drag meant, after being starved several months for one.

Several times at the old jail I tried to find out why they had me in the lock-up, and what were the charges. When I asked the Assistant Chief of Police Pang, he answered, "I do not know, you will have to ask the chief."

The Communists had proved very often that they do not need a cause to arrest and hold people, but I decided to ask Warden Lee what crime they had me booked for. He was more frank, and answered:

"I do not think it is much of anything, but during the land reforms, many people are brought in to avoid any possibility of their interference with, or upsetting the land-reform program. As soon as it is over, you will be let out, I am sure."

The land-reform work had been going on six months and was finished here in June, but the Communists go by the book and, before release, every prisoner has to write a document admitting crime, so they will have a written justification for their arrest and imprisonment. Even though in your eyes and in the eyes of a democratic government, your crimes are not real, yet you have to admit guilt if you want to get out, for a confession document is a *sine qua non* condition for release.

Not long before, I had told secretary Liu during interrogation that I was fed up with writing documents of confession and retraction. The one I had written I considered enough, but if they can get you to write more and bring out more offenses they did not know about, they are happy and their system is working out. I told them they would have to say what they wanted me to write for a confession and I would see if I could agree. They were not to ask me again to write their "frank and honest" bunk.

On June 10 and 11, the interrogators told me to reflect and prepare my confession document and perhaps I would be released. The land reforms were about finished here. On June 16, Interrogator Lin came to my cell with a written model of the confession of crimes they wanted me to copy and sign as my own.

Lin had a pointed ratlike face, small beady eyes, a cruel mouth and a receding chin. I had found him the meanest amongst the interrogators. It was very hard to be nice in the presence of his nasty, imperious remarks.

"Here is a model of the confession of crimes you are to write and sign, and then you will be released," was Lin's tempting offer.

"Let me read it over," I asked, without getting up from the bed where I sat.

To my surprise, the confession document they had prepared was short. There were only two points they wanted me to confess. First, that I had attempted to murder the guard with the cleaver-shaped vegetable knife; second, that I refused to let the guard at the bus station inspect the baggage in my jeep one day, and then threatened to kill him.

I handed back the paper, folded my arms, leaned against the wall and stated:

"I shall never sign a thing like that — lies, false!"

"*Lao T'ien* (old Tennien), you are the most obstinate person I ever saw, and cunning too."

I smiled, accepting this as a compliment from him, thinking someone else could be cunning. The prisoners hated him as an inquisitor and called him the cunning so-and-so.

"You have got to sign it or you will not get out of jail," he threatened.

"I prefer to stay in jail rather than sign," I said. "And now if you will excuse me, I shall take my morning gruel while it is hot."

But the order had come down to release me, and he was given the job of carrying out the preliminaries. He was given a mission, and a Communist must somehow carry out his assignment. The paper swung in his hand as he balanced his weight from one foot to the other, deciding what to do. He changed his tactics to blandishments and a tittering laugh, begging me to sign.

I took back the paper, got out my fountain pen and started to change his wording. I crossed out his "attempted to murder" and put "frightened the guard," and for his second phrase "threatened to kill him," I substituted, "I used menacing language when the bus station guard was impolite and threatening." We argued over the second point a long time. He begged me not to omit "menacing language" or the confession would not have any substance. This was harmless enough, so I agreed to put it down. However, it was only a half-truth, for, to be exact I had only threatened to report the conduct of the bus station officer to higher authorities.

My gruel was getting cold, but at his urgency, I copied out the corrected document in Chinese, and signed it. He had to take it back and see if the Chief of Police was satisfied. I intimated that I had gone my limit in admission of guilt.

The discussion with Lin had taken the edge off my appetite, and I was also thinking of some real food I could cook if they let me go back to the mission. A prisoner-carpenter was working in the yard near my cell door. I called him over to eat up my gruel and vegetables.

There was another snag to straighten out before leaving. A departing prisoner must get one of the shopkeepers to guarantee that he would obey the laws in the future. The "shop" in China is a store or any place of business. On June 10 and 11, when telling me I might be released, the authorities said I should send word asking a shop for the guarantee. This, I said, is impossible, and I told them that with my passport out of date the police had asked me to get such a guarantee six months before. All shops refused, saying they could not guarantee a person would obey the laws, for no one knew what the laws were, yet everyone around was being arrested for breaking them.

Warden Lee said he would take it on himself to find a guarantor, if I wished. Rules called for it and they must go by the book.

"Go ahead," I told him, "but it will be a surprise if you can get any of these scared merchants to guarantee me."

He went to a Catholic who owned a barber shop nearby and told him he should be my guarantor. People cannot decline when an official with a gun holstered at his side makes a request, so barber Paul Mok signed the papers for me.

Inquisitor Lin (the term inquisitor, rather than interrogator, certainly fits the man), returned from headquarters in about an hour. He directed me to roll up my blankets, that he was taking me back to the mission.

Warden Lee was near the outside gate, so I stopped for a word with him.

"Keep that cell reserved for me, I shall be back before long," was my parting remark.

The warden smiled graciously, but suspicious Comrade Lin questioned me immediately. "What do you mean by that; do you want to come back?"

"No, but with every one of your officials who carries a gun making arbitrary arrests for what he interprets as a crime, of course I shall be back."

Part Three

CHAPTER XI

House Prison Again

THREE MONTHS IN JAIL had left me sick and washed out. But even with my beriberi legs and puffing under baggage, the walk home outside the bare walls and depressing prison atmosphere was exhilarating. It was June 16. Out of the blackness I was surprised to see the rice grain high and colored in soft green. Flower shrubs were now in bloom along the roadside. The trees that were bare when I was taken away from the world in March now had leaves that waved in the June breeze. Birds still sang from the branches!

These things were a special thrill for a man from jail. Besides, my heart was gay, for I had been able to smuggle out the prison diary with me.

The last few days in jail I had worked out a plan. Prisoners released from jail were put through a search. But it was not thorough like the search at arrest. Guards cursorily looked through the blankets and baggage, then had the prisoners empty their pockets for an inspection of the contents. This gave me hope. Looking over the mud walls of the cell, I found a nail. I punched holes through the three notebooks of prison diary. Next, I punched holes in my shorts. I pulled out the string used to take up slack at the sides of the underwear and used it to tie the notebooks in the crotch. I kept the diary hidden there the last few days before my release.

The morning came when I was to pass out through the warden's office. Guards quickly looked over my baggage and blanket. My pockets had no contraband. When they found nothing damaging, I was allowed to pass. There was a letdown in tension as I walked out the door with the prison diary. For days I had worried that the searchers might find it and put me back in jail.

My wrist watch and cigarette lighter, which had been taken away upon my entry to jail, were not returned. After several complaints to the Chief of Police, he got these articles back for me. One of the Communists had been "holding them in safe keeping for me."

Back at the mission again, I was detained in the convent wing. The two police guards who examined baggage at the bus station were assigned to live at the mission and keep me in quarters. For three months dust and dirt had piled up in the empty convent. As our Vermont farmers say, you could grow potatoes in the place. The police had ransacked everything many times during my absence, though not many articles were missing.

The guards now allowed me to go to the bus station to buy vegetables and meat. It is the next building to us, though a hundred yards away and hidden by trees. When buses arrived, the guards were tied up there for several hours examining baggage and travel papers. People skipped in to visit me at these times and told me what was going on in the villages.

There are so many people sent by the Communists to

trick one into talking that great discernment and discretion were always necessary. After you live awhile under a suspicious government, you become suspicious and distrust everyone.

One priest told me that Communists had even ordered Catholics to ask questions in the confessional that would incriminate him. One of my Catholic teachers asked if it was a sin to kill the Communist land-reform men who were taking away their land. He might have been a plant, for all teachers have to undergo intensive indoctrination. I simply gave him the theology that one had the right to protect life or property even if he had to take the thief's life in doing so. Then I told him, according to his own conscience he could apply the principle to the case in mind.

Father W., a Chinese priest, paid dearly for his indiscretions. A Communist soldier visiting him asked:

"Why is it that the Catholic Church, after all these years here, has only a few hundred followers, and Communism in one year has the whole countryside following its doctrine?"

"Because you use guns, we do not."

Father W. was immediately thrown into jail and was still there the last I heard. And so I was determined to be suspicious and discreet when the people or officials stole in to talk to me, now that they had me under house arrest again. Communists were often sent to talk to us, claiming they were Catholics. They thought this was a way to get information or catch us in criticism. One day a Communist messenger confided to Bishop Paschang that he was a Catholic.

"And what is your baptismal name?"

"I can't recall," answered the fellow after a pause.

"Perhaps it is Lu-tsai-fa-erh" (the Chinese translation for Lucifer).

"That's right, that's right," muttered the man, while the Bishop chuckled.

Once again I could celebrate Mass each morning in the

room. Mass, that first morning after three months in the purgatory of jail, was a great joy.

There was still wheat flour in an air-tight can. Over the charcoal brazier I cooked the white altar bread and prepared for Mass. There was no server, no congregation — just a priest alone to meet God in this house prison. Time did not count in the rendezvous with eternity today. I took care to read all the prayers which rubrics would have us say from memory. The months in jail without Mass made me distrust my memory, and I wanted each prayer pure and without halt this morning.

After the consecrating words, I disregarded the hastening rubrics to linger on in God's Holy Presence. With caressing fingers I held the Host and talked and prayed and wept to be in His Presence once more. Sun rays crept across the altar until respect forbade me to hold the interview longer.

I took the Host in fervent communion, or better, union, which is love's consuming act. The sun rose high while I stayed on my knees at the end of the first Mass after release from prison.

We had been isolated since November last year, now eight months ago, when I last saw a priest for confession. During these months of arrest, necessity left me to unfold my wrongs with a contrite heart direct to God, while awaiting the solace of confession and absolution from a fellow priest.

Father Dempsey had been released from Jungyuen, next station to the West. He had been given a travel permit to leave China, three months after his request to go. On July 2, the bus he was on stopped here at Shumkai. Before departing from Jungyuen, he had been given written permission to call on me. The permit should have let him come to the house, or let me go out and talk to him. But the guards at the bus station warned him that no one could visit me. He stood in the road 150 feet away and we shouted a few words back and forth, which aroused the guards to action. I recited my prayer of contrition, while Father Dempsey raised his hand in absolution from the road. The guards rushed out, pointed a gun at me, and warned me to get back inside the door and stay there. Then they grabbed Father Dempsey to take him into Police Headquarters. On the road they met the Chief of Police. He looked at Father Dempsey's permit to call at the mission, which was in order, and told him he could go back and visit with me until the bus started. Then the Chief upbraided the guard for not reading and following written orders. Father Dempsey came back and we both went to confession beside the road while the bus made preparations to start. Five minutes later he was gone.

Since I had come back from the prison June 16, three weeks had gone by. Father Lynch was stationed at Blue Cloud six miles away. Although under house arrest, he had sent me three letters by messenger. Each letter the messenger brought told me our Bishop in Wuchow had directed all the American priests here to ask the government for an exit permit and travel orders to leave China. Father Lynch said that I was the last one of our diocese out of jail, and the last one to apply for exit.

This was disappointing news, though it was the only sensible thing to do if they were going to keep us under arrest and not permit us to do any mission work. However, I wished to stay, if only to be a thorn in the Communist's flesh. I wanted to force them to throw us out, which they boasted they would do in time, instead of letting them persecute us until we asked to go.

Bishop Donaghy was not long out, after his five months in the Wuchow jail, and his letters were not coming through. Two messengers, former Catholic teachers, arrived here from Wuchow and told me I should apply for exit. I asked one if the Bishop had given her a letter for me with instructions. She said he did not dare, with all the searches one must undergo on the way.

Then Father Dempsey on July 2 told me that all had applied for exit except myself. I thought over the move of requesting travel papers to leave China, for several days. The decision of Bishop Donaghy, though it had come through messengers, seemed quite definite in its direction, and there was nothing to do but obey. On July 6, I wrote a letter in Chinese to the Chief of Police, stating that my superiors had directed the American priests in this diocese to leave China and, therefore, I was requesting a travel permit to leave.

The letter was handed to the Chief of Police. Their attitude changed immediately. Annoyances to force me to ask out could be relaxed now that they had gained their point. I was told that clearance by Peking would take some time, maybe weeks or months. The Chief said I could call my cook back from the country to cook and carry water. He even told me I could move back into the priest's house, where there was a kitchen range for cooking and baking.

Guards who lived here at the mission to keep me isolated were called away, though they could see the mission from the bus station and were still under orders to prevent people from coming to visit me. With the guards busy down the road a ways, however, people could steal in to see me without much danger of being caught.

Word was sent to my cook that the police would permit him to come back and help me until the government approved my exit. Police thought their propaganda would frighten him from working for me. He came out immediately, but asked for two weeks delay to harvest the first rice crop and plant the second, for it was July. I was used to cooking and housework, so I did not mind the delay.

Between the tasks of housework, and late into the night, I wrote fillers for my diary that I had not dared write in jail. The pages that follow on Communist cruelty, deception, spies and suppression of religious freedom I could write now with few interruptions. Now that the guards relaxed their vigilance, frequent visitors brought me information, and I could walk through the fields near the mission and talk to the farmers about life under Communism.

Two weeks later, toward the end of July, 1951, my cook came and I moved from the convent back to the priest's house. My typewriter was useless to the Communists, so I found it there, but my razor had been lifted. There was nothing to do but let my beard continue to grow until I got to free land again.

The typewriter was dusted and oiled for the job of typing out my prison diary. Guards or the Chief of Police dropped in several times a day to see what I was doing or to see who had stolen in to talk to me. When I had visitors, I watched the road and saw the approach of police or spies, then quickly brought visiting Christians or friends to the dispensary room. By the time police or guards got to the house, they found me taking the person's temperature or handing out quinine, aspirin or some cheap salve. People leaving always took a few pills to show the questioning guards at the bus station why they were visiting the mission. The game went on with few catastrophes while I continued to get information.

While typing, I locked the door so as not to be caught unawares. A bang at the door or a shout from the guards was the signal to hide my diary script and slip a harmless sheet into the typewriter. When the cook brought the guards or police to my room, they found me typing some sentences like, "The cow jumped over the moon." Some knew a little English, so when they inquired, I told them I was writing for finger practice. Then I would write out their names in romanized script and hand them the whole sheet. This disarmed their suspicion and kept them from too many searching questions.

Each day I revised the text and pounded out the diary into type and paragraphs, or worked on an unwritten chapter.

Long sheets were torn from the binding of an old ledger and on both sides of these I typed the story, with one carbon copy. The problem now arose of how to get the script out of China. For eight months now I had lived in a news blackout, except for the controlled Chinese newspapers, which were scarcely helpful. A police censor in the post office still took away any letters or English newspapers addressed to me as soon as the bag was opened, informants told me. He also looked over the outgoing mail before it was locked into the mail bag, and took out all suspected people's letters. But there was a loop hole. The scheme was carefully planned and it worked. To tell more might bring punishment on those who helped me.

Thirty pages were now typed. The first letter got into the bag and was on its way to Hong Kong, I was told. Three more installments were mailed out at two-week intervals, but my incoming mail was still being confiscated so I received no answer.

In the quiet days of house detention, I typed on. I kept the original to try another way, in case the copy mailed out failed to reach Hong Kong. No word came, and I was left to wonder if the script ever got through.

Living expenses might have been a problem these last seven months, but I had made deposits with two trustworthy merchants in November the year before. In jail, I did not need food money, for the food bill there was supposed to be paid up on release. After my cook came back, he took a note to draw funds from the merchants, when I needed expense money. These times of trial proved my loyal Christians and friends when prison terms threatened dire punishment for their loyalty. From July to December, 1951, funds were plentiful, for the police who were ordered to pay me for goods confiscated did so in part.

Late in June or early July, 1951, orders had come through from the Government at Peking that any foreigner leaving China should be allowed to sell or give away his possessions before departing. The decision was to give us travel money, they said. Gradually they brought in money for the kerosene and other articles of value they had been taking from the mission. This turn was as unexpected to the local officials as it was to me.

One of my government friends visiting with me a few days later asked if I had any explanation why the seized goods were to be returned to me or paid for. I could offer none. He went on to say that everyone down at the Government Center felt sure that there would be no return of my jeep or anything else taken from the mission. Then he asked a startling question. "Do you suppose it is because of the reverses in Korea, the government is not so sure of its position now?" I knew of no reverses. Communist newspapers only told of victories. We were on dangerous ground, so I said I did not know. However, I did know the government people were boasting last December and January when Chinese troops were flooding down into Korea. Newspapers were full of their victories, and celebrations were held here as they took each large Korean city. One of the soldiers said to me, "It will not be long now, two-thirds of Korea is already liberated from the Americans." Then the counter-attack came, and the newspapers carried nothing of the Chinese reverses.

The postman brought the *Nan Chen Erh Pao* (*Southern Compass Daily*) to my house prison. Reading it helped pass the time and made a change from the fatigue of typing. Newspapers are, of course, government mouthpieces and are filled with the speeches of Communist officials, government decrees and directives, confessions of former non-Communists who now see the light, and such bunk, for the most part.

The public trials of "missionary spies" and "orphan-murdering Sisters" were given great space.

One day, in September, it printed that Father Robert Kennelly of Loting had just been tried by the people's court as spy, orphan-murderer and for other crimes. He had been banished from China three months before, as I already knew. In America readers write to correct the editor, in Communist China they do not.

Another day I noticed that a public accusation meeting was held against a priest. He had refused absolution to a Chinese girl who confessed she had joined the Communist party. He "stubbornly" stuck to his guns that the girl was excommunicated and must be denied the sacraments. This event gave the Communists columns of propaganda ranting against the "reactionary Catholic Church."

Papers carried no objective news of world events. Soon after the Communists took over, they closed down all newspapers that were neutral or anti-Communist. This caused a painful vacuum. An official came secretly one day to ask, "When they let you go to Hong Kong, will you send copies of *Time* air-mail edition to one of my friends? He will give them to me so I can find out what is going on."

"This is too dangerous for both of us," I said, fearing he might be trying to trap me.

But suppression of news has its pay-off. Rumors and supposedly authentic news flew from mouth to mouth, in spite of the arrests of rumormongers. One person came in later and told gleefully that Americans were using two thousand bombers day and night to blow the Chinese army apart and had already destroyed two Chinese armies. Another came in to say that the Chinese army had been driven all the way back to the Yalu River. The Chinese papers, which are controlled and manufactured, carried almost no war news now, which gave credence to the rumors passed around by "bamboo wireless."

Whatever reasons prompted it, the decision from the Peking government came, "Return possessions to all missionaries." The Chief of Police had pretty well wrecked my jeep, but they had it running again. He said he would like to buy it for a friend of his in Wuchow. Of course, this statement fooled nobody. After much dickering, we agreed on a price.

In Hong Kong I met over a hundred priests recently exiled from China. I found that I was one of the rare ones to receive any compensation for goods confiscated. Most of the men were forced to leave without any payment for property seized. Books, chalices, clothes, medicines, kerosene, movie machines, cameras and money were simply seized from the man leaving. The government had given the orders to pay, but, as so often happens, local officials interpret orders as they wish, and they took everything and gave no recompense.

After I applied for an exit from China, the police gave back the keys to the priest's house and other buildings, but they kept the church keys. Police told Christians they would not be permitted to hold any religious services.

CHAPTER XII

The Purge

WHEN I was sent back from the jail to house arrest, there was less danger in carrying on with my diary notes. For over a year and a half I had watched the working out of many phases of Communism. I had learned a great deal, but it was not prudent to write about the purge, the cruelty, their war on religion and their spies while I was held in jail. The guard for my house prison seldom came inside. He stood at the door or walked around the house. And so I had the opportunity to write about these vicious aspects of Communism in the chapters which follow.

It is only proper to note the Communists' own viewpoint in carrying out the purges. I merely state a fact which they coldly boast about as one of their aims for China's welfare.

"China has too many people, we must cut the population down by eliminating the bad ones,' officials frankly state.

Their strategy of war — "seawave attack" has been used

in China and Korea. This uselessly throws masses of men to be slaughtered. Interrogators and other officials inhumanely argue in favor of this, stating, "The losses do not matter. China still has one billion hands to strike down the invader." Such statements help explain their policy in carrying out the sweeping purges.

Two days after I was locked in jail, knowledge of the purge going on struck like near lightning to startle me. The fellow in the bunk beside me was called out for what I supposed was interrogation. When he did not return that evening, I asked innocently what had happened to him. Most of the prisoners gave the usual answer of Chinese who want to stay out of trouble, "I don't know." But one prisoner near me had his arms folded. I felt a little nudge and saw one hand pushed out where I alone could see. Then he worked the trigger finger with several pulls that told me the answer. The departed man's quilt, rice bowl and extra clothes rested in a little pile beside me, and the empty bunk would be filled with a new prisoner tomorrow. Nobody talked about the event except in secret. Some of the old-timers, who had seen this repeated many times and knew the routine, folded the departed man's baggage and put it near the cell door. Next morning the trusties going around on their usual pick up at the different cells, asked for the baggage of "Student Liang." Through the bars I silently watched the group of trusties carrying about a dozen quilts towards the shed out back.

The baggage of the departed is piled in a shed which we pass through on the way to the toilet. There it awaits relatives to come and claim it. One morning I tried a quick count of quilts as we passed. There were over 150 in the pile not yet called for.

After the second day I knew that when a prisoner was called out without baggage and did not return, someone somewhere was soon digging a grave for him. When prisoners are told to pack up their baggage and come out to the

· 193 ·

office, it means either they are to be released or they are assigned to the labor gangs, which have cells apart.

The labor gang was supposed to be the graduating class in our indoctrination school, and there one is slated for possible release. Going on the labor gang means that your crime is comparatively light, and after a short expiation you will soon be home. Just to cross up the slate, it seems, the Communists arrange an upset. One of the ex-guerillas in our cell was transferred to the labor gang after a month. Two months later, without any explanation, he was brought back to our cell, then one morning called out without baggage.

If the prisoners are told they are to be returned to their country district for trial, but are directed to leave their baggage until they return to the cell, it means they are marched back near their homes to be shot. Police accompany the prisoner on a one-way walk back to his native village. There he is shot. This saves his people the expense of carrying the body back home in a coffin.

The prisoner who worked the trigger finger beside me that second morning, whispered to me later on, "I came to the cell a month before you, and I have seen eight prisoners leave the cell without baggage." In the next thirty days while sojourning as a prisoner, I kept count of the number who went out without baggage. Seven out of the original twenty were liquidated in that time.

Working on the percentage of executions from this cell for two months, I figured that in this prison alone 170 prisoners are liquidated each month by the firing squad. Some time later when Comrade Liu had me up for interrogation, I stated, "I see you are liquidating five or six prisoners each day here."

"Not five or six — we are shooting between ten and fifteen prisoners here every day." Hence my estimate was far too low.

After I was transferred from jail to house arrest in June, 1951, the guard always permitted officials to come to the mission dispensary for medicine. These visits gave me a chance to get much information. One of the officials forced to work with the government gave me more accurate figures on the purge. I had been a friend of his family for many years, so he told me confidentially while I wrote down the notes. In the county of Shumkai during the first six months of land reform 1,400 people were executed by bullet. In the whole province of Kwangsi during the same six months they executed by bullet between 180 and 190 thousand. The population of Kwangsi, according to the government, is just over 13,000,000. This means that out of every thousand people, fourteen were shot during the first six months of land reform. If the same proportion holds, it means that in all China nearly seven million people were liquidated in the first six months.

Land reforms have been undertaken in only half the districts of Kwangsi. When the land-reform teams move in to these other districts, there will be another purge of similar magnitude. Fourteen million purged in one year of land reform in China is indeed a sizable figure.

Priests from North China believe this figure of seven million purged in six months is only a fraction of the real number shot. When the Communists were struggling to get control and held only a few provinces in the North, they slaughtered wholesale to consolidate their position. Kwangsi was one of the last two provinces to come under their control. When they held all China and were quite sure of their power, the executions were comparatively small. But they are watching the thousands of ex-Nationalist soldiers, the minor functionaries of the former government and the many thousands of persons they are not sure of. If an invasion is launched against the Communists, or another world war threatens their position, everyone knows there will be wholesale slaughter undertaken here.

A Catholic schoolteacher stole in to the mission to see me one day here at my house prison. He comes from a village of eight hundred people. During our conversation I asked him how many of the village inhabitants were shot by the Communists during land-reform months. He answered, twenty. This also would indicate my figures for those liquidated was far too low.

I tried to estimate the number of people sent to prison by the Communists, based on some three thousand prisoners in our small mountainous county of Shumkai. But prisoners are a floating population, and the number is hard to estimate. Under the Nationalist regime the Shumkai prison averaged one hundred inmates. The Communists have built new jails and converted old buildings into jails both here and in the country districts, and they now hold over three thousand prisoners. As near as I can figure it, for all China, there were more than twenty million people sent to prison in the first six months of Communist rule.

People talking to me have often remarked that it makes little difference whether we are in jail or outside. China has become a national prison with the loss of freedom, and everybody is looked on and treated as a prisoner of the regime.

One prisoner in our cell was given a forty-day stretch when the Communists first came. At that time one felt a stigma and shame at getting out of jail. But doing his second stretch a year later, he said with the wholesale arrests the people viewed the Communists as the criminals not the victim. And so he would walk out, this time with his head high.

Starvation brought on indirectly by their land reforms and general program does not seem to be part of their planned pogrom. Father Lynch, from Pittsfield, Mass., was my nearest neighbor. He lives in a rice-producing valley and saw the thousands of residents, in this second year of Communism, hungry, sick and starving in the worst year they had ever known. He contends that for every person shot in the purge, fifteen died of starvation.

A Shanghai businessman of Polish nationality sat beside me on the train, the day I came out of Communist China. Formerly he had been a journalist. I asked him about the official announcement the Communists put in the newspapers, that between May 1 and October 1, 1951, the number of counter-revolutionaries executed in Shanghai was 1,742.

"Don't believe it. I know from men on the inside that the number is over 40,000," he answered me.

The Deputy Governor of Kwangtung, the next province to the south, gave out for the newspapers in China: "Between October, 1950, and August, 1951, 28,332 counter-revolutionaries have been executed." Here again, I am only reporting, and one can draw his own conclusions about the real number executed.

A letter from Brother Francis Wempe in Hong Kong, dated May 14, 1952, gives later news. He takes the one-hour train ride each day to the Communist border to meet missioners expelled from China. He states:

"People arriving from Shanghai say that a thousand people commit suicide each day now in Shanghai . . . Those from Canton say the Communists closed the public park in that city, for they found a number who had hanged themselves from the trees each night."

Bishop Donaghy, in May, 1952 (he is now under house rest, the only American left in the whole province of Kwangsi), wrote Brother Francis of the great increase in suicides there. "The wife of our Catholic Action Leader cut her throat attempting suicide after torture. A Catholic teacher here took his life by poison after torture. Father Tennien's most outstanding family, husband, wife and daughter, went to reward by their own hands after two years of torture."

I have transposed from the Bishop's Latin letter written in ambiguous terms to get by the censor. He gives a long list now in peace "*a manibus suis.*" He concludes by saying men of the New China evidently believe "You can change the world," and they have stepped up their process in the last few months.

When Communism had control of only about half of China, the Nationalists claimed that the Communists were planning to cut China's population down by a hundred million. At that time it sounded like one of the wildest claims propaganda could manufacture. After seeing the Communists at work for nearly two years, I am ready to congratulate the Nationalists for their merciful understatement.

CHAPTER XIII

Spies that Snoop

SOON AFTER the advent of Communism, we saw for ourselves that everybody was trained to be a spy. Newspapers and youth magazines carried accounts of the "vigilance" training for the Communist youth, which taught them to search out reactionaries and counter-revolutionaries. Youngsters were apt pupils for this training. Teen-agers and children went at sleuth work with enthusiasm. Those not afraid to denounce their parents or who cleverly eavesdropped on private conversations were lauded in the newspapers as glowing examples for New China's youth.

In a police state one expects to find an elaborate spy system. But I was astounded to find them giving universal training in spy work for all Chinese. During land-reform meetings I heard the Communist leaders drilling every citizen to spy and report on everyone else. The papers carried "Regulations dealing with the Purge," and article 19 stated: "Any person has the right to expose and denounce counter-revolutionaries . . ."

There was an intensive campaign worked up in 1951, which I saw and heard from my house prison. Speakers to the group in the church read out long government documents and directives for spy work, "to eliminate criminals, bandits, counter-revolutionaries and *spies*." Detailed directions were given on how to carry out the snooping.

Speakers gave the reason: "There are active and passive opponents to the Chinese revolution, who undermine the morale, the economy, and the Korean war effort against the imperialist aggressors. We must search them out." In spite of their purges, Communists were admitting that counter-revolutionaries still existed.

Meetings, speeches, slogans and songs excited the citizenry to a hysterical nation-wide witch hunt for counter-revolutionaries and criminals of all sorts. Children took the task to heart and got a thrill out of snooping under windows, infiltrating market-place crowds and reporting even against relatives and parents. I saw guards, plain-clothes men, boys and girls stealthily carrying out their task. Spying was so widespread that it was generally obvious, but it succeeded in throwing fear into everyone.

There was every evidence that the government was dealing with opposition to the regime with determination and vigor, though they admit it is a long term job. The government "Report on Political and Legal Work," issued in May, 1951, stated: "This is a long complicated struggle, and must be carried out continuously. It is necessary to continue the suppression of counter-revolutionaries persistently, and the opposition to complacency and imprudent emotion . . ."

Communists are unceasingly urged to carry out orders without emotion or sentiment. One of their often repeated slogans is *Pu yao k'e ch'i* (do not stand on ceremonies). People are taught to snoop into your house, your private effects and your secrets, that they have equal rights with you in your possessions. In China today one soon realizes that no secret is safe.

Snooping by the people was surpassed in zeal by the snooping of the police. The police started their night snooping ostensibly to see that no house lodged an unreported guest. But this sudden night visiting was designed principally to search for plotters and revolters against the new regime. Between nine o'clock and midnight they came periodically. One week they inspected us five nights. All had to get up for them to count noses. They would search the servants' quarters, then search through my house, trying to discover unregistered guests or visitors, they said. After snooping through everything and asking many questions, they would leave. In the morning before dawn they often came again for another inspection.

Soldiers were often billeted in the people's homes. They pretended to be servants of the people in this new regime of "people's government." They carried water and helped with the work so as to be taken into the people's confidence. But their searching questions soon revealed they were there for spy work.

People in the villages nearby told me the police or soldiers patrolled silently among their houses at night. Where they heard people talking they broke in on them. Each person was taken aside and asked what they were talking about. If their answers varied, they were run off to jail, suspected of plotting against the government.

The father of one of my lady doctrine teachers was a Wangpo Military Academy student under Chiang Kai-shek. After the conquest by the Communists he returned to his village. He was a wanted man, along with a number of others in that village called Feng Mu. The Communists stationed a squadron of police there to eat at the expense of the wanted man's family. They figured this rice-bowl pressure would force the people to turn over the wanted man. At the same time the Communists made attractive promises to the one who would betray him. They got a youngster aside and worked on him. This lad finally agreed to lead them secretly to the hiding place. Late in the night he led the Communists to the hideout, and they shot the man in his sleep. Relatives of the victim told me it was an adopted son the officer had taken in and raised from childhood, who had betrayed him.

A ragamuffin youngster from the neighboring village was hanging around the mission door for a while. Though only about twelve, he was playing his part as silent observer and listener quite well. I pretended to think he was a beggar, called him one and ridiculed him for "non production," a great sin in Communist eyes. His pride was hurt and he zigzagged slinkingly away and didn't come back.

I had a great deal of jockeying with the police over the baptismal records. All the other missioners had the same pressure put on them. The police asserted that this was routine and they wanted the records only to know how many Catholics there were in the district. I had seen enough to make me wary, and if they planned to persecute the Christians at a later date, it would not be through any disclosure of mine.

They came many times during the next six weeks with the same demands, but left each time without success. Finally they had their own operatives in each village ask who was Catholic and got an incomplete, inaccurate list that way.

The house was quite prepared for their snooping. Account books had all been destroyed, so their search was in vain to find out how much money was being sent from America for the mission work here. When they questioned me, I stated it was never the same; when works are active I receive more, and when they are inactivated, as they have been since the arrival of Communism here, I do not need funds, except a little to buy food for myself.

After my arrest in January, they searched and snooped high and low for information and contraband numbers of times. They looked into the medicine bottles of the dispensary, and even into some of the cans in the storeroom. They believe every missionary is a spy harboring radio sending sets and startling secret records.

Several times the help was called to the police station. They were queried to find out who my friends were; they were asked if I had a gun, sending set, etc. They asked the cook what I ate and how much I spent on food. They often sent men to talk with the help, snooping for information.

In the Watlam mission the person employed as head man was a clerk in the court under the old regime. The new government held this as a sword over him, but left him to carry on working at the mission for their own advantage. Each day he had to go for questioning and make his report to the police. They asked who visited the mission, what the priest said to them, what were the priest's viewpoints and so on. It was rather amusing, for the priest and the rest of the help knew he was the Communist spy among them.

Much of their spy work is not sly; it is just puerile and amateurish, but it holds the people in fear and subjection, and does get many results of value to them. But people who are wrapped in their own aims revolve in their own orbit. Cut off from the views of others, they make very bad estimates. Thus, they underestimate the secret hatred people have for them.

The most dastardly snooping spy work which I saw was the assignment they gave Father X. Father X had been ordained five years ago in a North China province, where the Communists have been in control for at least half a decade. The religious work there was limited because of Communist control, so he came to help in our diocese. In 1949 he was sent to Shumkai to be my assistant.

Father X, tall, thin, and bony, was an exceptionally bright student. Though from North China, he learned the local dialect in a few months and spoke it with singular perfection. However, his meekness was overdrawn and made him a timid soul, who was troubled by fears of things that might happen. He had been arrested several times and suffered prison and the torturing grilling of the Communists before he had come to this sector to work with us. And so his worries and timidity may have been based on the realities of a Communist going-over.

To divide the work up with him I asked him to care for the Christians in a region six miles out, where there were eight hundred Catholics. He made his residence at the Catholic school in Virtue Village. It was not long after he came here to help us that the Communists invaded and took over control. How he was picked up, while taking a trip with me in the jeep, I have told earlier.

When the police released him from jail after that episode, it was with the condition that he live at the mission and report to them daily. He was to report what I said, who visited the mission, and any other information he could pick up. He had majored in history at the University in Peking. The Chief of Police saw that he was a man of many qualifications, whom he could use on his staff where there were so many illiterates. Since Father X knew not only the Mandarin language of the Chief, but was also facile in speaking the local dialect, the Chief suggested that Father X might soon become his assistant and interpreter.

Father X told me after his release what was in the wind. He could not sleep nights, worrying about the perilous and embarrassing position he was in. We decided that because he was Chinese and subject to their drastic punishment, or even shooting at their whim, his usefulness here was over. We decided on a double cross for the time being. He would go to the police station daily and report visitors to the mission and other harmless details we could think up. After three weeks of this he told the police that his work and place of residence was out in Virtue Village. If he did not soon return, I would begin to wonder why. The police agreed with this and told him he could go back to Virtue Village. He was, therefore, ordered to visit the Christians on his usual mission duties, but every ten days must come in and report anything they had said against the government. He was drafted for their service because a priest has access to all the villages and the confidence of the people. He could be their spy and pick up any dissatisfaction, plotting, scheming or talk against the government. Father X came back to the house badly upset by the interview.

"I am no Judas, I wonder what they think a Catholic priest is," he told me in a voice that trembled with fear and anger.

The farmers' chairman in Virtue Village had given him a travel permit to go to Wuchow, and he had not been back to report in and return the travel order. With this he could get away, so one morning before dawn, instead of going back to Virtue Village, he took his bicycle and pedaled toward Wuchow fifty miles away. In Wuchow he changed his name (he had learned something from the Communists) and got a travel permit to return to North China.

When the Communists first came, they were allowing us to carry on religious services. On Sunday mornings when they saw the crowd coming in for Mass, it was a common occurrence for soldiers to stand in the back of the church watching the ceremonies or listening to the sermon. Although they were always quiet and respectful, the task of preaching under such circumstances is painful and trying. It also served to intimidate the people and let them know they were being checked and spied upon.

The confessional, whose sacred precincts no one can invade, is an object of dark suspicion for them. In certain places they demanded that confession be public or not at all. One Sunday morning before Mass two of the soldiers worked their way to the front where I was hearing confessions. They edged near to see and hear what was going on, in good Communist snooping fashion. I stepped out and politely requested them to have a seat down back. They begged pardon and went back.

It was not uncommon to see Communist soldiers or officials break into your office, dining room or bedroom unannounced, for in the new regime there are to be no secrets — no one stands on formality. Usually I would ask them to go to the guest reception room and they would go. One Sunday morning I was vesting for Mass when the server told me the Assistant Chief of Police and a companion were snooping around upstairs in the house. I asked the server to escort them to the reception room. As usual they paid no attention to the help, and said they would wait up there on the upper porch. I took off the vestments and marched up in my cassock.

I appeared and spoke in a severe tone, asking them to go to the reception room where guests waited to see me. Right now, I told them, people were waiting for Mass. My words were unfortunately spoken in temper. They immediately went down and out the front door. Probably they derided the imperialistic American who did not understand that in the new classless society of Communism there are "no formalities;" "all property is common to everyone."

Besides the snooping spies, the interrogators, threats, promises and lies, they have developed many other sources of information. One of them is a mailbox-shaped affair marked "for secret reports." They have them in the different government departments. At the prison one hung in the dark alley on the way to the toilet. Prisoners are encouraged to drop in a word of what they see or hear from other inmates; any information that is against the government, or the indoctrination progress each prisoner is supposed to make in the Party Line. A prisoner ostensibly was scribbling away with a fountain pen one day and nudged me to follow the pen. I had been saying what I thought about the government. He wrote a Chinese word in each corner of the sheet, then scribbled over it. The message when he got through said: "Here one should keep mouth shut; dangerous; your words grave crime; many tattlers report secret box; maybe gun silence you."

I gave the fellow a smile for the warning.

The Communists who want to know and control every thought and action of their subjects, have developed reports (*pao kao*) to keep them informed of every phase and movement. At the prison we had to call out to the guard "report to the Comrade," then "I want to throw out this water, lift the rice into the cell, wash my teeth," or even "turn over in the bunks," when certain guards were on night duty. Each cell chief and head of the Study Committee must report each evening to the warden and the head committee, the progress of the cell mates in indoctrination. The interrogators have to report each night to a committee; government officials have to report anything out of line and their progress in the Party Line. School children, country folks, laborers — in fact everyone — are told to report, to snitch on their fellows whatever they hear. They are taught it is their glory and advancement in merit with the Party, to tattle.

This doctrine is the direct opposite of our Western ideals of Christian charity and loyalty. We loathe the tattletale, the stool pigeon, the snitcher and the sneak-spy as despicable sordid individuals. And we are in the habit of making excuses for, or keep silent about a person who makes a slip against virtue or law. Evangelical charity of "hate-the-sin-but-help-the-sinner" was taught us in example by Our Lord. But the Communists are of the other camp. They berate such charity and laud and reward the person who searches out and reports every slip.

In our cell there was a simple country fellow with a bad temper. He was already wearing iron anklets as punishment. One morning he got angry and blasted one of the cell mates — even threatened to fight. When it was quieted down, I said to the cell chief, "Do not report the poor fellow, he is already in a mess of trouble." He answered, "I have to; if I do not report it, someone will turn in a secret report on me for neglect of duty."

One laments this passing away of chivalry and etiquette

in the ceremonious and polite Chinese people. The Communists ridicule and berate the old ways and teach in their place barbarous behavior imported from the Russian Reds. Some say the old China is dead, but I like to think it is only dormant, and with the turning of the years their better sense and character will again come to the fore.

The practice of self-criticism and criticism is used everywhere. It is designed to uncover secrets and believe me no secret is sacred there. At our criticism hour in jail I was shocked and disgusted by the disclosures. One prisoner might confide his past to another, his sex life or his desires. The one hearing it was sure to reveal the sordid tale at criticism hour. According to good Marxist teaching, a free sex life shows emancipation from bourgeois restraint and is perfectly all right as long as it does not interfere with one's duties. I have heard prisoners tell about disclosures at criticism hour in their village that would make a pervert blush. With the authorities smiling at free sex life, old China's customs and restrictions are being swept away for people to wallow in the mire of a pig sty. In time such license, if it goes on unchecked, will wreck any government and its people.

This government of contradiction, paradox and about face leaves one with head spinning when he tries to understand it. The people are not permitted to have a secret, yet officialdom strives to keep every act, thought or design wrapped in secrecy or covered by deceit. People must be "frank and honest," but the foxy government lives on trickery and strategem.

My Christians and teachers told me that when I was in jail and police were searching for accusations against me, they held inquisitions in all the Christian villages.

"Does the priest have radios, guns, gold, foreign currency or any valuables cached in this village?"

With guns rapping the table and threatening jail sentences if the people did not tell all, they asked hundreds of questions to search out secrets. Questions were asked that would soil the paper if I wrote them down. My friends always sought to reassure me, saying, everyone is subjected to this soul searching now in China.

Their devious methods in finding out everything and prying open every secret are effective. A psychoanalyst could not beat their interrogators in getting to the bottom of a man's locked interior. But, of course, terrorism is the great lever bar the Communists use to dig out hidden facts. People "voluntarily" tell where they have hidden gold, "voluntarily" confess their statements and actions against the government, penitently admit their former wicked affection for the Nationalist government.

Since coming out of China, people often ask me why the Chinese do not resist and rebel against a system that is so contrary to man's nature. One reason is because the subjected, enslaved and dispirited citizens are defenseless as sheep. As a Nazi general expressed it, "The wolf does not care how many sheep are in the pasture."

People outside China, who have not seen the citizenry roped up and tied like a steer for branding might think there is an underground resistance to Communism from within. There is none! It has been completely crushed and wiped out. Missioners who came out from all parts of China in late 1951 and early 1952 are unanimously of the same opinion. Along the Burma and Indo China borders are the only notable exceptions, where there is refuge and a source of supply. But in Communist China there is no place to hide now.

In the first few months after Communist conquest, Nationalist guerillas fought well and suffered a terrible toll at the hands of the conquerors. I saw also the stretchers, the wounded and the dead Communists carried in from the mountain battles. And this went on for the greater part of a year all over China. But guerilla supplies were used up and there was no way of replenishment.

It is wrong to say there is no heart for resistance and rebellion. But it will not arise until a mighty invasion from the outside gives promise of sure success.

The Communists in their first year of rule have stripped the countryside of guns. They tricked the guerillas into surrendering their arms, then shot most of them after their organization was completely crushed. With their system of enlisting and encouraging everyone as a spy, they went after village people who had guns for their protection. Some informer was sure to tell on every person who ever had a gun. Threats and torture brought them out of hiding. Country women brought up before a gun or a shot close to their heads told where the men had buried the guns. Some were frightened to death during the ordeal, but the Communists got their results, of unearthing almost every buried or hidden gun.

After that came the searches for opposition, the snooping spies and the grilling of interrogators. At the end of that first year came the new and largest mass arrests, the crowded jails, the widespread punishment and torture and the wholesale purge taking its toll from every village. The carrying out of their system left a populace that was cowed and cringing with fear, ready to accept the Party Line and mouth its slogans and propaganda. From what I have seen happen, I am convinced that the nation is completely powerless in the fist of Communism. This is not because the Chinese are easily regimented; they are not. It is not because they have no courage and fight; they have. It is the system of Communism that applies fire to the soul and breaks the spirit of a people.

We cannot blame the Chinese for falling into the trap; it was too well disguised. We cannot blame them when they were hopelessly enmeshed and ceased to fight back. They are human. And now, having seen Communism take over and enslave a nation, I do not hold with those Americans who naively say, "It cannot happen here!" For it can!

CHAPTER XIV

This "Freedom of Belief"

I N COMMUNIST CHINA the government carried on a war against each one of its citizens. But the campaign against the "beliefs" of the people was carried on with special intensity while their newspapers, posters and slogans claimed at the same time that there was "Freedom of Belief."

During each session I had with the interrogators while I was in jail, they repeatedly insisted that Communist China allowed absolute freedom of belief. They were indignant when I questioned or disputed this claim. Comrade Chen said assuringly:

"When you are released from jail you will see; anybody who wishes, will be absolutely free to practice religion."

Their claims were mouthed so often and the interrogators were apparently so sincere that they had me half believing their assertions. This was in spite of the double talk I had often heard, in spite of the warning a Chinese priest gave me after his many years under Communism:

"Never trust them, never believe them!" And then he would repeat the treachery and deceit he had seen.

The Saturday afternoon I was released from jail the guard took me, at my request, to see the Police Chief's Secretary, Comrade Liu. During the interview I said:

"Tomorrow is Sunday, and I would like to inform the Catholic families here on the street that they are free to come to Mass."

"Certainly, certainly, you may." And he ordered the guard to accompany me while I called on the families.

Sunday morning early a devout widow was the first to arrive. The guard on watch was the same one who had accompanied me the day before. He ordered the widow to the guard's quarters for discipline. The window of the guard's room was open and I could hear his insults poured out in an angry voice. It was a long diatribe, and I'll give only a few bits of it:

"Religion is useless, an opiate to fool the people! . . . You kneel to pray; don't you know that in our new classless society nobody is to kneel; it shows inferiority . . . with all the teaching of indoctrination you have not changed your ideas . . . you must *kai nao chin* (correct your outlook)."

Under his infuriated yelling I could hear the woman's sobs. Then he started to inveigh against Americans:

"Why do you associate with this American at all? . . . Imperialists, aggressors, cheats, capitalists; how can their religion be any good? . . . We must have nothing to do with them, ignore them, keep away from them."

When he had used up all his venom, he ordered the widow to go home, and told her she would not be permitted to attend Mass. He gave her orders to tell the other Catholics not to come, for they would not be permitted to see me or attend Mass.

The scene hurt me deeply, for I had brought on the widow's suffering and humiliation by my readiness to believe the Communists. The woman was sent home sobbing.

As she passed by my house prison window, I said in a low voice to console her:

"God bless you, you have a martyr's merit for this morning's suffering."

"And God bless you too," was all she could say between sobs.

On July sixth when I had applied for the exit permit from the Chief of Police, he was frank to a surprising degree.

"You know about our three points on religion in our new religious program; it must be self-ruled, self-supported and self-propagated?"

"Yes, I have read about these conditions in the newspapers."

"Very well then, you know we do not want you Americans here."

That was good plain talk that one seldom gets from a Communist. It was probably due to the straight talk I had given him on many occasions.

"That is clear — we understand each other better that way," I answered.

It needs no clairvoyance to realize that the Communists' three conditions are designed to cut off Chinese Catholics from the Universal Church. Not very skillfully hidden behind these conditions is the Communist aim to make the Chinese Church independent of Rome and subservient to the government.

These conditions were first published in the newspapers at the end of 1950. Simultaneously in all the larger cities, the Christians were called upon to hold "Oppose America, Help Korea" meetings and parades. This move calling on their nationalism brought the Christians together for the rallies. Once there, the Communist speakers harrangued them on the new program of a self-ruled, self-supported and self-propagated religion for China. The gatherings were anti-foreign and anti-religion rallies, though the latter issue was subtly concealed.

The people were asked to pledge support for the "three autonomies" religious program, and embrace China's "Oppose America, Help Korea" effort. Combining the two issues on one ticket, so to speak, was a move to push the Christians into a corner.

The Protestants were forced to go along with the plan without too much trouble. But they found that the Catholics who were better disciplined and better instructed in doctrine, for the most part, were hard to push into a corner. In many places Chinese priests attended the meetings, and after much discussion the Catholics refused to subscribe to the Communists' three-point religious program. Other groups where the priest was not present maintained that such questions must be taken up with their bishop or parish priest. None refused to embrace the nationalist issue, "Oppose America, Help Korea."

I followed the newspaper accounts of these meetings and parades. No Catholic bishop had attended any one of them. Even from the Communist version of the news, it was apparent that their three-autonomies drive was a failure. News articles of bitter criticism assailed the reactionary Catholics for failure to take up the three-autonomies movement for religion. It smelled of heresy, and the faithful were wary and reluctant to adopt the program. The outcome of their rallies could not have been very encouraging to the Communists.

However, they twisted reports of rallies to lead people to believe that Christians and priests all favored their viewpoint. When the Papal Nuntio, Church Representative to China, was expelled, the Communists ordered Christians to mass meetings everywhere, for approval. At Canton, Bishop Tang sent his Vicar General to represent him. Father Chen was called on to voice his approval for the expulsion of Rome's Representative. He said, "If the crimes are what we read in the newspapers, the government is justified in expelling the Holy Father's representative. But I do not know the facts in the case so I can say no more." With this he sat down. That is what he had told me when I saw him later.

Next day I read in our daily: . . . "Father Chen speaks for Bishop Tang. He says the 'government is justified in expelling the Papal Nuntio.' " The article reviewed the crimes and the trial, then declared the Catholics, clergy and bishop, all had praised the government's action.

One thing their program and meetings brought into the open was that under Communism, the foreign missioner in China is through. Whether they frame us before expulsion or crowd us out by persecution, or discourage us by forbidding the people to associate with us, it all comes to the same thing. They are not going to tolerate us. Without the personnel and extra finance from the outside, it means there will be very little expansion and growth of the Church. Indeed, it will be a struggle to hold its own.

Father R. Moulin was expelled with five other French missioners from Kunming, West China, in May, 1952. He wrote me on May 19 from British Hong Kong stating:

"Two of our missioners, Father Harrie and Griffon went insane (perdient l'usage de la raison) under the ill treatment. . . .

"The Communists found an American flag in our mission at Kunming. This made a beautiful picture in the newspaper . . . it was proof that I was a spy for Mr. Truman and gave them an apparent reason to expel me.

"Bishop Carlo, whom you know, died under the ill treatment of the Communists in Kweiyang. Bishop Valentin of Tatsienlu is still in prison. Only four foreign priests, all in prison, are left in the Kunming diocese. Let us hope the Communists will be stopped soon before the Church in China is entirely destroyed."

The Church is not too badly prepared for a holding operation. Some three thousand Chinese priests and their bishops, and four thousand Chinese Sisters will be left to look after the three and a half million Catholics. When I left China, about one third of the Chinese priests were in jail or under house arrest. The others were under difficult restrictions in carrying out religious work. Many were tilling the land for livelihood. Some were acting as roving peddlers or doctors. This gave them travel permits to visit Catholic villages and do a limited amount of religious work in secret.

Their lot will be hard, but no one under Communism will have an easy lot. Subtle and constant pressure will continue in order to force the Church into subservience to the Communist state. Just how well the faithful can resist, and how much the Communists in China can harm and bleed the Church, only God knows. Looking back across the centuries, we see that tyrants and puppets and blasphemers are a flash that quickly passes. For the present, Chinese Christians must pass through a dark night, but dawn has always come to give surcease from tyranny.

The religious freedom of the Communists could well be studied in Shumkai. Shumkai mission was started the end of 1946, at the invitation of a village called Blue Cloud. The thing caught fire and swept from village to village. On the waiting list for instruction there were always several thousand ahead. These people from many different villages signed petitions asking for doctrine teachers to come and prepare them for baptism.

Expansion was limited by lack of trained personnel. Gradually teachers were brought in and others were trained until we had an organization that was bearing fruit. Over a hundred men and women instructors were at the task. But building the faith in each soul takes time, and a group of men and women instructors were kept in each village a year for the evening study and instruction classes. For the three years up to the end of 1949, over a thousand converts were baptized every year. The first six months under Communism the number dropped to three hundred and forty converts. However, the drop was due primarily to the confusion and upset of fighting and troop movement. As the Communists settled down here in 1950, their pressure on the Church started.

In the country villages the Communists ruled that teachers from outside the village could not live there to carry on evening instruction classes. The officials required a roster of names of everyone studying, and the attitude of the officials was one of scorn and smear, to discourage the people from studying.

These steps frightened any new groups away from starting instruction. For the latter half of 1950 there were only seventy new converts. These had most of their instruction before the Communists started to bear down, and thus had sufficient faith and courage to go through.

Since our trained staff could not live in new villages, I picked better educated people from the local residents there and brought them to the mission for an intensive course. Then they were to go back and instruct their own villagers. The course went on from February to May, 1950. Then one day police came to tell those studying at the mission they could stay no longer. When I asked the reason, the police said that people away from their villages for study, interfered with their program of increased production. We had to settle for that, even though everyone knew such a reason was preposterous.

Prior to that move, the authorities had thrown in many difficulties to stop the classes here. Every person studying at the mission had to register at police headquarters; there was inspection and searches and counting of noses at night to see if all were registered. All these petty annoyances failed to halt our work so they ordered it stopped. This was happening months before war in Korea had started at all. And so it was not an anti-American move; it was anti-religious. So also were their other moves, like stopping the people on their way to Sunday Mass for search and questioning, often ordering the people to go straight back home. Their cold war tactics were now being used against the enemy — religion.

Here is a circular that I translate to show the subtle deceit at its worst. The Communists were passing it out to the Christians. A copy was given to our Chinese Sisters at the convent:

Dear Friends.

Jesus came first and then later Communism. Communism was born out of the social spirit of Jesus' doctrine. The realization of Communism therefore may be said to be the fulfillment of the hopes of Jesus, and even more truly, the establishment of the kingdom of heaven on earth.

Then the complete impoverishment and helplessness of society, and all sufferers, will be fully liberated. At the same time Christians and, even more so, the pastors will be able to lay down the heavy burden of preaching and of striving with their whole heart and soul to establish the kingdom of heaven. For the sick will be few, and there will be no need for so many doctors.

This is not to say, however, the love and doctrines of Jesus should not be preached; but when the work of Jesus has been accomplished, everyone can rest a little. It will be the period of reward for all. It will be like unto the seventh day when the Spirit had created heaven and earth, the rest was a reward upon the completion of the work.

It may be claimed that between Christ and Communism there is no contradiction. The Roman Catholic Pope, however, today is tainted by despotic class distinction and capitalism. The heart of love has been blinded. Heaven knows that to protect his own present interests and despotism, he has forgotten the sufferings of the flock. To continue to speak of loving others as oneself is laughable. God (lit. Spirit) hopes to really enfold the beloved disciples of Christ. Think about this and quietly meditate on it.

As for Marx, he was born in 1818. His father was a Jew. He also was a descendent of the ancient religion, but was converted to the new religion of Jesus. Very many of the ideas of Marxism are largely drawn from Christ. This is a historical fact. He who does not believe this should examine the complete life of Marx.

Believers in Christ, arise! Together let us establish a new world. The old social order is outworn. Extirpate it root and branch. Create a new China. To set up heaven on earth is the destiny of the people.

When the government placed all the priests of the diocese under house arrest or in jail at the beginning of 1951, they gave as the reason — during land reform religious activity must be suspended. And so all our churches were closed, and most of them taken over by the government.

For the eight months before I was writing this chapter in Shumkai, the church there had been used as a meeting hall for the Communists. Police guards kept the Christians from coming near the church or near me. The church's once sacred walls that heard the voices of prayer, love and penance, now echoed day and night with the speeches and cheers of hatred and revenge. It is absurd in the extreme to listen to the Communist speeches inside a church they requisitioned by force, asserting that Communism allows freedom of religion. They even had the effrontery to argue with me that this is true. Such double talk and double dealing must be quite incomprehensible to people unfamiliar with Communism. But here one sees it is the normal routine for Communists who must swallow the Party Line with never a word to the contrary. Contradictions do not seem to trouble the logic of Communists!

The authorities would like to have believed that their propaganda and threats might keep the faithful from trying to see me, but they were without success. Since the Police Chief let me move back to the priest's house in July, I fixed a small room into a chapel, and kept the Blessed Sacrament reserved there in a cupboard. A number of Catholics would steal in each day for the sacraments. In times of persecution the fast before Communion is not required, so people could receive Holy Communion at whatever time of day they could get in to see me.

When the guards were busy at the bus station, people dodged in. Some were caught and brought to the police station for lecture and warning. One day three children stole in for the sacraments. The guard at the bus station happened to see them and came rushing in. He found the three youngsters kneeling in silence, making their examination of conscience. Off they went to police headquarters for a reprimand and warning to stay away from the mission. Later that same day two of them were able to get back while the guards were inside the bus station, and I gave them Holy Communion. Afterwards I went out to watch and gave them the all clear when it was safe to cross the fields and go back home.

It was always painful to see them caught, scolded or punished, while I went scott free. It is because there is a deference toward foreigners that the Communist hardness and cruelty toward us is somewhat mitigated. Otherwise, I could not speak out so freely. While I was in jail, some of the prisoners remarked, "All they will do in your case is expel you from the country, but if we spoke up to them as you do we would be shot." This is true, for we saw many a prisoner shot for things far less offensive than my talk. Others were tied up or put in chains or starved or beaten for words far less bold.

Indeed, I am sure that the ropes and torture would have broken my resistance and made me cry for mercy just as the Chinese did. It just happened that the Communists' full savagery was not turned on me, and I refused to be silenced by the threat of it.

Why this deference toward us? Why do the higher and

more responsible officials use caution and restraint in handling foreigners? Communist China is seeking recognition by foreign nations, and hoping for admittance to the United Nations. They frankly admitted this in their newspapers and other propaganda. And hence it was not the time to show their uncivilized conduct toward foreign nationals. They must act with some semblance of international decorum.

When the Chinese priest Father X and I were arrested together, I was released after about six hours of grilling. Though they had no justification for it, Father X was thrown in jail. I argued with the Chief, "I am the one to be locked up if there is reason for it; not Father X simply because he happened to be in the jeep with me. You should let him go and put me in jail." In spite of my arguing, Father X was left in jail, and I was sent home to the mission. Next day the Chief of Police told Father X they had to be careful in dealing with foreigners so as to avoid international complications.

After November, 1950, when China entered the war in Korea, restraint in jailing foreigners was cast aside. The Communists' chances for recognition or entry into the United Nations were thrown to the winds and there was no need of playing the game any longer. In the next move for wholesale arrests foreign missioners all over China were scheduled for jail or house arrest.

It is significant that foreign businessmen who were in the large port cities were not interfered with and carried on as before. But of course they did not have the large following of the Chinese populace as did the missioners. Until 1952, the period I was still in China, there had been very little rough treatment of foreigners in the large port cities. And pressure against religion in these cities had been comparatively light also. "Face" with the foreigner and propaganda value explain this. It was in the interior places that they bore down hard.

In December, 1950, the Communists started their intensive

program to bring all religious work to a halt, saving the large port cities for later attention. During December and January, every one of the thirty-two priests in the Wuchow diocese, both Chinese and foreign, were jailed or put under house arrest. The same thing happened all over China at this time, I learned from the missioners expelled from different provinces, when I got to Hongkong a year later.

The blow was smart and well planned. With bishops and priests out of the way, it would be easier to crush out or weaken religion, they calculated. Religious services were automatically stopped, the churches were taken over and used as meeting halls while priests looked on the ruin from their house jail or prison. Catholic and Protestant schools were taken over by the Communists; hospitals and dispensaries suffered the same fate. Seminaries for training Chinese clergy also came under the ban.

The closing of our seminary illumines Communist methods. It must be run by Chinese priests was the first requirement, so the only American stopped teaching. It must receive no financial aid from abroad was the next requisite, so the seminarians had their rice and funds brought in from their homes. When it continued to function and struggle along, the Police Chief called Father Lai, the Rector, and ordered him to close the seminary and send the boys home to work the land for "increased production." The only seminary still open in all China is the one in Shanghai. This may be looked on as the churches left open in Moscow — something to show foreign visitors and for propaganda.

Needless to say, with the three thousand foreign priests now almost all forced out, with the Chinese clergy in jail or laboring under prohibitive restrictions, with the seminaries closed, the churches and institutions taken over, and the Christians tied up with numberless prohibitions, the Communists have struck a telling blow at religion. One wonders how long religion can last under these conditions.

Figures are dull but they are instructive, so I must give a few. In 1949 there were almost 3,000 foreign priests working in China. Communist pressure to force them out was stepped up in 1951, when 1,368 foreign priests and Sisters were pushed out. In January, 1952, only 1,250 foreign priests of the original 3,000 were left in China. Only 440 foreign Sisters were left of the 2,000 there two years ago. It is only a matter of time when they will all be out, for the average number of priests and Sisters expelled during 1951 was 150 a month.

Without seminaries and training schools, the 3,000 Chinese priests and over 4,000 Chinese Sisters now in China are doomed to slow extinction. They cannot work underground where the suspicion and spy system leaves them no place to hide. Materialistic and anti-religious Communism is ready to counter and undo any religious work they attempt. It will generally be in a subtle indirect way while the Communists contend all the while there is freedom of religion. That is what it has been and that is what it will continue to be until world-shaking events step in to overthrow their power. Religion has a hard and uncertain road ahead, with a dark and troubled future for the clergy left there to carry on. This is the universal opinion of all the men now being forced out of China. The optimists have all been converted by the reality of life under Communism.

It is not my scope to give the thousands of cases of religious persecution and torture of religious personnel that were going on around me in China. My aim is rather to give a picture of conditions and note the trends. But a few examples here and in the pages on Communist torture will illustrate what is going on in China.

On the train with me from Canton to Hong Kong was a large group of missioners also forced out of China that day. French, Spanish, Polish, Italians and Americans from every part of China told the same story of religious persecution and torture of missioners and Christians. The movement, therefore, was not anti-American, it was anti-religious. Each group of Nationals claimed that the Chinese clergy working with them were getting harsher treatment than they received.

Late in 1951, added to other things, came the Communist blackmail racket. On the way out a priest told me the Communists made demands on the French Bishop Jantzen of Chunking for the equivalent of forty thousand U.S. dollars. He sold the house and one church to pay. He was left to wonder what they would demand tomorrow. In Kweiyang the Communists demanded sixty thousand U.S. dollars from the French Bishop Larrat.

A person is inclined to doubt the Communist government would stoop to underworld holdup methods, for one thinks of Communist China as a responsible government. I listened to the many tales wondering how much could be believed. On December 3, 1951, five days after I reached Hong Kong and freedom, a letter came in from Bishop Paschang to the Maryknoll House. He is St. Louis born, the Maryknoll Bishop of Kongmoon, about 100 miles from Hong Kong in China's interior. I quote the words of his note; explanation in brackets is added:

"Yesterday [November 30] I sent a telegram asking $40,000 Hong Kong [$6,000 U.S.] at once. I was entertained as a lord of the earth [judged and condemned by the people's court as a landlord with the usual beating], and if I do not pay up in seven days, I shall be entertained again. I have a nice shiner and bruises; I feel my age all over. Such a life!"

On December 5, a telephone call was put through the military line to Canton, then connected over the commercial line to Maryknoll Hong Kong. A voice that trembled under the strain of being forced to speak was evident as Bishop Paschang talked:

"They have agreed to reduce the demand to $22,500.00 if I pay immediately. Will you send it?"

"Both Maryknoll and the U.S. government have forbidden us to give any ransom money," answered the Superior.

He gave the guards the answer and was led away. In the few weeks following, before I left Hong Kong, Chinese priests sent messages out to say that Bishop Paschang was taken out twice more to be beaten up by the mob.

Although his treatment during 1951 prior to the "people's judgment" was quite normal, it does indicate the Communist attitude toward religion. Bishop Paschang's house, the cathedral, the seminary, the convent and Sisters' training school were all taken over by the Communists and everybody ordered out. The Sisters were released from their vows by Bishop Paschang, disbanded, and sent home to their families. Seminarians were sent back to their homes. Most of the fourteen Chinese priests had to go back and live with their parents until they could find work and devise ways to carry on their religious profession in secret.

Communists took away all the property and buildings from Bishop Paschang. Then the people's court in the "settling of accounts" ruled that the bishop had paid too little for the property thirty years ago. He was forced to pay the sellers' families about 40,000 pounds of rice, even though the government had now taken over the property and buildings with no compensation. Bishop Paschang's American Maryknoll priests are being forced out at the rate of four or five each month. Orphanages, dispensaries, the leper asylum and missions were closed and taken over by the government. Yet in every one of these cities and towns the Communists are shouting their propaganda — "Communism allows freedom of religion." One priest commented, "Then, of course, the only countries free of Communism are where Communists are in control."

Bishop Paschang's story could be duplicated with little variation for every bishop in China. And yet people outside

China have been telling us for years, "The Chinese are not real Communists; they are only carrying out agrarian land reforms!"

Shrewd and calculating minds in the Kremlin know that the greatest obstacle to their conquest is religion and they are already warring against it. Capitalism, the love of freedom and the rest are petty opponents compared to the firebrand of faith in a man's heart.

Their campaign against religion now might be called the preliminary skirmishes against the great enemy religion which they must hit broadside later. Their attack is so well organized and far-reaching against belief in God that we see they know the measure of their enemy. The systematic suppression of religion in China, as in every Communist country, follows the same routine. Break the power of the Church, a Church submissive to the government and a dead Church are the steps.

If they could manage an autonomous or independent Church for China, which would be submissive to the government, it would hasten their program. Independent churches have forever been doomed to slow death, and that is what they are trying to establish now in China. The autonomous movement is meeting with little success, but Communists are patient and relentless and no one should hazard a prediction for the future.

Of course the Communists overlook one factor in their program. And that is God. Even in our short time we have seen the rise and fall of architects who would build a new world without religion. The Chinese sage Confucius wrote, "The plan of a thing rests with man; the success of a thing rests with heaven."

CHAPTER XV

Cruelty

MENTAL CRUELTY is a weapon the Communists apply unceasingly to break people to their way of thinking. It is so important I run the risk of repeating thoughts I touched upon in the chapter "Indoctrination Course," in order to bring out the meaning of mental cruelty. It is something that one must experience to really understand, for it cannot be adequately described.

The Communists know a mind can be changed by a subtle prodding attack, just as a child instinctively knows he can change his parent's mind by teasing, hounding and repeating. They have perfected the science of mental cruelty and use innumerable ways to confuse, upset and torture a man's mind until it gives in to their way of thinking, or is driven off balance in the attempt.

Their way of thought and outlook is so different they must "reform the mind." People must be trained to follow the Party Line unquestioningly. This means, to follow the directions and decisions of the top Political Bureau without criticism or independent thinking. Their Party Line song, translated earlier, states:

Tear to shreds as vain and false,

All contrary thoughts to the Party Line.

Their process of training a man's mind is directed to cleanse it, change it and mold it for regimented thinking. They give names to the different phases of the process, such as "brain washing," "reorientation of the thoughts" and "remolding the brain." These terms are heard so often — especially during indoctrination — that they sound like bell vibrations that never cease ringing in a man's head. Repetition, nagging, prodding and threatening are parts of the mental torture ceaselessly applied to everyone, in order to change over the mental process to a new way of operating. The Communists' indoctrination, carried on with mental cruelty, aims at reducing a man's mind to something less than human. The dehumanized person is then ready for machine thinking and acting without sentiment, courtesy or charity.

That process of extracting the human characteristics of a man is a major operation and results in numberless casualties. Many suicides end the agony, great numbers gone insane have been delivered from mental torture, but the masses with no escape who must live on for continued mental arrangement or derangement are the ones to be pitied. For some, the course turns their minds to ice-cold, hard, relentless Communists, and no demon could teach them anything new in the ways of madness and torture. They are zealots, graduates in mental torture, the most devastating and cruel science on earth.

In a small way I felt the mental torture; in a big way I saw it going on all around me. It started with the first day of the Communist invasion when their imploring, demanding and threatening at all times of the day and night worked me up and kept me under a constant strain and tension. My nerves soon became taut with the strain, and after a while the only way to get any rest was by taking sleeping tablets. These gave only that heavy, deadening, unrefreshing sleep. The army went through, then came the police, the party workers and government officials, who pressed for some demand or other again, all day and all night. It was so constant and repeated I wondered if it was a campaign to break me down to their way of thinking or drive me mad. They needled me with those demands for the jeep, medicine, furniture, household supplies, tools and permission to take my house and church for living quarters. I tried to be accommodating, but refused their unreasonable demands like jeep trips in the night and long trips that would keep me away from the mission on Sunday. When they made their demands appear so important and pressed with such intensity, I began to ask myself; is their perspective off balance or is mine?

People told me I was only one fly in the web, that they were subjected to many more demands than I was. In three days the Sisters in the convent were called upon twenty-eight times for one demand or another. When they were scolded for not answering the door soon enough in the night, one took up watch while the others slept with their clothes on. After a while one comes to learn that much of this torment is to create a mental atmosphere of cringing fear and obedience in the "broken" subjects.

The Communists come to the house day or night to demand the most unreasonable things, then argue, threaten, cajole and shout to wear you down and break your resistance. A man gets so tired of fighting and arguing, he wants to say, take the house, take the mission and anything else you see, but get out and let me alone. Their torment rubs the nerves so raw that after a few weary sleepless nights one is ready to explode at a word. I prayed and prayed that I could hold my temper and avoid a blowup — which is what they wanted, so as to put me in jail, then throw me out of China in a dishonorable ceremony. That is just what happened to several missioners.

Father Francis Keelan of Boston was working in the same province 250 miles from me. He came out of China a day ahead. In Hong Kong we discussed this mental torture, and he said, "If I were to go through that two years again or be shot immediately, I would much prefer to be shot as a lesser punishment."

The mental torture tried us so cruelly that one priest went to the jail twice and begged to be locked up, hoping to be rid of the constant pressure and stay sane. For me the jail was a welcome relief. Everyone living under Communism is a prisoner, so it makes little difference — in or out of jail. If one could get enough to eat in jail (the dirt and all the rest would be gladly tolerated), the life inside would be much preferable to their kind of "freedom" outside.

Right after I was returned to the mission upon release from jail the callers were hounding me again. Soldiers passing banged at the door and got me up at 1:15 A.M. Others banged again at 3:30 wanted me to open the doors and let them in to sleep. After long argument they went on to the billets where they were supposed to go. When they were gone I sat on the porch smoking cigarettes, trying to cool my nerves so I could get to sleep again. This psychological warfare day and night finally made me conclude "jail was better than this." But of course if they think you want to go to jail, they will keep you out as a torment. I begged the Chief of Police to put me in jail again, but he refused.

Every day and every evening after my transfer from jail to house arrest again, government officials or other Communists held meetings in the chapel. Their speeches of hate and revenge, of down America and down capitalism, battered my ears like the music of savages. Nine days out of ten, one can ignore or laugh at their silly lies, but maybe on the tenth day their falsity changes one to dynamite. I was afraid of exploding and kept my door locked against the mob. Before the meeting or at recess time, the mob, doped up by propaganda, often gathered below the porch and challenged me to come out and argue with them. When I would not come, they threw stones and called names in anger except when the guards or police were around. They lived in fear, like everyone else under Communism, and one word from the police cowed them. This teasing was a strain that demanded a constant fight to hold one's temper. It was better for me to be back in jail or out of China, and yet their delay on my application to leave, was running into months. This was just another device to worry a person and leave him hanging, it seemed.

Missioners living alone, especially those who were not jailed, carry the ugliest scars of mental torture. Many were nagged until they were no longer normal. The two months I was in Hongkong after leaving China I saw several priests come out of Communist China completely off balance. It was tragic. These poor victims claimed Communist spies were following them around Hong Kong. They said they heard the barber, the clerks in the stores, and people on the bus recounting their crimes against Communism. When left alone, they heard voices accusing them. But it is not like hereditary dementia. After a week or two of rest their wild imagining and hallucinations ceased and they were quite normal.

This mental derangement was common among the Chinese when the heat of mental torture was on. Christians who stole in to visit me in my house jail told of people in their villages who were talking *luan hwa* (muddled words) or *fei hwa* (words of a mad dog), as they express it. I shall report only a few cases that throw some light on the cruelty of mental torture. Physical torture is sometimes used as we have seen, though it is unlawful and ruled out by Communist craft. It is not subtle enough and is less effective than mental torture, as these artists in breaking the spirit have learned. However, they are sometimes combined as in the case of Dominic Leung.

Dominic Leung had worked for the mission as a doctrine teacher for fifteen years. He was living in a village near Shumkai with his family, instructing a class of over a hundred people for baptism when the Communists got control here. Peter So, whose uncle is a priest in Kongmoon diocese, was assisting him with the instruction. Old-time staunch Catholics as they were, they no doubt spoke their minds on Communism to the village people. This made the Communists want to crush them.

One day when Dominic Leung went out to the market town for supplies, he was arrested. It was July, 1950, seven months after the Communists took over and wholesale arrests were starting. Peter So, whose family was at home about four hundred miles away, got wind of Dominic's arrest. He jumped on a bicycle and came to see me. I gave him travel money to skip and get home. He hid out in a Catholic village fifteen miles from where he had been teaching until the search quieted down, then took the mountain road back to his home, some ten days' walk.

Dominic was put through a grueling interrogation for days, and was left tied up in the July sun between times. They tried to force him to admit he was a secret agent engaged by me to do spy work for the American government. He held out against all their tricks, telling them to go ahead and shoot him, but he would never admit such a false charge.

His elbows were tied behind his back. From the ropes around his arms they strung him up until his feet were about a yard off the ground. Two full nights after all-day questioning, he was left hanging in this gruesome agony. After a short time, he told me later, he lost consciousness, and came to his senses again some time after being let down. Then he went insane and with his delirious talk they could get nothing by their questioning for the next month.

Dominic has a wife and five children. When his wife went to inquire of the officials about the reason for his arrest, and ask if she could bring food, they followed their usual practice of denying they had even arrested him, and claimed they did not know where he was. But news like his passes quickly from mouth to mouth, so she knew where he was and what he was suffering.

In August after being worked on a month in the country, Dominic was brought under guard to the prison here in Shumkai city. He gradually recovered and his mind became quite normal again. But the grueling which the interrogators put him through in prison after his recovery began to affect his mind once more. He got to imagine things and went through spells of morose weeping. At times he thought his children were in another part of the jail and that he could hear them screaming under torture.

He had been in the prison six months, and when the authorities saw that his mind was getting worse, they had guards bring him back to the village where his wife and children were, for release. Before long he was quite normal and sane again. A couple of weeks after his release I was put in jail where prisoners who were with him told me the story. Then when I was transferred back to house prison, Dominic stole in one day and gave me an account of the whole experience. He seems quite sane again, but is a nervous wreck, talks rapidly and sometimes without sequence. This torture both mental and physical is going on all around, and when I have thrown it up to the Communists they say it is a lie, and that they inflict no torture.

When I left China the end of November, 1951, I sent word to the Christians not to see me off. This was to save them later punishment for showing friendship to an enemy American. But Dominic Leung could not be stopped. He and a small group of teachers were at the bus station to see me off. They might break his mind but they could not crush his heart. He told me he would visit the Christians often and strive to keep them strong in the faith. As we shook hands, tears ran down his cheeks. A painful lump filled my own throat. In the background Communists looked on with hatred in their eyes, coldness in their faces, grimness in their lips and revenge in their hearts. These men whose doctrine stresses retribution and retaliation in their "settling of accounts" were sure to make him pay for his rashness. But people with the stuff martyrs are made of do not count the cost.

One of the sad deaths brought on by Communist torture and mental cruelty was that of Dr. William Wallace, head of the Southern Baptist hospital in Wuchow. Dr. Wallace was famed for his surgery and medical work, but most of all for his kindness and devotion to the sick and poor. His whole life was medicine and charity.

Dr. Wallace would be called a strange fellow by the hustlers, bustlers and seekers of wealth who people the world today. They would call him stupid and impractical, for when people asked him the charge for services he would usually answer, "Forget about it." His canceling of charges drove the treasurer's staff to despair, for he was all charity; a sort of mystic walking on clouds and looking for the stars. Earthy worldings who spent so much time figuring nickels and dimes walked far below the plane of Dr. Wallace. If you tried to talk world events or politics with him, his mind was far off and not interested.. But he would talk medicine, surgery and all its latest techniques, and all the newest medical discoveries for hours on end.

I knew the man well, for I was stationed in the same city of Wuchow, from 1939 to 1942, with him. He was tall, but carried himself with a little stoop that often goes with humility, and made him seem less towering. Running up and down five flights of the hospital from 6 A.M. to 8 P.M. kept him thin as a distance runner. His hair was the color of ripening grain when the autumn sun is turning it from a faded green to pale gold. A high forehead shaded the serene, deep-set eyes, and looking into the eyes of Dr. Wallace one thinks of the poetic lines: "blue bells in a sunken garden." Worn to weariness by overwork, the eyes carried their part in a smile that was no less warm and engaging than the smile of his lips.

Dr. Wallace had the soft voice that one looks for in kind men. He never lost his Tennessee drawl, and when you talked to him he would drop a polite "yes suh" or "no suh" into every pause like a musical accompaniment to what you were saying. His long slender fingers that worked at surgery every day were the marvel of Chinese doctors learning the art from him. Six months after his death a Chinese doctor who studied under him said to me:

"Dr. Wallace was a master in surgery, we shall never see his equal again."

The Japanese advance toward Wuchow in the last war separated us. I was assigned to Chunking. Dr. Wallace was not folding up his work. He calmly packed hospital equipment and staff on boats and moved five hundred miles to the interior to carry on at Poseh all through the war. Before they had packed to go, the hospital was hit by bombs. A sky hole was blown through the reinforced concrete roof. Window glass was strewn over every floor. Lines of wounded were being carried in from the streets with limbs or bodies torn apart. Inside I saw Dr. Wallace working like a machine, but comforting like a man each unfortunate casualty.

Strange enough in this world of boasters, you could never get Dr. Wallace to criticize the enemy's actions, or even talk about his difficulties or troubles in Wuchow and Poseh. One of his fellow mission doctors told me when the last war was past, he and the Mission Board were annoyed with Dr. Wallace, for Dr. Wallace told them almost nothing of his troubled experiences. It was simply duty and charity with him, and in his code those are to be done and not talked about. Troubles and accomplishments were kept as his own secrets. In this world of advertising and being advertised, we find it very hard to understand a man like Dr. Wallace.

The year 1949 passed and with it the National government that had been host to Dr. Wallace for almost twenty years. He did not run from the new Communist rulers, for he had a job to do, which cut across no political lines. Each month of 1950 brought a tightening down on missions, and when his own mission people found they could do no work, most of them packed up and left China. No one can justly blame them, for they were family people. But Dr. Wallace chose to stay. He had never taken a wife, for he was married to his work here in China, and this claimed all his affection, all his time. No, he was not the kind to divide his love, he kept all of it for his work.

One day after most of the Baptist missionaries had left Kwangsi, he was visiting the Catholic mission in Wuchow. Bishop Donaghy asked Dr. Wallace:

"Are you going to stay?"

"Why yes, Bishop, you men are staying, aren't you?"

"Yes, but we are expendable," he jested, to take away any show of heroism.

"Well, if you people can stay, I guess I can too," he smiled.

The Communists were smarting under the popularity Dr. Wallace enjoyed. Their propaganda got nowhere in ruining him. He was running the most modern and best equipped hospital in South China, and the city of Wuchow was still his domain of loyal admirers. The Communists were jealous of both these assets and planned new measures to crush him. Yet these shameless fellows had been using the hospital and demanding the services of Dr. Wallace for most of a year. In their life of contradictions and savagery, they saw nothing indecent in using a man for all he was worth and at the same time hating him and trying to destroy him. And yet the Doctor forced praise from them. He was the only American other than American Communists I ever heard them speak well of. Comrade Lee, an old-time Communist from North China, was a political commissar in Shumkai. He was taken seriously ill and, like all difficult cases, was brought down to Dr. Wallace for treatment. After his recovery and return to Shumkai, he came to my house prison to snoop and chat one day. He remarked:

"That Dr. Wallace is not only a good doctor, he is also a good man."

This praise from a Marxist, trained to show no courtesy, no gratitude and no praise for anyone outside the Communist orbit, astounded me.

The end of 1950 brought another period of wholesale arrests. Father Justin Kennedy, a New York boy, was in Blue Cloud mission six miles away. He wrangled a travel permit and went to Wuchow. Released from the Wuchow prison nearly six months later, he was brought back to my house jail for three days while police completed arrangements to get him out of China. He recounted events and details of the Wuchow episode, which I wrote down.

On the morning of December 19, Bishop Frederick Donaghy of Fall River, Mass., was visiting with Father Kennedy. A rumpus at the gate interrupted them. Communist police pounded at the gate as though they were attacking a block house, and shouted, "Open up immediately." They flooded into the house and scattered out for a search.

Those who were accompanying the bishop, later brought him back to his own room, for now the plants were fixed. The house boy stood by gazing around. He noticed a package on the clothes-closet shelf and started toward it, saying:

"What is this package, it was not here when I cleaned today?"

A police slapped down his reaching arm and shouted:

"Get out of here, go back to your room."

The officer in charge turned to the Bishop and said:

"We now come to the search of this room."

It was not long before they "discovered" the gun concealed in the clothes closet, which they had planted a few moments before. A scene followed. Accusations were shouted at the bishop that he was an American spy with a hidden gun in his house. Why had he kept a gun when everyone had been ordered to surrender firearms? He was tied up while they searched Father Kennedy's room. There the police "discovered" more contraband — bullets in his baggage — so he too was roped up as a spy.

At the same time another group of police were at the convent. One of the officers asked the cook which was the Superior's room, then dismissed her. When they brought Sister Rosalia around to witness the search, the police "discovered" a large package of opium hidden in her bed. She was accused of opium traffic, arrested and tied up.

The Pastor, Father Peter Reilly of Boston was also in the priest's house. But the police who go by the book had orders to arrest the bishop and the one priest at the Catholic mission, and they had dropped the bullets in Father Kennedy's bag, who had just come in that evening as a visitor. It was their good fortune that Father Reilly was detained at the mission for he could send food to the jail each day.

The search was completed, the "discoveries" made. Now the bishop, the priest and the Sister with hands tied behind them were marched through the streets to jail. Police carried the evidence in this exhibition of the captured criminals. At the jail they met Dr. Wallace who had been arrested that same night. He was the spy chief, for they discovered not only hidden guns, but radio gadgets for his secret sending set. The whole spy ring was now rounded up.

A photographer at the jail placed each "criminal" behind a table. The "discovered" proof of each one's guilt was placed on the table for a picture. This was a scoop for their propaganda mill, to justify their acts in the eyes of the people and rouse them against America. The absurd show could have been funny if it were not so tragic.

The bishop and Father Kennedy were locked in a cell

beside the one that held Dr. Wallace. Sister Rosalia was locked in one across the way. Next morning bulletin boards all over the city published the capture and the crimes of the mission spies. Chinese doctors and nurses at the Baptist hospital saw these wild accusations. They wrote a petition to the police vouching that the accusations against Dr. Wallace were not true. This was a bombshell and only set off more woes for themselves and Dr. Wallace. A mass meeting was called for the city people. One of the Communist masters of invective harrangued the mob for six hours, denouncing Dr. Wallace most of the time. Anyone used to Communist speeches knows the nasty, disgusting language they use. A certain type of extravagant language is a tag that usually reveals a Communist anywhere.

At the jail interrogators were prodding and driving at them individually, trying to force them to admit their crimes. But they were putting more pressure on Dr. Wallace. If he could ignore the absurd accusations, laugh at them, or fight back and throw his own accusations in their faces, he might have retained his mental balance. But he was highly sensitive and so thoroughly honest that their wild accusations bewildered and upset him. The accusations shouted at him over and over again, allowing no defense, no answer and no excuse, worried him. Using these tactics, the interrogators were probably able to bring on a sense of guilt in Dr. Wallace, as they did in so many others.

The Communists had conjured up a list of crimes that Dante's demons could not improve upon. It hurt the sensitive doctor to hear the accusations that his incompetence in surgery had murdered Chinese patients, and his negligence had caused the death of many more. The interrogators claimed they had the proof from other doctors and the people were now calling for his punishment. It pained him to hear he was the master spy for America, working against the Chinese, when, as a matter of fact, he had given his life and his talents to help them. The prods and digs of the interrogators were at his mind, to confuse and upset him, to force him to admit their catalogue of crimes.

Dr. Wallace, who walked the ways of truth, was inexperienced in wickedness. Under the mental torture to break his mind perhaps he began to believe the accusations they repeated and painted so darkly to him. When they threw some sordid accusations at him, which modesty forbids repeating, he must have wondered if he was in his right mind. He told Sister Rosalia:

"If they keep this up, I'll go out of my mind."

After a few weeks in the cell, Dr. Wallace broke down and cried each time the interrogators turned the heat on him. Soon he began acting queerly. Periods of delirium started, and Father Kennedy said he could hear him wail:

"God, I've got to get out of here . . . they are driving me mad!"

A prison interrogator asked Father Kennedy one day:

"Why does Dr. Wallace cry when he is brought up for interrogation?"

The priests knew that Dr. Wallace had been driven off balance now, and Father Kennedy, answering, tapped his head:

"When a man cries like that there is something seriously wrong."

Nothing was done about it and the interrogations went on. Singing, shouting, crying or uncontrolled laughter was now heard from the doctor's cell, for the mental torture had driven him past the point of sanity. The guard had a bamboo pole to ram between the bars and jab noisy prisoners as a punishment. When they tried this on Dr. Wallace, he only screamed louder. Guards called Bishop Donaghy and Father Kennedy over to quiet him down. They had little success, so a guard asked Sister Rosalia to try.

Sister Rosalia had a way with people. She had already obtained a favor, hardly less than a miracle. And this through a Communist guard, trained to show no sentiment and grant no favors. American prisoners could send out no note in English. But Sister Rosalia got around the guard and sent a note to Father Reilly at the mission. The note gave directions for sending daily Communion to her.

A small loaf of unbaked bread or a roll was to be cut open, the Sacred Host inserted, then placed in the oven to bake.

A messenger from the mission was allowed to bring her food to her cell each day. She reverently took the bread, broke it open and received Holy Communion hidden within. This brightened the days of her five-month imprisonment, before she was exiled from China.

When others failed, Sister Rosalia came to quiet Dr. Wallace. Her gentle ways and soft voice calmed him for a while. But he got worse and worse and did not seem to recognize her. For some time he could not eat and refused all food.

On the morning of February 9, 1951, Dr. Wallace's cell was quiet at last, ominously quiet. A guard peered in through the dim morning light and announced that he saw a lifeless body hanging in mid-air. Rest and quiet had come to the tortured mind and wracked body in the darkness of a cell where they had been killing him slowly.

Communists immediately peddled this story: "During the night, Dr. Wallace had taken one of the sheets brought from the hospital for his bunk. He tore it into strips for a rope and tied one end above his head, then hanged himself."

Guards rushed to bring Bishop Donaghy and Father Kennedy to the cell of tragedy. They were reluctant to take down the body as the guards ordered. But they went ahead, thinking there might still be life present. The body was cold and stiff; he had died long before and any effort to revive him was useless.

Father Kennedy said he was puzzled. No discoloration or marks of strangulation were evident. His first thought was that Dr. Wallace must have died of heart failure if he tried to end his life. But Communists who had planted evidence and manufactured accusations could have rigged it to look like suicide after their torture had killed him. They alone know the answer, and in any case they still have to answer for his death. For torture that drives a man to insanity and the brink of death, then keeps on until it pushes him over, is murder.

Officials at the jail were worried. All manner of pressure was put on Bishop Donaghy and Father Kennedy to sign a statement that Dr. Wallace was a suicide. They refused absolutely and held out. But they did certify that Dr. Wallace appeared to be insane before his death.

Friends at the hospital were told to come for him. They could have the doctor now, a ruined, murdered corpse. The head nurse came. She was forced to sign a statement that Dr. Wallace committed suicide before they would release his remains. She signed the document as the only means to keep Dr. Wallace from an unknown grave, and to give him a decent burial.

A Chinese wooden coffin carried all that remained of one of the world's truly great men, along the West River. A grave was dug in one of the lonely valleys near the city. The grave is cradled between high mountains that leap toward the sky. His soul is God's, but his heart he gave away long ago to the Chinese people he came to help.

Dr. Wallace's Chinese friends contributed in secret and bought a monument to mark his grave. A stone, tall, slender and square points from earth to heaven to show the world his way. The words of St. Paul are carved in Chinese down one face: "To live is Christ."

Maybe Dr. Wallace had never read the life of St. Francis of Assisi, but he had many of the saint's ways, and much of the saint's grace and charm. I expect he knows St. Francis now, for he fulfilled the law; he loved God and he loved his fellow man.

When reading these words of Vesper prayer for St. Francis' feast, I think of Dr. Wallace: *Beatus vir qui inventus est sine macula et qui post aurum non abiit, nec speravit in pecunia et thesauris. Quis est hic, et laudabimus eum? Fecit enim mirabilia in vita sua* (Eccles. 31:8-9). It translates: Blessed is the man that is found without blemish; and hath not gone after gold, nor put his trust in money, nor in treasures. Who is he and we will praise him for he hath done wonderful things in his life.

I shall take space to write up only a few of the hundreds of other cases of Communist cruelty that were happening around me. The threats, pressure and fright caused the mission washwoman to take her life by jumping in the river. The sister-in-law of one of my doctrine teachers went crazy after weeks of strain and torture, then killed herself. Almost every large village reported a like casualty.

The landlords and people of any means who were not shot were sent to an early death after being treated like dogs. In the market of Shumkai a few of the men were classed as landlords. They were forced to crawl on hands and knees through the streets for ridicule, then through mud and dung, while the torturers commanded them to bark like dogs.

A professional man from South Ferry, the next big market town sixteen miles away, told me the same torture was carried out there. He said they kicked the crawling victims, then stepped on and ground their wooden shoes into the legs and feet of the sufferers as they crawled along. For the big laugh, they got the toilet buckets saved by each family for the fields and dumped them over the victims. All the while they jeered and cheered like a circus crowd.

This is part of the Communist process to dehumanize the people and brutally carry out the program without feeling or sympathy. One shudders to think about the future "New World" and "New Society" they boast of, with people trained that way.

The number of people who have been killed by fright and fear adds up to an appalling figure, though it is impossible to estimate the number of millions. The professional man from South Ferry talked with me one day about it. He said his old mother and his aunt both died of fright. The Communists held them at gun point and demanded their gold and rice grain. They were supposed to be well-to-do, and perhaps had hidden their wealth. After several days of shouts and threats, those old women died of heart failure.

Planned starvation is a sinister method of death. One of the men in the government here told me that in this county of Shumkai three thousand persons, who are the heads of families, were adjudicated and condemned as landlords. Here in China married boys live with the family — only girls move out, so families average at least eight people. After robbing these landlord families of everything they own (Communists call it requisitioning their wealth), the Communists limited each person in the family to two ounces of rice per day, the official told me. This is one way of killing off the people who had wealth and land.

Father Joseph McDonald, my neighbor in Yunghai, the next district east of Shumkai, had a harrowing experience under Communist cruelty. Father McDonald, a big-framed Celt of six feet three, has all the charm of the Irish. His big frame carries a big heart. He is gay, hospitable and generous almost to recklessness. Added to this is the courtesy and polish of a "proper Bostonian," for Boston is where he was born and schooled. This blends with his Irish humor to make everybody like him. But, make no mistake, there is fire under the ashes, and when stirred up, Father McDonald is like the old Irish patriots, ready to fight the world.

The first year of Communist occupation he underwent the repeated search of his house, the suspicion, the questionings, the accusations and the frequent calls to police headquarters for alleged breaking of their rules. He was regularly called up during the night and hounded during the day by their importunate demands. Their demands and pressure multiplied and restrictions tightened with the start of the war in Korea.

When the Communists started the land reforms, they threw off all restraint. Father McDonald was confined to one room of his house under guard. The Communists took over the rest of his home and all other mission buildings to house the mobs they brought in for indoctrination. They took over the church to use as their lecture and assembly hall.

Interrogators accused Father McDonald of being a spy, and an imperialist American, sent here to keep China in serfdom. Not satisfied with this, they forced the people of the town to sign a petition telling the American priest to get out; he was not wanted. He made no move to go, so the Communists started printing manufactured charges in the newspaper. The ugliest charge printed was that when he baptized a class of converts he made the women disrobe.

Added to the interrogations, accusations and demands, was the noisy mob studying all around him. They were being indoctrinated, and the songs, speeches, lectures and discussions going on day and night kept him from sleep. A man's nerves have limits, and human nature can stand torment only up to a certain point. He realized he could not hold his temper much longer and asked the officials to take him to jail. They refused.

One day they were at their political meeting in the church. The Communists had taken his church by force. Over the statue outside, they hung a picture of Mao Tse-tung. Above the altar they had hung another large wall picture of their leader. The anti-religion, anti-God speeches aroused him. Their insulting slogans, shouted in unison like college cheers, fired his anger.

Father McDonald got a ladder and tore down the picture

over the church door. He walked in through the meeting and placed the ladder beside the wall picture. Rung by rung he climbed up, then reached out and tore the Communist leader's picture to shreds.

Pandemonium broke loose, and a free-for-all followed as they yanked him off the ladder. The odds of two hundred to one were too much for Father McDonald. He went down unconcious under their punches, kicks and clubbing. They got ropes and tied him up outside the chapel. That afternoon he still had not regained consciousness. He was left bound and put in a tiny room under guard. Next morning he was only semiconscious. The Communists wanted him alert to force a confession of crime before the mob.

They were getting ready to dip him in a water tank to restore full consciousness. Now something intervened. The Chief of Police of Wuchow six miles away heard of the incident. It was not long after the Dr. Wallace tragedy, and the Chief was worried. He sent a message to cease the torture and take the ropes off the priest.

They unbound Father McDonald and ordered him to confess and ask pardon before the crowd, even though he was semiconscious. Father McDonald got out of China late December, 1951. He laughs about the confessions which neighboring Christians told him he was forced to make. He says, "I must have been punch drunk, for I cannot remember it."

After the episode he continued under house arrest, but their torment was relaxed. His Irish sense of humor saved him and with the fire of anger burned out he could see the funny side of his experience. The guards who went out to buy Father McDonald's food liked to watch him cook. He could always make it a show and they became quite friendly now. One taste of his cooking was enough for the guards, but Father McDonald would flip the leathery fried cakes and tell them, "This only proves I am a better missioner than a cook."

CHAPTER XVI

Narrow Escape

TIME was running out for me as a prisoner of the Communists when October, 1951, was torn from the calendar. The village sickles hacked at the tufts of rice to gather the autumn harvest. Fields were dotted with farm folk swinging bunches of grain against the inside of threshing boxes. The thump, thump, thump of farmers beating off the kernels of grain boomed through the valley like signal drums to herald the coming of winter. The straw was stacked, the sun was yellow and summer had gone. Lazy oxen were lashed and cursed as they dragged plows to turn the soil for winter wheat.

November was passing, and I grew impatient with the Communists' delay in letting me go. When I gave them the letter requesting an exit travel permit in July, they assured me it would be cleared in a few weeks. Two years under Communism, one of them as convict and prisoner, were wearing me down. Now I was worried at the delay in release.

Perhaps they would not make the mistake of letting me go, for they had already made many mistakes.

It was a mistake to let us stay in China after the Communists took over. It was a mistake to put me under house arrest where I could see and hear the Communist meetings in the church; a mistake to leave me as eyewitness to the land-reform meetings, the public trials and public beatings held in the church; a mistake to sentence and shoot the landlords in plain sight of the "foreign spy." After months of eyewitness observation from the house prison, it was another mistake to put me in jail with five hundred prisoners, where I saw too much for their pleasure. It was a mistake to give me the indoctrination course, but they found out too late. It was a mistake to let me have my fountain pen in jail, for I kept a written diary of what I saw and heard. It was a mistake to let me smuggle the prison diary out of jail. It was a mistake to leave me my typewriter at the mission. Under house arrest after the jail term, I could type out my prison diary in double copy for a book to expose them.

After all these blunders I began to wonder if they would make the final mistake of letting me get out of China. If they arranged to have me conveniently die, it would correct all their mistakes. I was more worried as time slipped by. On November 15 a friendly police officer visited me. I asked him to press the Chief of Police to get an answer from Provincial Headquarters on my exit. They had had nearly five months now to look into my case. Next day the officer told me an official letter had been sent in to urge for action.

Later in the afternoon, November 23, the police officer came in smiling. He announced they had received clearance from Provincial Headquarters to release me. Tomorrow I would be escorted to have pictures taken for a travel permit and fill out the necessary papers. But he warned that I must leave the day after, for travel orders were restricted to the four days necessary to get out of China. It would not be my fault if I did not get across the border by November 28, I assured him.

He came for me early next morning. There are no secrets in China, and Christians were already stealing in to say farewell. The officer abruptly ordered them away. We started the procedure so as to be ready to set out next day. I was bolder now and sent word to the military asking for payment or return of the mission telephone, gasoline and other things they had taken from the mission while I was in jail. The Chief of Police was requested to pay for the drum of gasoline he had taken. My requests and protests brought no results.

A big decision faced me as I packed my foot locker that night. I picked up the copy of my prison diary and wondered if it was foolhardy to try and bring it out. During the recent months in house jail after my prison term, I had been revising and typing it. Many daring chances had already been taken to try and get a copy out to Hong Kong. Although the manuscript had been smuggled into the outgoing bag, my letters might still be caught when the mail went through the big centers like Wuchow and Canton. And so I lived in fear and expected a jail sentence or something worse if my letters were caught. But my luck held and nothing had happened up to now. Tomorrow I was to start the journey toward freedom. Perhaps it was crowding my luck too far to carry the dangerous material with me.

But no word was received from Hong Kong to say that the manuscript had arrived. All incoming letters were seized and kept by the police censor in Shumkai. Brother Francis wrote from Hong Kong in riddles which would give the desired answers if letters could reach me. But they were all stopped.

I decided on a big gamble, to take the manuscript with me. It represented many months' work and contained statistics, translations of documents, songs and other things that could not be reconstructed outside. The long ledger sheets, typed on both sides to reduce bulk, were clipped together with wire staples. Elastic yarn was slipped under the staples to tie the sheets tight, half around each leg. A string inside my belt held each pack from slipping down. Documents concealed on the person were sure to condemn me as a spy if they were discovered. I thought I could get by without discovery. Concealing the script was my mistake, not the Communists'.

In the morning five police came to take me to the bus station. My cook, Martin Neep, had stuck by me through all the Communists' ridicule and ugly epithets. He helped carry my baggage to the bus station for inspection.

"We start with a search of your person," announced a police officer. "Let's see what you have in your pockets."

My heart jumped with fright and sent a sharp pain through my chest. Now was the time for quick thinking. I spread the contents of each pocket on the foot lockers, and at the same time pulled the pockets inside out. The police searched through everything; they even pulled cigarettes and fountain pen apart to look inside. As I pushed my pockets back in place the Secretary to the Police Chief slipped his hand into my pants pocket. His fingers felt the top edge of the manuscript sheets, though it was hardly higher than a seam.

"What is that under your pocket?"

"My underpants, of course!" and with that I dropped to one knee and fumbled with the keys to open the foot locker. This put his hand out of danger. Now I had to try and talk myself out of a tight corner.

"Open up the small bag first," ordered one of the police.

"No, no, search this one first; it is open now."

Communists insist on having their orders followed, so I started a heated argument, while dumping things out for their inspection. The Secretary was distracted in trying to settle the argument and he seemed to forget about my pocket. I stayed down on the one knee for nearly an hour watching the baggage search. When they took my camera and pictures, it gave me an opportunity for violent protest. Fortunately I had smuggled out many pictures beforehand. In my own mind the argument was a secret plea for freedom and perhaps for life, so I turned on the heat. I was not angry, but I was scared enough to put on a good act. The argument and ceaseless talk kept them on the defensive. It distracted them and stopped any more dangerous questions.

Finally the search was over and I was left to repack my baggage. The Police Secretary had completely forgotten about the crease under my pocket. I stayed down on one knee and dallied with the packing until the police wandered across to the bus station. Then we quickly loaded the baggage on the roof rack of the bus, and I climbed inside to stay away from frisking hands.

The bus delayed another hour, waiting for passengers and freight. I looked at the wrist watch or held it to my ear every few minutes, wondering why it moved so slowly. Dominic Leung and a group of doctrine teachers arrived to see me off. I got out to shake hands with them and with my loyal cook, but dared not stay long with police across the road.

The driver's assistant cranked away at the 1940 Dodge. He poured a few precious swallows of gasoline into the carburetor and after several tries the engine started. The driver changed to charcoal gas as soon as the engine was warm. But going up mountains he would have to open the gasoline valve again to let gasoline trickle in for extra power in climbing. The buses have a boxcar body to carry either freight or passengers, usually both. We had only a few passengers, since people cannot travel much under Communism. Everything is controlled under the new regime so our bus driver was ordered to take on pigs at villages along the route. Planks were thrown across to make the required number of seats for passengers. Baskets of chickens were tied all over the roof. The pigs and the people rode inside.

With the grinding of gears we chugged into motion. I waved farewell to the group waiting to see me off, then sat down in thought. It was hard to leave these thousands of new converts without a pastor, but it was useless to stay and watch their persecution from a prison window. My heart was heavy with sorrow, but it was running fast with fright, for I carried on my person a story to tell people outside of this inferno.

Every few miles the bus stopped to load more pigs. They had to be weighed, freight and taxes had to be collected and papers filled out for the bus union, the farmers' union and the government. Loading and squeezing the pigs into place also took time. The procedure took about an hour for each stop. After five stops the bus was cram-jam full with pigs piled on top of one another in bamboo crates. The crates were cone-shaped, and a pig crowded into one head-first cannot move. I sat with ten passengers on the two planks in front of the pigs. The hog snouts or rear ends bumped against our backs over the rough road. The rest is left to the imagination.

The fifty-mile trip to Yunghui across the river from Wuchow should take only three hours. But today the many stops had held us on the road from ten o'clock in the morning until almost six in the afternoon. I stormed heaven with rosaries and ejaculatory prayers during those hours. The police had sent word ahead and I faced another search by police who were to meet me at Yunghui. There was no way of unloading or destroying the manuscript tied around my legs. Passengers or the bus driver would report it if I tried. The only way out was prayer.

Darkness was falling as we drew into Yunghui at six o'clock. No police were in sight. It was mealtime and they were all inside for evening meal. I asked the driver to stop a little ways short of the police station and unload the baggage. Coolies were quickly hired to carry the baggage over to the mission. We walked right by the police station. Oil lamps inside showed the police with rice bowls and chopsticks in front of their faces as they ate. With prayer in my heart, I walked by brazenly.

We reached the Catholic mission without incident. Youngsters guarding Father McDonald let me in after inspecting my travel papers. Father McDonald's room gave me an opportunity to get rid of the dangerous manuscript tied around my legs. Then I went directly back to the police station and marched in saying:

"I came in on that bus with the pigs and was told to report here."

"We must inspect your baggage; where is it?"

"The coolies did not see anyone outside, so perhaps they took it over to the mission."

The officer called three police to his desk and ordered: "Go to the Catholic mission with this man *k'wai k'wai* (quick quick) and inspect his baggage."

Probably he thought we could overtake the coolies, but they had been gone from the mission almost ten minutes when we got there. The police searched through the baggage an hour and found nothing to complain about. Unlike the usual cold, officious searchers, these men were chatty and pleasant. They addressed me when the search was over: "The inspectors at the river are finished for the day! No boats are permitted to leave for Wuchow until tomorrow morning, so you cannot go now. Since you are here at the mission, we permit you to stay for one night only."

These fellows were reasonable so I chanced another request. Father McDonald had not been permitted out the door for months.

"Very well. The priest here has cooked his meal and done the dishes, and I have had nothing to eat since morning. Would you permit him to guide me to some restaurant for a meal?"

The officer thought this over for a moment. He consented with the proviso that we return immediately after, and so informed the guard.

That evening we compared experiences, and then Father McDonald read some of the manuscript brought out of hiding. He commented, "This is dynamite; burn it immediately and rewrite it when you get out of China. If the Communists find you with this material, you will be shot or left to rot in some jail."

His comments were given long consideration. But I had wiggled through two inspections, so it seemed best to keep going like a back-field runner until finally brought down.

Father McDonald had been in jail a few months, then isolated in his room for the remainder of a full year now. He was his own cook. Perhaps I better say he was trying to cook for himself. The kitchen was a low, soot-covered shed where he cooked and ate. Breakfast came due, and I witnessed the interesting operation. Father McDonald hacked away at a pine stick for kindling to start the fire. War surplus coffee, bought five years ago, was boiled into a black mysterious potion, stronger than Tennessee moonshine. The eggs the guard bought for him were supposed to be 1951 model. But he broke each egg into a saucer first to see whether he had an egg or a chicken inside the shell. His morning commentary was better than the breakfast. Here he remarked, "The Chinese have salted eggs, preserved eggs and one-hundred-year-old pickled eggs. When you taste these you can decide which they are."

His pancake batter looked good as he started to whip it up. But then he added a pinch of this, a dash of that, and a drop of the other thing until I wondered what he was producing. He flipped one over in the frying pan and the bottom was black.

"The black is an added touch to make it taste better," he said.

We sat down to attack. Charity kept back any remarks

· 254 ·

about the food. But he sensed my reaction and explained, "You know, I studied four years at Holy Cross College, then four years of theology at Maryknoll, and half the things I learned are of no practical use. Why didn't they give me a course in cooking?"

Washing down a belabored mouthful of the leathery stuff with mud-syrup coffee, I answered:

"Yes, I guess they should have."

It came time to leave. A new device had to be figured out to try and slip through with the manuscript. I put the typed ledger sheets back in the original book cover. Clipped together and fixed with wire staples, they looked like printed pages of a book. At least they should be far less dangerous or suspect than sheets found concealed on one's person. Father McDonald watched me pack the ledger between books in my foot locker shaking his head. Once again he named it dynamite.

Coolies carried the baggage down to the river police for another inspection. I whispered, *"Deo Gratias"* when they passed everything without serious interrogation. The coolies loaded baggage on to the sampan hired to take me to Wuchow. Father, mother and children stood at the oars. This "floating palace" was both a home and a means of livelihood for the family. The sampan was about thirty feet long. An arched roof of woven bamboo, with layers of leaves stuffed between the trellis work, covered the middle of the boat. The top was varnished with wood oil to make it rainproof. Before stepping onto the grass mat of this "living room," I took off my shoes — a must in Chinese courtesy. When I squatted on the mat, the sampan was shoved off. Up ahead the father stood at a sweep oar for one side, his two children worked an oar for the other side. The mother, with an infant strapped to her back, pushed an oar in back and manipulated the rudder stick with her feet.

The rhythm of rowers started us on our six-mile journey to Wuchow. Two steps forward for each stroke of the oar, then the bare feet pattered back to start again. When each oar broke the surface, spatter and spray were caught by the morning sun and sparkled like a diamond-studded comb. When the oars dipped, they brought little whirlpools of caress to waken the sleeping water. For over twenty years I had traveled China's rivers on these little boats. Today was the last ride. An exile was leaving like the water pushed out to the ocean; water that had made the rice grow and the flowers bloom.

I waited until we were far away from the listening ears on shore, then asked:

"How are you making out under the Communist regime?"

"Things are harder now than I have ever seen them in my life," the father commented, between strokes at the oar. "They organized us into a union, then set a low price for fares. They collect the money, as you saw, and each sampan has to go in turn. Money is divided — a small bit comes to each of us, the end of the month. We used to eat white rice but now all we can afford is rice gruel. I dare not let my own people hear me say these things for someone would report me."

Yes, I understood. Boat people hated the system like every other group and wailed the same words, "But what can we do?"

In an hour we drew up to the police wharf outside Wuchow. The boatman presented his papers and waited for the search. Police were expecting me and three came on the boat to search my baggage. I watched with alarm when they started looking through my books. In the dictionary was a sheet of paper with doodle drawings which I had traced out when looking up words. Police turned it to study from every angle then one handed it to me.

"What does this mean?"

"It means nothing," and, laughing at my own crazy drawings, I tossed the sheet overboard. This electrified them with excitement. Police were ordered to fish out the mysterious sheet of evidence which the foreign spy had tried to destroy. An angry interrogation followed when I was forced to make sense out of doodle drawings. Try it for mental exercise if you do not think I was on the spot. Finally they accepted my explanation but kept the sheet. It had to be sent to the higher intelligence branch for study. If Communists have a sense of humor, the decoding expert would get a laugh from this.

Thanks to the long delay over doodle drawings, police searchers glanced cursorily through the other books. The ledger was passed over as just another book, so I relaxed and breathed normally. One of the police was on the telephone to announce that the expected foreigner from Shumkai was here. The search was over, so he asked the Chief what to do next.

"Take him to the Canton boat," was the instruction relayed to me.

Our sampan was ordered to row down one hundred yards to the Canton boat now loading. It was only eleven o'clock. Sailing time was not until 5 P.M., so I planned to run up to the mission and see Bishop Donaghy. Alas! I found two guards assigned to watch and keep me on the boat. Every argument was used against them. I had to get my spare glasses and clothes kept there at the Wuchow mission. Guards phoned the Chief, who said no, nothing could be added to the baggage. Next I argued vehemently that I had to leave surplus coffee and jam I had brought for the mission. Communists, trained to wear down their opponents by argument, found me outdoing them in persistence. At last the guard phoned headquarters again. He came back to put me off by saying, "If you go, you will have to hire coolies to carry all trunks and baggage back and forth."

"Very well," and I beckoned coolies to pick up everything.

"No, no, it is too much trouble," said the guard.

"Aren't you men of your word? You said I could go if I took the baggage along."

"All right, we'll go." They could not lose face before the crowd after committing themselves.

They took me to police headquarters with baggage and let me sit there an hour and half. The Chief was busy, they said. I hounded everybody about Communists not keeping their word. They wanted to get me out as a general nuisance. Assistant Chief of Police told the guard in a disgusted voice:

"Leave the baggage here and take him to the mission. Watch every minute to see that he picks up no maps, photos or anything else."

The guard sat watching while I visited with Bishop Donaghy an hour. We had to figure out some way of handing over my extra money not needed for travel. Communists were taking up all currency at the border before exiles were released to cross into Hong Kong. I told the guard I had to go to the bathroom. He followed me to the door, but I excused myself and turned the key to shut him out. In a few seconds I put all unneeded funds in the cupboard over the washstand. Mission accomplished! Coffee, jam and even hidden funds left for the bishop, neat as an air drop.

The guards escorted me with all my baggage back to the boat. It was what is called a "junk," a large wooden boat over two hundred feet long, towed by a steam launch. Eighty first-class lower and upper bunks lined the large room back of center. Two hundred more passengers could be accommodated in the second class and hold below. The space on the bow of the boat was for hundreds of pigs, chickens, or ducks in bamboo crates.

An hour before sailing time police came for search and baggage inspection. Shoes, stockings and clothes right down to underwear had to be taken off for their search. Fortunately the manuscript was not tied to my legs then. They went through my baggage and replaced the dangerous ledger as just another book. A box of writing paper puzzled them. One of the police was holding each sheet to the light. He said to me, "We have no chemicals here to examine this paper for secret writing, so we must take it away."

"Chemicals!" I repeated sarcastically. "Here, take the box along if you want the writing paper." The stupid fellow did not like ridicule before the crowd so he dropped the writing paper back into the trunk. When the police left, I thought, "Another hazard past; maybe I shall get through with the manuscript."

The boat started for Canton at 7 P.M. It would take twenty-four to thirty hours, depending on tides. The kitchen was a cubbyhole in the bow of the boat. A steward took each passenger's meal order without writing anything. Flunkies deliver a tray to each bunk at mealtime without a mistake in the order. This trick in the steward's trade is quite a feat when the passenger list is large. If you insist on fresh eggs, the boys reach into the chicken crates for fresh eggs the hens have dropped since loading that day. If it is chicken you want, they pick a nice one from the crates and kill it.

Only fifteen passengers were in first class. All except myself were government servants, who bunked together on the other side. One of the boat officers leaned his back against my bunk and talked over his shoulder when no one was near. He remarked:

"It is too bad when Chinese and Americans are such good friends, we have to pretend to be your enemies."

"Yes, I understand. How is the boat business now?"

"You can see for yourself. Formerly four full loaded boats left for Canton every day; now there is only business enough for one, and we must wait and go only when our turn comes. Look around, fifteen passengers for eighty places. People cannot travel under Communism. Business is dead."

"Don't you have plenty of freight to compensate for loss of passengers?"

"Look at the plank walk outside the boat — four feet above

water. We are lucky to have one-third capacity load. When loaded full, the plank walk is down to the water."

The boat officer looked round to see if anyone was casting glances our way. Then he talked even lower, with one hand shading his mouth to hide lip reading.

"Under the old regime we made money and ate well. Now we can afford only rice gruel, and we are forced to say times are better and people are happier under Communism. But do not talk to any of the help on the boat, for someone is sure to report what you say."

He got nervous and walked away before anyone noticed him talking to me.

I read myself into drowsiness with a detective story. At the first big city next morning, police came aboard for another baggage inspection. They came to mine and passed everything without serious question, even the ledger which held my prison diary manuscript. One policeman confiscated the Chinese newspaper I was reading.

"You cannot take that out, nor anything else written in Chinese."

"I don't want to take your newspaper abroad. If you take this I'll have to buy another when you leave the boat." He threw it back on my bunk rather than look silly.

Sunday evening about nine o'clock our junk tied alongside the wharf in Canton. Police guards supposed to meet me were not around. I went to the hotel across the street. After breakfast in the morning I reported to police headquarters and caused more excitement than a hand grenade tossed at them.

Accusations were poured at me — "You break our laws, you refuse to follow our regulation of immediate report. We were here even if the boat police were not at their place to meet you. You stayed overnight without first reporting to the police. This is against the law for everyone. You are a stubborn, incorrigible criminal . . ."

Every excuse I tried to give was shouted down. When I

shut up they accused me of being sullen and resentful of correction. Questions were yelled at me: "Where did you go last evening, whom did you talk to, where did you eat?" and a thousand other queries. When they exhausted their abuse, they ordered me to bring all baggage from the hotel to police headquarters for search. These lads were even uglier than the usual run of Communist police, so I began to fear my luck had run out.

When the baggage was brought in, three police started the search. One of them knew a little English, so he started to look through my books. First they ordered me to confess if I had any secret documents or anything else that should be surrendered. It would go hard if I did not tell them now, they said.

"There is nothing concealed; you will find only books, diary and personal effects."

The search went on for hours. Cold sweat soaked the palms of my hands. When the officer picked up the ledger, I waited tensely for the explosion. Sweat under each arm ran down the flesh under the nervous strain. Thank God the policeman knew only a little English. He struggled half an hour trying to understand the first page. All my talk and all my devices failed to distract him. Outwardly I remained calm. I spun idle talk to keep the fear from showing. The inspector turned back to a page discussing Communist economy. Here he walked on thin ice and was sure to break through.

He came across a passage stating that Communist cut-throat methods in their government stores were driving private merchants to bankruptcy. The examiner jumped up and screamed in my face:

"You say Communists cut people's throats. Did you see that done? When and where did you see it? How many throats did you see them cut?" When he ran out of breath from a stream of questions and a flood of abuse, I tried to would look further. There were the chapters on "Communist explain "cutthroat methods" of underselling. Government stores could undersell because of tax exemption and large scale buying. He "lost face" before the other police when I proved he did not understand the English terms used.

The fuse was burning close to the powder keg. I dragged incessantly at vile Chinese cigarettes awaiting the crash. The reader came to words stating: "Communists call their soldiers 'volunteers.' But their system has brought about a total economic collapse forcing men into the army. If they want to eat, there is nothing left for young people except government service or the army. A subtle way of forcing men into the service."

My doom was sealed. The officer ripped the whole manuscript out of the ledger. His face darkened with anger. Blood vessels bulged on his forehead; his voice went up to a high-pitched yell that drew two hundred other police over from their drill.

"You calumniator, you liar, you slanderer. You dare to write this way about our volunteers. You are a spy, that is certain."

After a string of vile names that would even surprise an Australian sailor, he and two interrogators started to work on me. They were out to force me to admit, then sign a confession that I was a spy. These sessions were the worst I had ever been through. It was astounding to hear so many false accusations hurled at a man. But I held out all day.

It was imperative not to irritate these interrogators when fate held a tragic sentence over me by a thread. I contended · that the script was a diary account to show my folks and friends. It was not concealed but left in the open for police to inspect if they wanted.

"You Communists are told to keep a diary. Why shouldn't I keep one?"

One possibility troubled me. Suppose the police officer who struggled to find two comparatively harmless sentences Cruelty," "The Purge," and "Snooping Spies." I shuddered to think the officer might take the manuscript out to one of the bankers who had studied in America or England to read for him.

Fortunately a large crowd of people were on the way out of China that day. A few had come in on different boats. Later the train arrived with several hundred from Shanghai who were lined up for baggage search and examination of travel papers. The inspectors had to leave me to process each group. It was a relief to see the officer lock my manuscript in a drawer after each session. He had not thought of taking the material out to someone who could read and understand the contents. The officer who was so inadequate in English had no time to study two hundred pages he found in the ledger. Between groups they spent all their time interrogating me, trying to force me into a confession of espionage.

They left me standing while they examined incoming groups. It is safe to say that I never prayed more intensely, more pleadingly, or more fervently in my life. Only God knows how many rosaries and ejaculations poured from my lips that day. With my heart racing madly, I thought of the numbers who died of heart failure under the Communist ordeal.

The train from Shanghai brought over fifty foreign nationals and stateless persons. A barrel-shaped White Russian woman of seventy hard winters was in the line. She spied my Cossack beard and waddled over. Her rich smile compensated for the poverty of an old shawl, the tattered coat and cloth shoes. A flood of Russian words poured from her lips. When I gestured "no understand," she looked at me in surprise. This motherly old lady pointed at the beard and repeated, "Ruski, Ruski." I tried out sentences in half a dozen different languages. Now she gestured, "no understand."

She motioned me to sit beside her on a bench nearby. The police did not interfere. With her hand on my arm, she told me what I presumed to be all her troubles. From an old cloth bag she pulled out documents and travel papers for identification. All I could do was nod and smile. Then I made the sign of the Cross. She squeezed my arm and blessed herself the Russian way, right to left. I wished I could comfort her with my thoughts:

"Lady, you think you are in trouble, but it is nothing. Look at the mess I'm in."

The interrogation went late into the night. It ended where it started, with the accused refusing to confess he was a spy. My travel permit expired tomorrow, and they had to get me on the one train for Hong Kong — seven o'clock in the morning. The interrogators wanted to get some sleep. One of them motioned an officer to seal up my baggage, a sign that I was to be passed. I breathed a prayer of thanks at pulling a little ways out of the hole.

"You go back to the hotel. If you stop anywhere or talk to anyone, you will be arrested and never get out of China," cautioned the police.

"Very well."

"This diary has lies and slander about Communist China, so it is hereby confiscated. Any objection?"

"No objection." And I saw him lock away the precious document that cost me sweat, tears and almost blood.

At four o'clock in the morning police summoned us to the railroad station. The same ugly inspectors that worked on us yesterday were there to search the person of every passenger leaving. They started with me. Off came coat, shirt, shoes and stockings before the crowd, while the inspectors frisked and looked everywhere. Each person was subjected to a similar search. Although it did not happen to me, other missioners told me they were taken into a room for rectal examination.

As the trains pulled out, crowds at the station sang Communist songs. They had groups on the train to sing and give Communist lectures. I breathed easier leaving the station, but the danger was not over. It was a five-hour run to the Hong Kong border. Police might now have time to take my manuscript to someone facile in English. They could still wire the border police to bring me back.

When the train reached the border station, I listened for my name and looked for police to nab me. I stood in line over two hours nervously waiting my turn to be searched. This gave me an opportunity to tear up the currency I had left over rather than let searchers take it away. It was the usual search, the usual questions over again. We had been there since noon for examination of travel permits and baggage search. At three o'clock I was released to pass over the railroad bridge to the Hong Kong side and freedom.

The Hong Kong police smiled and chatted jovially. Across the bridge Communist police stared with looks of suspicion, grimness and hatred. I knelt to kiss the free earth and then in scriptural style stamped the dust from my boots against the Communists who had forced me out. The policeman of free land laughed heartily.

Brother Francis and a group were there to meet me. In the station restaurant we had beer! And sandwiches! And American cigarettes! I hurled the Chinese cigarettes that tasted like moldy straw across the tracks and reached for a real smoke. It was all like a dream come true. People here talked freely without looking over their shoulders to see who was snooping. Voices rang out without restraint. Carefree laughter startled me to look up in surprise. There was no fear and dread in peoples' eyes; no slinking in their walk. This was another world, something I had almost forgotten about through the years under Communism.

Filling my lungs with free air, I told about the narrow escape to freedom. But the manuscript which wore several years off my life was gone. Reticent Brother Francis listened with a twinkle in his eye until I asked:

"You probably never received the manuscript copy I sent out by mail, did you?"

"Why yes, three large envelopes reached me."

"Just say that again, Brother, and break it slowly; I can't stand so much good news that fast." It was hard to keep back an Indian yell. The nerves, like high-tension wires, could now rest.

Yet this big change of atmosphere was a danger, even for a phlegmatic man like myself. One of the priests, who held his grip and fought through five months of prison and public trial by the people's court, broke completely when he reached Hong Kong. He told me he went to the chapel sobbing and crying for an hour before he could get hold of himself. When the impact of freedom comes bursting in all at once, right after the surcease of Communist tyranny and cruelty, it is too great a shock. The overstrained nerves snap and men are liable to go to pieces under the sudden change.

In Hong Kong I settled down for six weeks' rest at the Maryknoll rest house. Next morning a message was flashed across the Pacific from our seminary at Maryknoll, N.Y.: "Welcome to freedom, approve book on your experience." This was an order in polite language, so I set aside four hours a day for writing. It was my good fortune that three out of four packets of the prison diary had slipped through the mail to Hong Kong. Here was the framework. The fourth part could be reconstructed without much effort.

Brother Francis had saved Time magazine for 1950 and 1951. After two years blackout from dependable news, I read all the war news, and some other articles to catch up. I felt like Rip Van Winkle struggling to get back in the current of life.

On January 21, 1952, a slow freighter took me out onto the Pacific for three weeks, far away from Communist China. Except for the morning hours with the pen, I could forget the experience under a tyrannous, nerve-wracking system. But we cannot and must not forget the unhappy people trapped under Communist power who live on, in agony and despair.

Appendix

THE TRIAL of five Canadian Sisters was broadcast from Canton five days after my release from China. In Hong Kong we listened to the ordeal, which I add here as an appendix to give an idea of Communist legal procedure.

Missioners who ran orphanages were a special object of Communist cruelty. The orphanage furnished a fine pretext for propaganda, accusation meetings, and people's judgment against the missioners, who were "killing Chinese babies," they asserted.

Poverty, famine and the low standard of existence in China have perenially driven many of the poor people to abandon their babies. Missions established orphanages to receive these unwanted, abandoned children. They saved and reared what they could of these newborn waifs. But the death rate was high in this group of sickly, dying infants that were left on the streets or at the mission gate.

During my house arrest, the Communist daily paper brought me news of missioners all over China who were sentenced and expelled for the murder of orphans. Every mission that had an orphanage was an easy target for the trumped-up charges. Priests and Sisters in many towns were forced to dig up the orphans' graves, and the bones of the "murdered" children were then exhibited to the people's court as evidence of guilt.

The trial of the five Canadian Sisters was only one of many. You may well ask why the Communists broadcast their atrocious procedure of trial by people. It is hard to find logic in anything they do, but we may say that a public trial over the radio is good propaganda for home consumption. And it is the people under their domination that they aim to convince. It is also true that Communists are so confident of world victory that they often ignore world opinion. They are well aware of American indifference to their program and often told us so. A police officer said to me the day before I left China, "Say what you want about Communist China when you get to America, it will make no difference."

December 3 was the morning set for the trial of these Sisters from Sherbrooke, Quebec. Rehearsed accusers and a mob of over five thousand people was herded into the Chungshan Memorial Stadium. This was to be a spectacle not unlike the extravaganzas held in the Colosseum of Ancient Rome.

The mob was whipped up to a frenzy of hate by the Communist songs, cheers and speeches. Between times announcers described the scenes like the excited announcers of a football game. The crowd was divided into several sectors with a cheer leader for each group. This plan was followed at all the big meetings and public trials I had seen before. Each leader and group tried to outdo the others in rousing enthusiasm and hatred, driving out all possibility of sane judgment. Speeches, songs, cheers, and shouting slogans in unison worked the crowd to the proper pitch.

Five white-robed nuns were marched in by armed guards. One after the other came: Sister Alphonse of St. Dorothée, Que.; Sister Marie Germaine of Prosper, Que.; Sister St. Germain of Pont Rouge, Que.; Sister St. Victor of Nashua, N. H.; Sister Ste. Foi of La Baie de Fêbre, Que. They were ordered to kneel and bow their heads in shame while the crowd jeered and ridiculed them for their crimes. Cheerleaders called on the spectators to repeat after them, "Down with the murderers, down with the spies, down with the imperialists," and a long list of other slogans. The nuns who were allowed no words except to admit their guilt, knelt in silence. They had knelt other days at their mother's knee, on the prie-dieu in the chapel, on the cold floor of the prison cell awaiting trial, while they prayed. Today they knelt in prayer while the rabble prepared to judge them as murderers. They no doubt prayed for the multitude before them who were as helpless as they were in this process. Their fingers crept over the rosary beads hanging from their cinctures. Their eyes were fixed on the crucifix over their hearts.

The charges were explained to the assembly. For twenty years before the Communists got control, the Sisters had run an orphanage there in Canton. Records showed that some twenty-three hundred infants had been received. About two thousand of them had disappeared. Where had they gone? Psychological tension had been so worked up that accusers actually screamed their charges like people gone mad. "The Sisters murdered them!" came one accusation after another. Others charged that planned, deliberate neglect had done away with the Chinese children at the orphanage. Servants helping in the orphanage claimed they were underpaid and treated shabbily by the "imperialist" Sisters.

Communist democratic process wants unanimous accord and after each accusation or suggestion the leader would call on all to agree. The hands went up and voices shouted agreement as directed. The bedlam went on until the mob which constituted the people's court was called on to name sentences. Three of the nuns were sentenced to be expelled from China. Two were given jail terms of five years each. Everyone agreed. All that was left now was for the Sisters to sign confessions of guilt and the routine was completed. The two five-year sentences would, of course, be remitted and changed to expulsion, by the "leniency" of the government. This change was habitually made for all foreigners sentenced to long jail terms. The government in this way got rid of the foreigners and police guards escorted them to the border in ignominy and shame.

The Hong Kong people listening to this horror show only two hundred miles away were shocked. Next morning, the English language newspapers all carried editorials condemning the travesty of justice. The Chinese press, except the Red-controlled journals, joined in to show the revulsion and indignation of all fair-minded people against this burlesque on truth.

Mr. C. S. Kwei, editor of the *Hong Kong Standard,* met me for lunch next day. This American-educated lawyer and journalist said:

"I blush with shame to see our Chinese people taking part in this brutal, inhuman perversion of justice, even though they do it under force.

"These Sisters left your land of comfort and convenience and came to the raw hard life of China to help us. They picked up abandoned babies left on the city dumps to die. They took them in at their free dispensaries when mothers wanted to be free of the sickly youngsters. They gathered up the unwanted infants left at their door each night by mothers too poor to keep them. And the Sisters gave all these care and a home. At the trial no one was permitted to say that most of the newborn babies left with the Sisters are sick and dying. Our poverty-ridden Chinese mothers know that their dying infants will receive a respectful burial if left at the orphanage."

During the tiffin he later commented:

"If the Communists did not want the Sisters, they should order them to leave and thank them for their work. This is common decency. But instead they forced the people's court into an indecent show to judge them murderers, so they could drive them out as common criminals. The affair is shameful for China, and I hope the world can judge the Chinese by their hearts and not by their actions in these sad days."